VIBRANT WATERCOLOR

A creative and colorful exploration into the art of watercolor painting

GEETHU CHANDRAMOHAN

Colourfulmystique

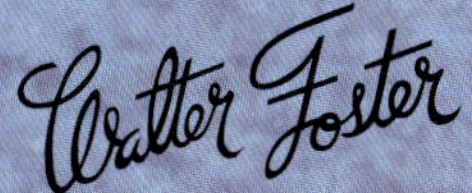

Quarto.com
WalterFoster.com

© 2024 Quarto Publishing Group USA Inc.
Text, Photos & Artwork © 2024 Geethu Chandramohan

First Published in 2024 by Walter Foster Publishing, an imprint of The Quarto Group,
100 Cummings Center, Suite 265-D, Beverly, MA 01915, USA.
T (978) 282-9590 F (978) 283-2742

Walter Foster Publishing titles are also available at discount for retail, wholesale, promotional, and bulk purchase. For details, contact the Special Sales Manager by email at specialsales@quarto.com or by mail at The Quarto Group, Attn: Special Sales Manager, 100 Cummings Center, Suite 265-D, Beverly, MA 01915, USA.

27 26 25 24 1 2 3 4 5

ISBN: 978-0-7603-8487-9

Digital edition published in 2024
eISBN: 978-0-7603-8488-6

Library of Congress Cataloging-in-Publication Data is available.

Design: Megan Jones Design
Page Layout: Megan Jones Design

Printed in China

CONTENTS

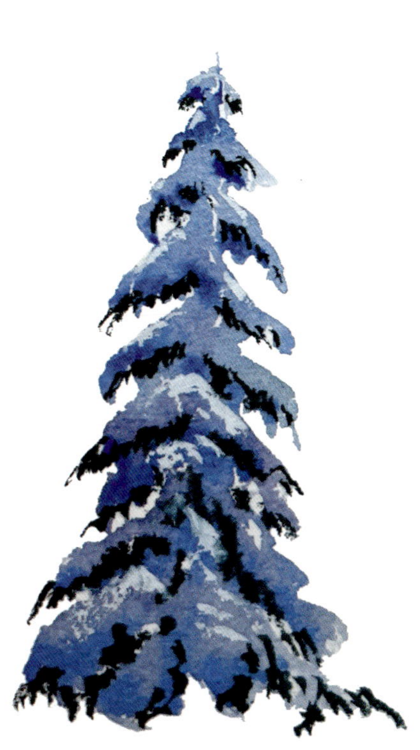

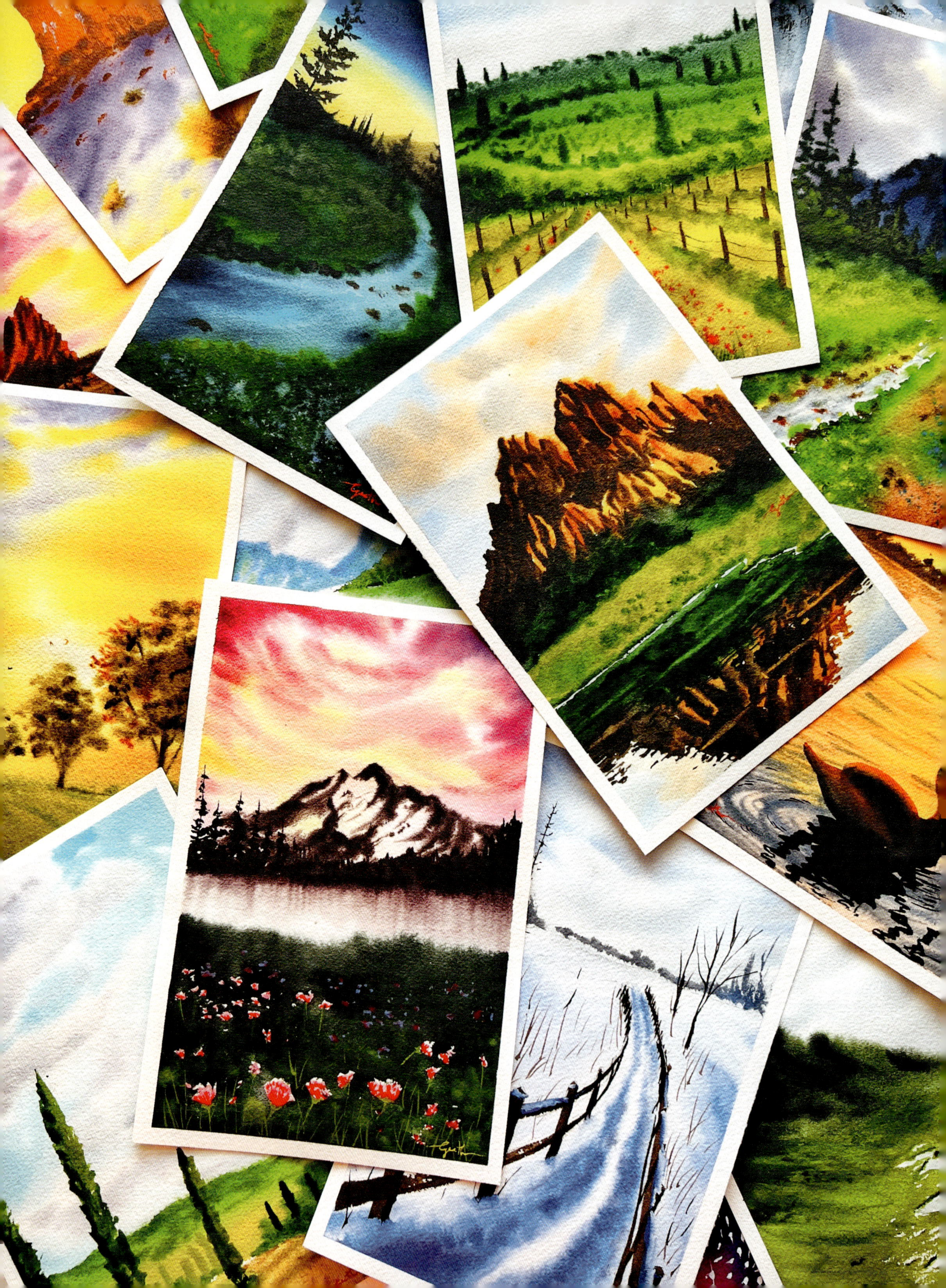

INTRODUCTION

I know that watercolor can be quite intimidating for a beginner, and without the right guidance and support, you might end up frustrated. But let me tell you one simple thing: there is no right or wrong way with watercolor! You can paint in any way that you prefer and still end up with your own unique style. Every artist dabbling with watercolor has gone through this phase and curated their own palette and found their creative style.

Being a self-taught artist, I know first-hand the challenges faced by a beginner and how it would make the learning process easier if there was a simple guide to demonstrate the necessary techniques, color mixing, and factors influencing a painting like composition, perspective, etc. But don't worry! I have curated every single one of these things that I have learned over the years into this book so that you can start painting with watercolor seriously.

This book is divided into two sections—the basics and projects. The basics will give you all the tiny details and everything you need to know before starting with watercolor. The projects consist of step-by-step instructions for painting gorgeous vibrant landscapes. The basics section builds the foundation for each of the painting projects.

Right from the tools and materials required for watercolor paintings, this book covers the different watercolor techniques, color theory and color mixing, building perspective, light and shadow, and composition in the basics section. The projects range from landscapes, waterscapes, and cityscapes.

Each of the watercolor techniques discussed and the color theory lessons in this book will provide you with the most essential skills for building your knowledge with watercolor. Following along the step-by-step projects will help you move from a beginner artist to an advanced-level watercolor artist.

I have shared the general steps involved in painting the projects and by following along you will notice that you get the creative freedom to experiment on your own and build your own artistic style with watercolor paintings. By the time you are finished with this book, I am sure that you will be more confident in your strokes and build a connection with some of the watercolor techniques that will later become second nature to you.

I am eager to see your creations! You can use the hashtag #paintwithmystique if you would like to share your paintings with me on Instagram or Facebook.

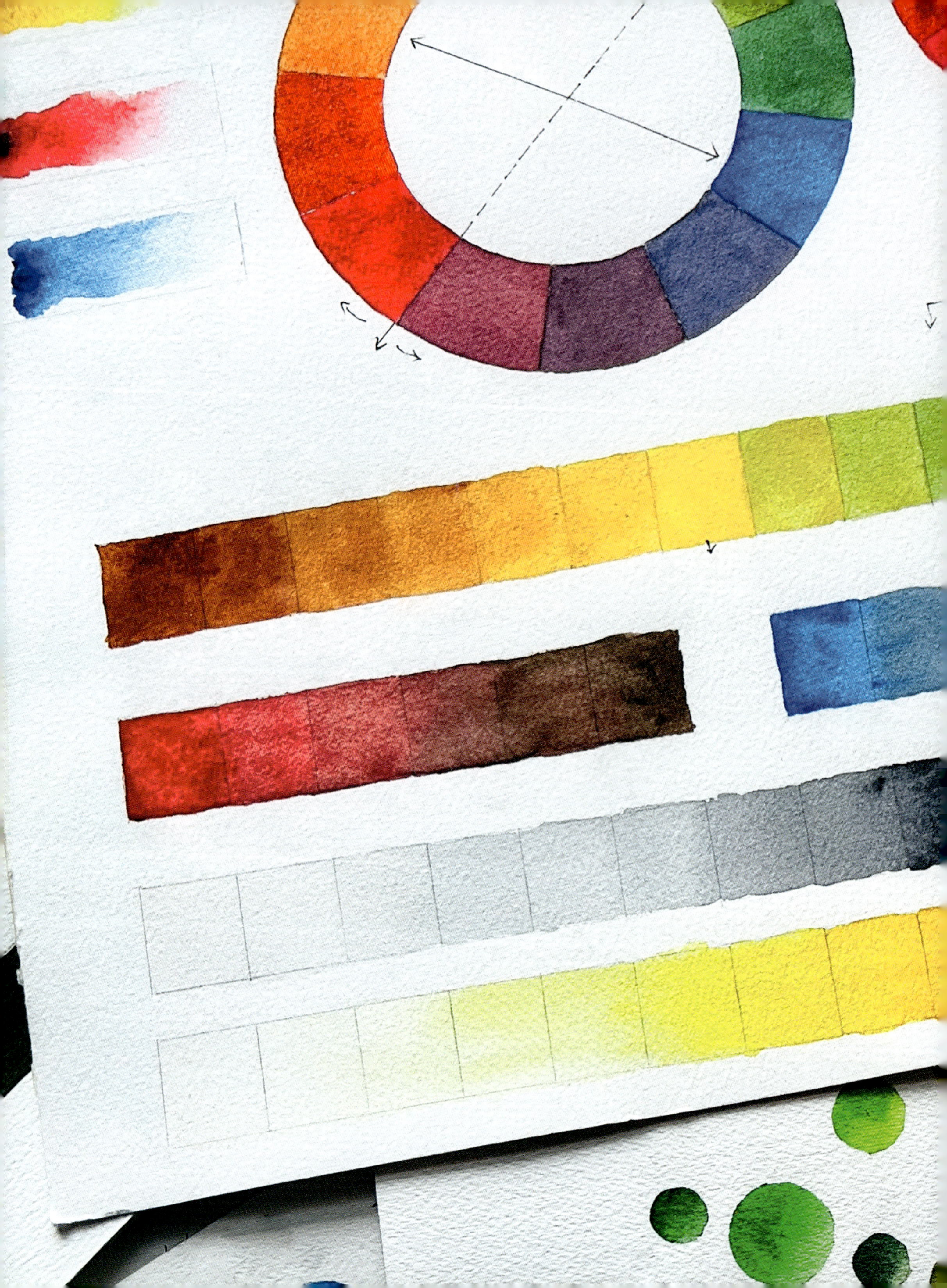

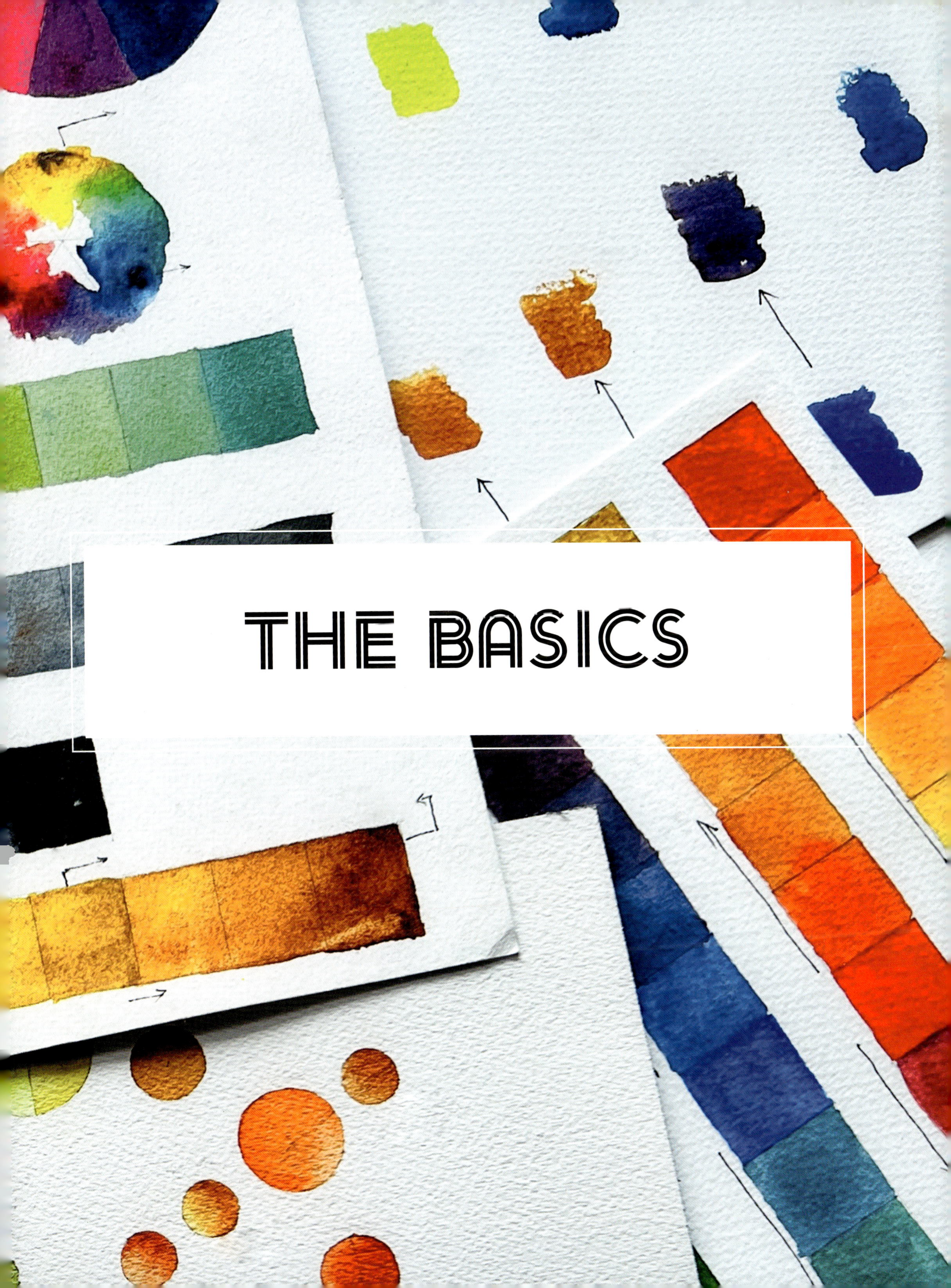

THE BASICS

TOOLS & MATERIALS

When it comes to watercolor paintings, the supplies you use make a huge impact. Just like most people, I started out with cheaper-quality supplies, only to realize later that my techniques, strokes, and everything turned out better with professional-quality materials, even if I was just using a basic primary color palette or handmade rough paper. Thus, from my personal experience, I would advise you to invest in professional-quality supplies so that you can thoroughly enjoy the process of painting. Having said that, you are welcome to use your own palette of colors and the other supplies that you own.

In this section, I have shared my recommendations for each of the supplies. My color palette and all the materials listed in this book are carefully curated by my experiences; with practice, you will also reach a point at which you can choose your own set of favorite materials.

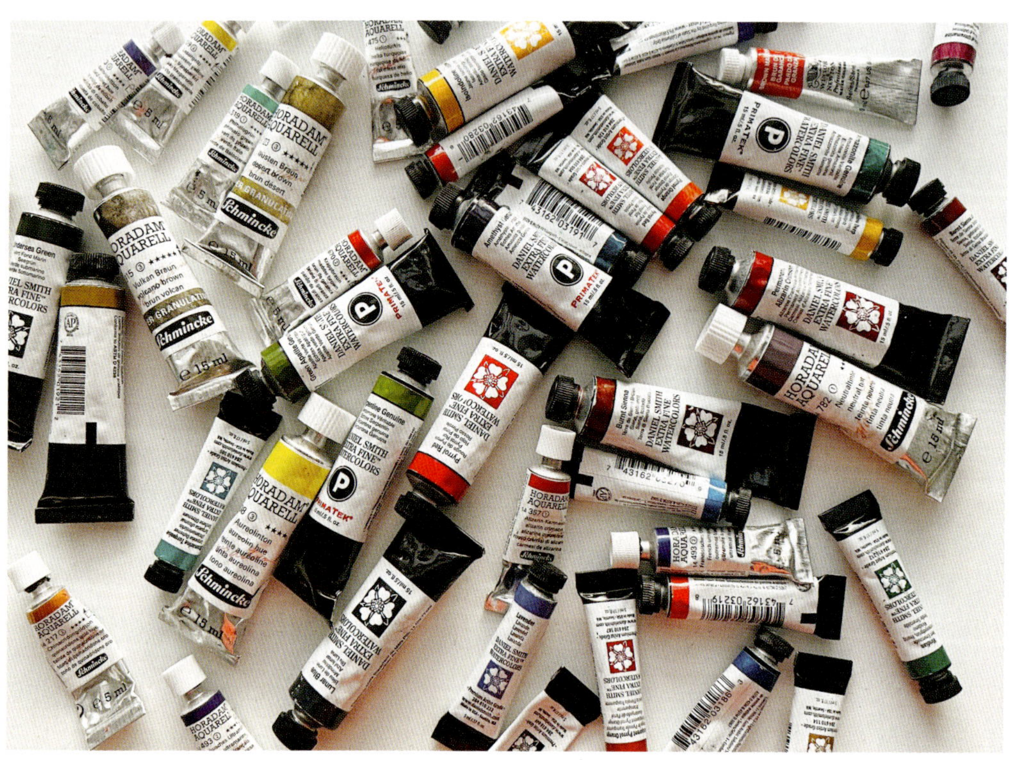

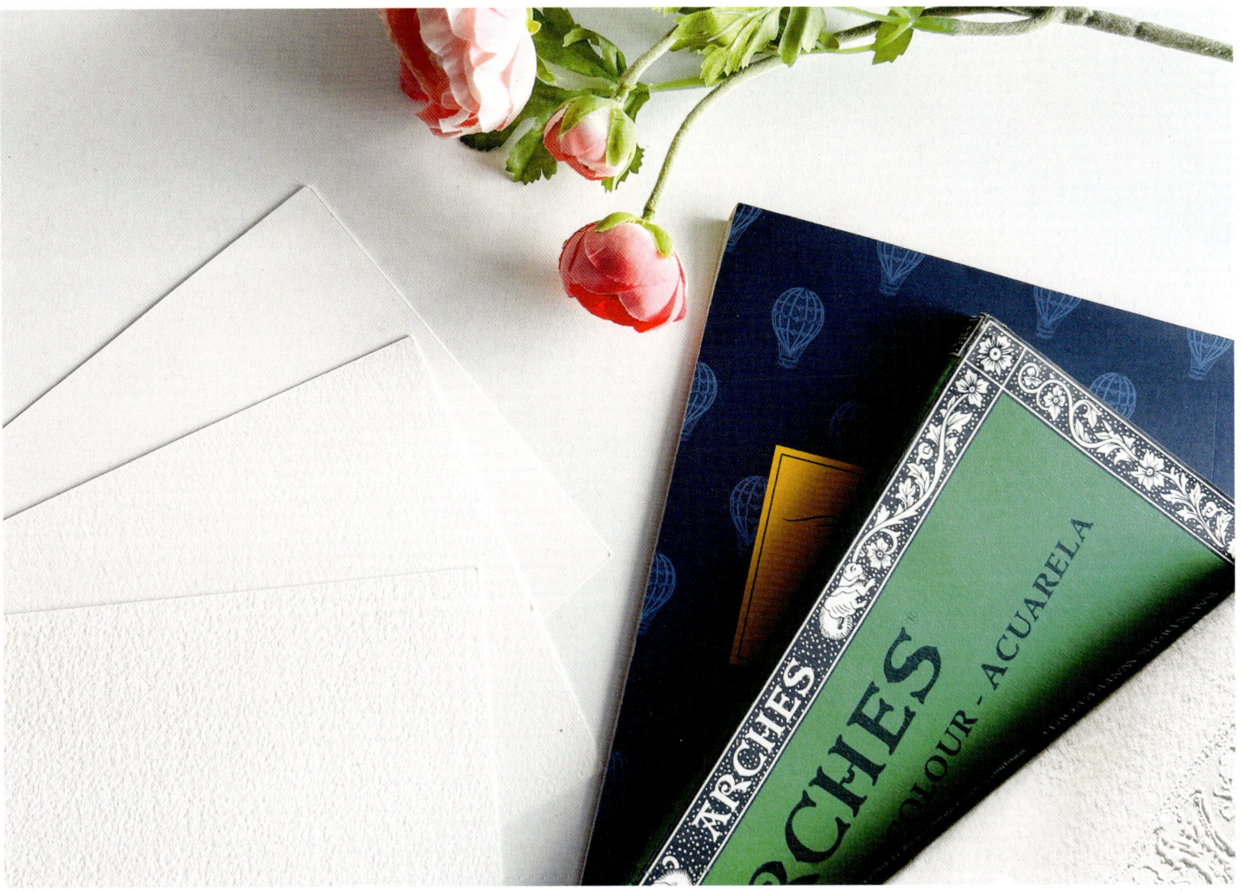

WATERCOLOR PAPER

Paper is the most important material to bring out the full potential of your various watercolor techniques. I would advise investing in good-quality paper right from the start. Even if you were to compromise on watercolor paints or brushes, it is of utmost importance that you practice your artwork on paper that is made to withstand the techniques and wet washes used in this book.

A watercolor paper is defined by its material or composition, density, texture, and the way it was made.

Material/Composition

Usually, watercolor paper can be made from cellulose, cotton, or a combination of both.

- **Cellulose paper:** Cellulose is the least expensive of all. Even though this paper does not absorb the color well, it is good for practice works and color studies.

- **Mixed paper:** The price of the paper increases as the cotton content in it increases. This paper is ideal for mixed-media techniques where other media, such as colored pencils and markers, are to be used along with watercolors.

- **100% cotton paper:** The water and color absorption capability of this paper is the highest and hence it is the most preferred choice for watercolor paintings, especially those featuring multiple washes. The cotton content in the paper increases the stability of the paper and keeps the paper wet longer.

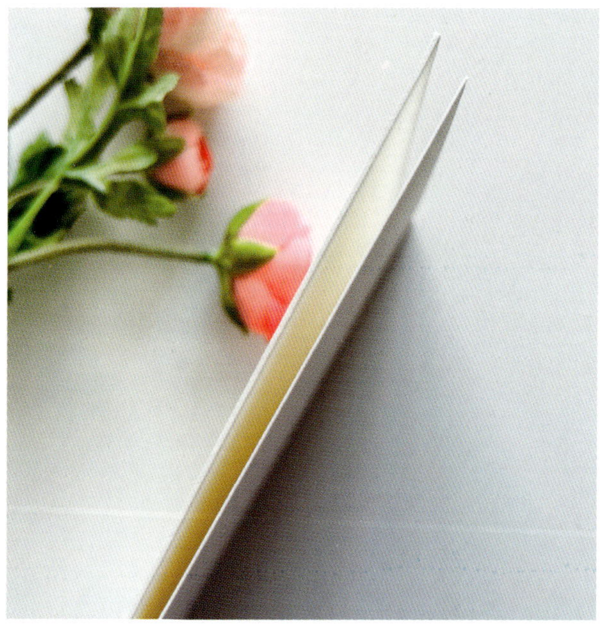

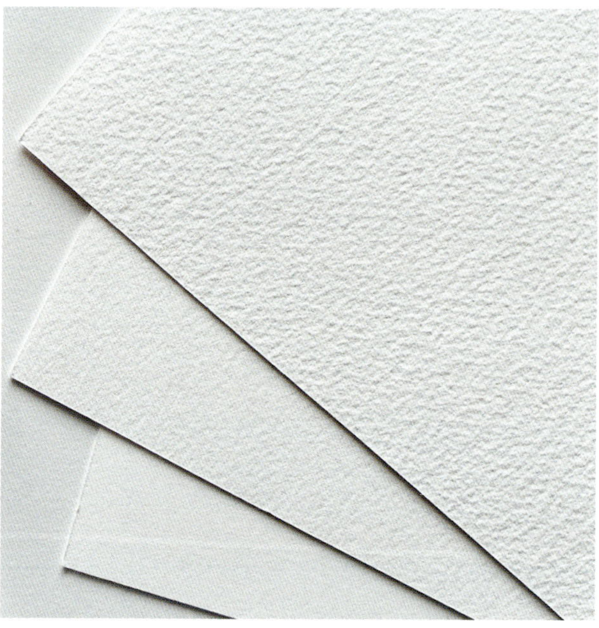

Density

This is the thickness of the paper measured in grams per square meter (gsm) or pounds per square inch (lbs). Watercolor paper is available in varying densities from 185 gsm to 640 gsm. 300 gsm (140 lbs) is considered the optimum weight to work on.

Texture

Watercolor paper can be hot-pressed, cold-pressed, and rough-surfaced. Hot-pressed is the smoothest of the three; the paint dries faster and the paper is suitable for extremely detailed paintings and botanical works. The more texture the paper has (i.e., the more crevices in the paper), the more time the paint takes to dry. Cold-pressed paper is the most-used paper for painting with watercolors, as its medium-grain texture is suitable for almost all watercolor techniques. Rough-surfaced paper has a heavy grain texture and is also widely used.

How It's Made

Watercolor paper can be either handmade or machine made. Hot- and cold-pressed papers can only be made by a machine, and handmade papers are usually heavy grain and rough-textured.

MY RECOMMENDATION

Arches Aquarelle or St Cuthberts Mill's Saunders Waterford are both cold-pressed, 100% cotton, 300 gsm papers.

WATERCOLOR PAINTS

Watercolor paints can be student grade and professional grade. As evidenced from the name, student-grade paints are cheaper quality, contain lesser pigment, and have other fillers that make it impossible to mix the desired colors; this results in faded, muddy, or chalky mixtures. Professional-quality paints, on the other hand, contain pure pigments and a binder, thus delivering rich colors and an enhanced color mixing experience.

I would recommend investing in some basic shades from a professional-grade brand rather than buying several shades from a student-grade version, only to realize that they don't give the desired results.

Watercolor paints are available in tubes and pans. Most professional artists prefer paint in tubes, as they are already wet and take less time to reactivate. Paints in pans are lightweight and in small amounts, which makes them ideal for painting outdoors.

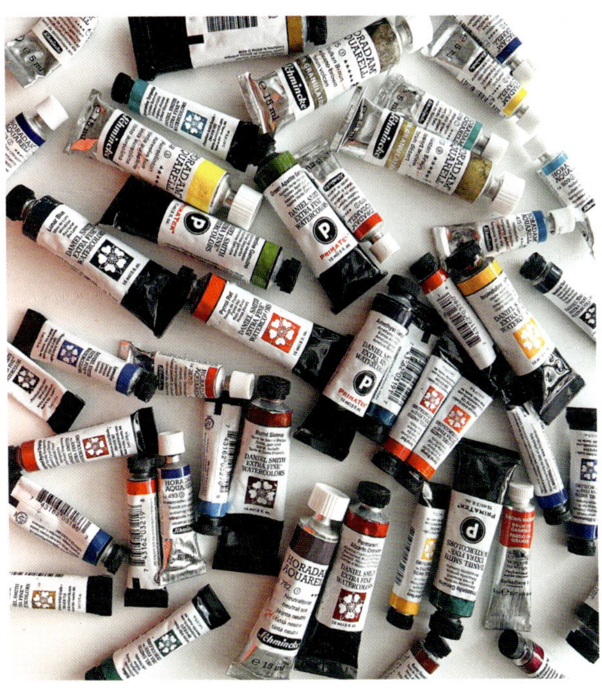

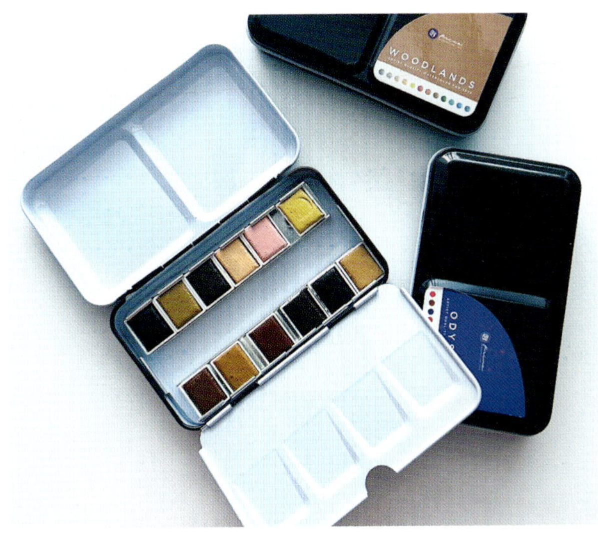

WATERCOLOR BRUSHES

Choosing the right brushes for watercolors can be quite tiring and intimidating owing to the variety of choices available. However, it is important to note that each brush shape is designed with a specific purpose; as a beginner, you do not need all these shapes and sizes.

Brushes can be either natural hair or synthetic. Natural-hair brushes hold a lot of water, release water and pigment well, and have a long lifespan. Synthetic brushes, on the other hand, are perfect for details and are less expensive.

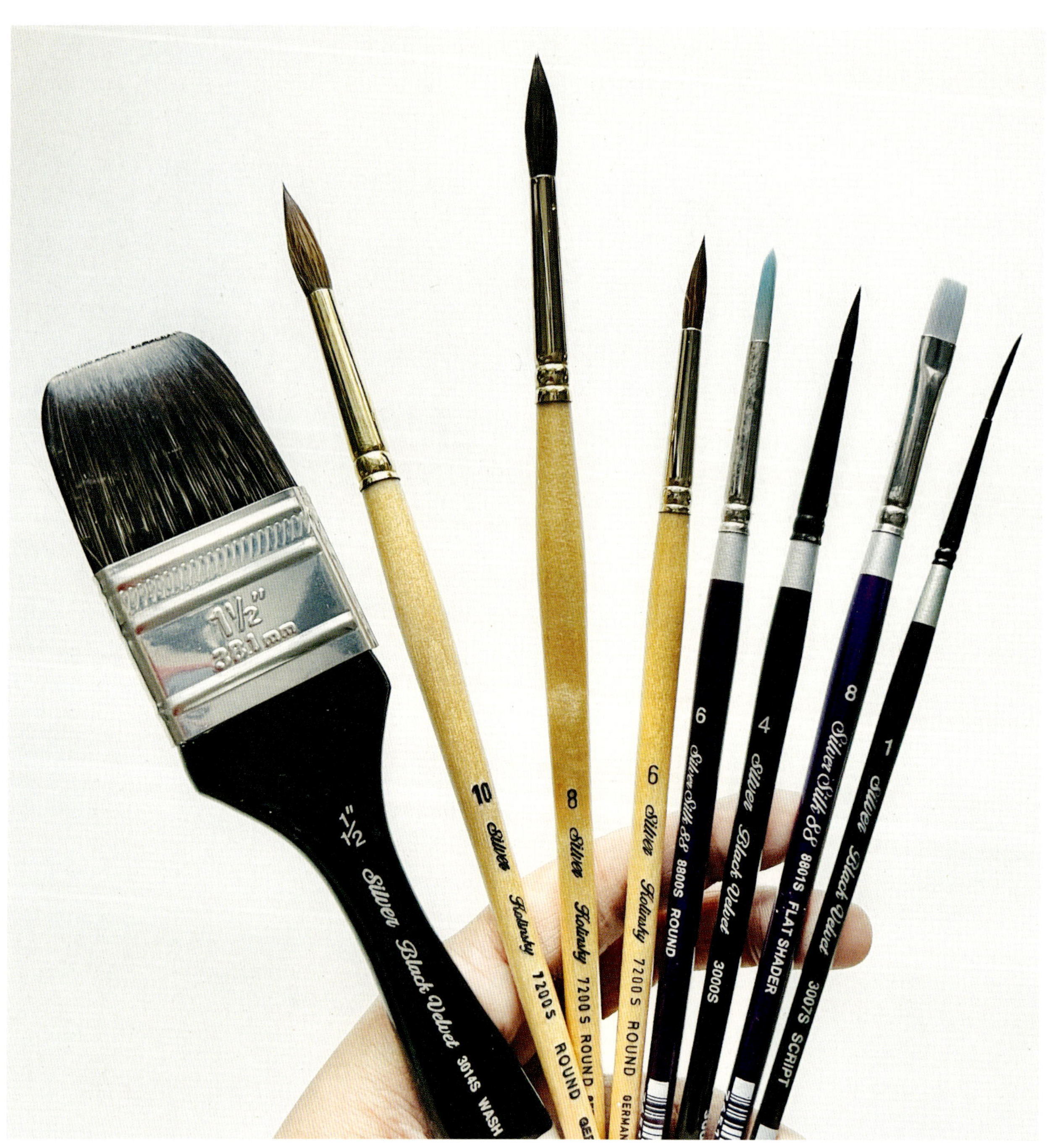

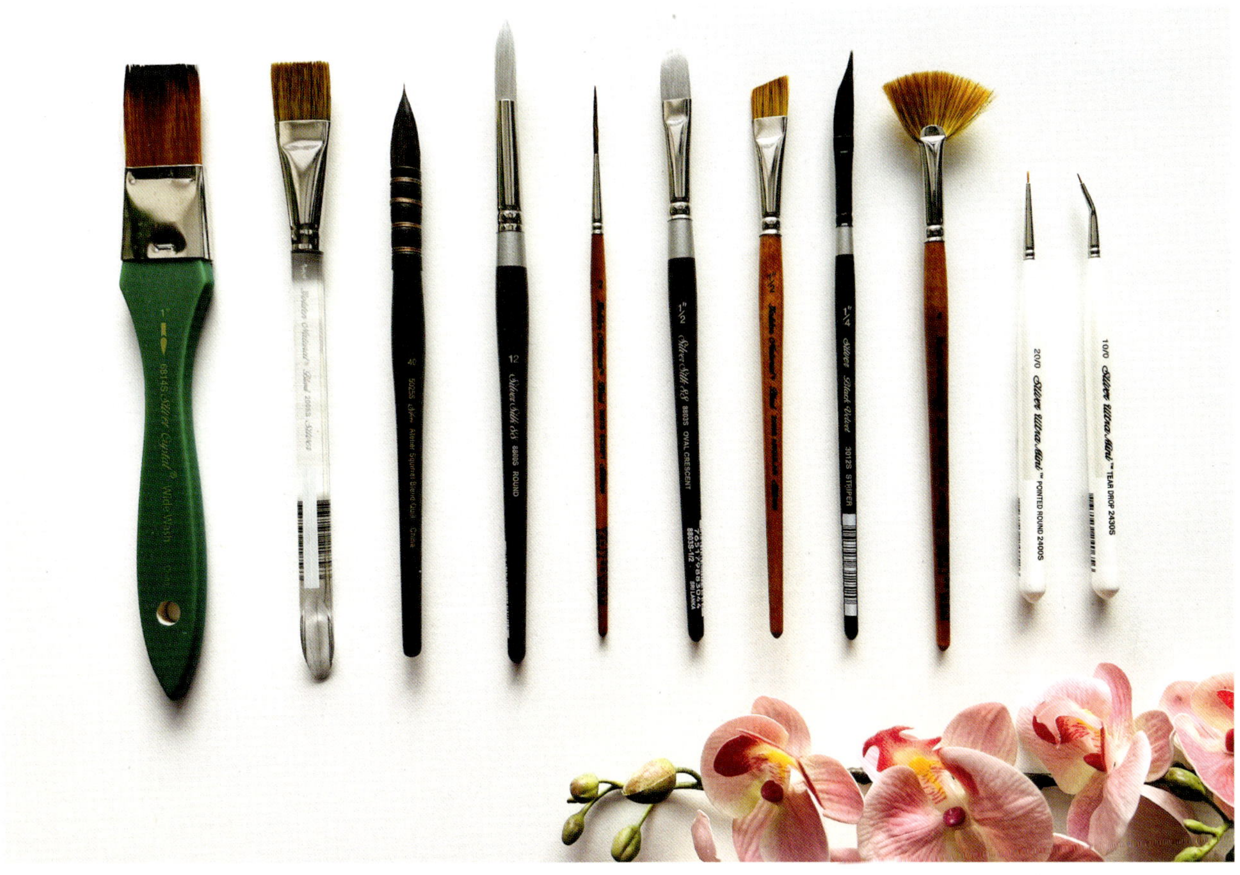

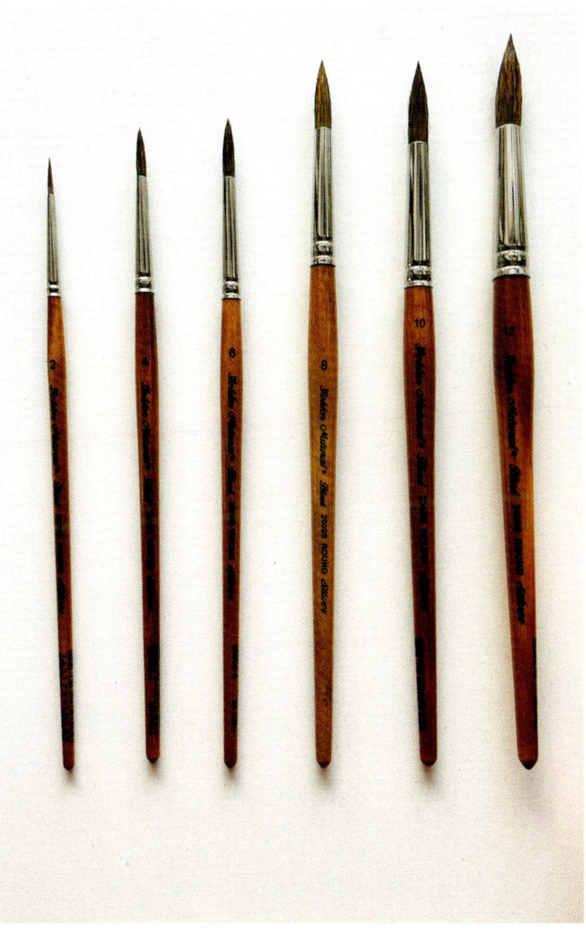

MY RECOMMENDATION

My favorite brushes are from Silver Brush Limited. Below are the brushes that I find myself going back to for almost all of my paintings.

- Atelier flat wash size 20 or Black Velvet 1½" (3.8 cm) wash brush

- Most regular strokes: Kolinsky pointed round size 8, 10, or 6

- Dry details: Silk 88 round size 6

- Smaller details: Black Velvet round size 4

- Flat lifting: Silk 88 flat shader size 8

- Long lines and minute details: Black Velvet script liner size 1

PALETTE

When working with watercolor tubes, you need a palette to mix colors. The palette should contain enough space for you to squeeze out the pigment from the tubes and large wells to mix the paints. You can also use large ceramic palettes where you can squeeze out desired pigments as you need them. Watercolor pans usually come as part of a small set with a designated mixing space.

Pictured below is my extended watercolor palette of 36 colors that I have curated after a lot of trial and error with different shades. Every artist will gradually create a unique palette that caters to their needs and style.

There are also different ways that artists prefer to arrange the colors in their palette. It could be based on color theory with the warm colors on one side and the cool colors on the other side or it could be completely random. Over time, you'll learn how and where you prefer your colors to be on your palette.

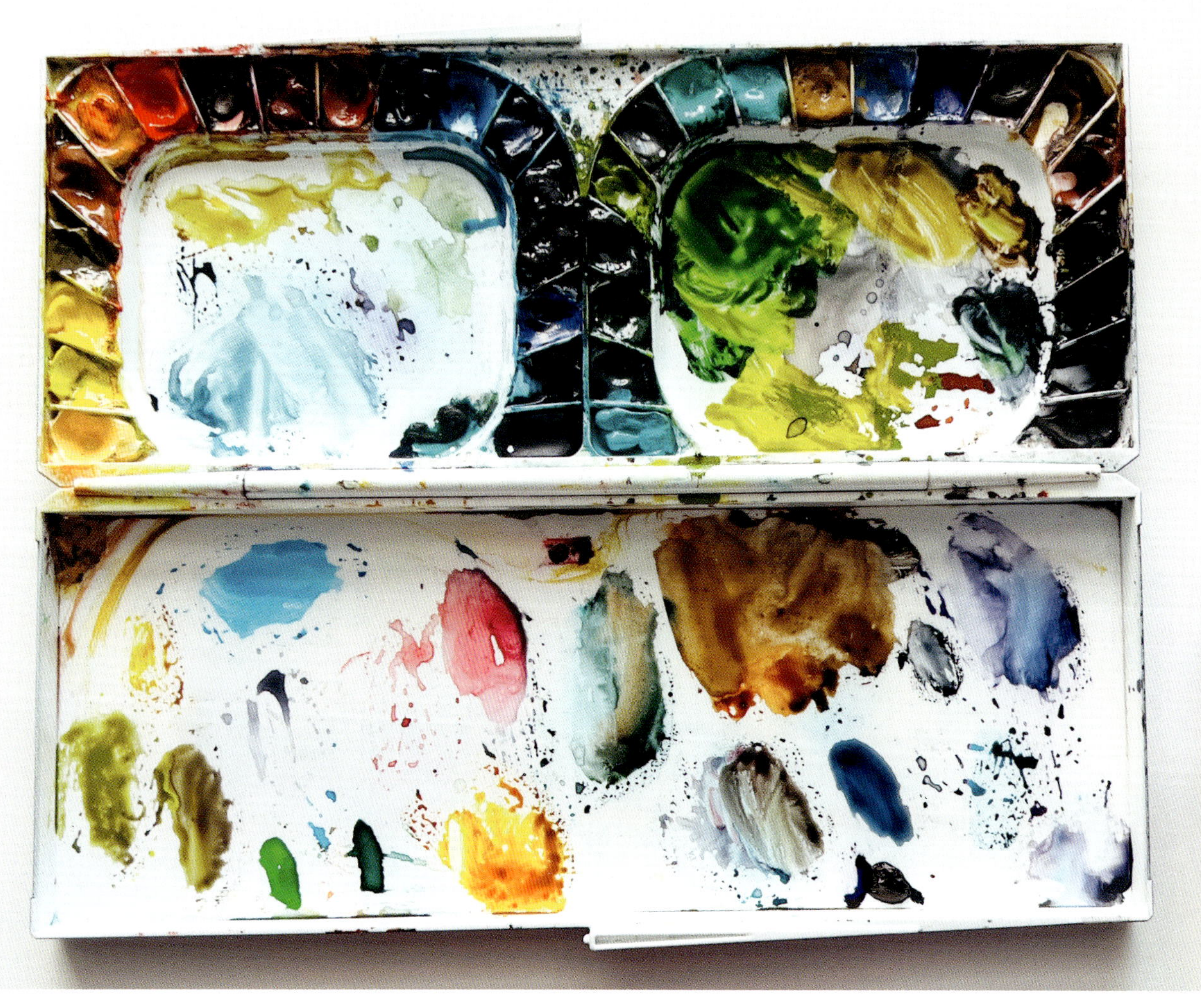

ADDITIONAL MATERIALS

Two Jars of Water

I usually use two jars of water, because once you start painting and repeatedly wash the brushes, it turns the water muddy. So, I use a second one for the wet washes on the paper or for picking up fresh color. Make sure to always to rinse off your brushes in the same jar to keep the other water clear.

Masking Tape

I use a ½" to 1" (1.3 to 2.5 cm) width masking tape to get clean edges for my paintings. You can also use cut-out shapes of masking tape to mask areas in your painting. MT washi tape is a good brand to use. From my experience, it is always the paper that is the culprit if the masking tape tears the paper when peeling it off after the painting process.

Pencil

I mostly use a mechanical pencil with a 0.5mm HB lead so that I don't have to keep sharpening it for rough sketches before I start painting. You can use a normal pencil as well.

Eraser

Erasers are important to remove any mistakes as you sketch. I would highly recommend using non-dust erasers, as eraser dust can settle into the troughs of the paper—especially if you are using rough paper—and can get in the way of painting. Also, remember to be gentle with erasing; harsh erasing can damage the sizing of the watercolor paper, rendering it useless for painting.

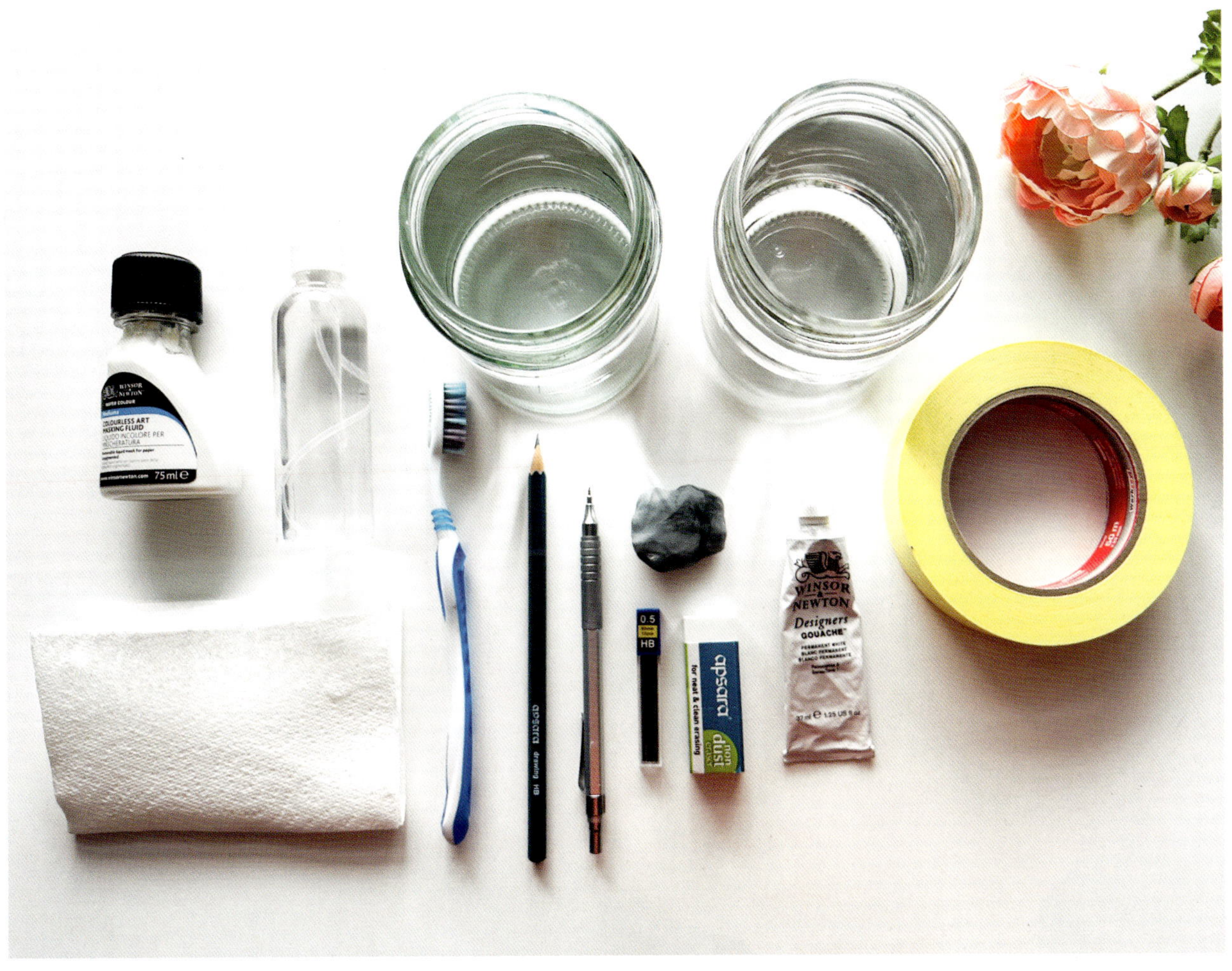

Kneaded Eraser

You will notice the paper getting graphite marks as you sketch. A kneaded eraser is useful to rub off these graphite marks. Also, if you have made very dark pencil lines, this eraser can be used to lighten them up.

Spray Bottle

A water spray bottle is useful to re-wet the paper when it starts to dry or to enhance the moisture on the paper.

Masking Fluid

This is a rubbery fluid that is quite useful to mask certain areas of the paper from being painted on. You can peel it off later and that area remains white; you can leave it that way or paint over it.

White Gouache

Gouache is an opaque water-based medium; light colors can be layered over dark colors. This makes it highly useful to create white accents or highlights in paintings. You can also use other gouache colors if you would like to layer over the top of watercolors.

Toothbrush

A toothbrush is useful to create tiny splatters on the paper, which is otherwise a difficult process. I mostly use the toothbrush to create white splatters.

Paper Towels

Paper towels are useful to absorb extra moisture from the brush while painting. You can also use a cloth for this purpose.

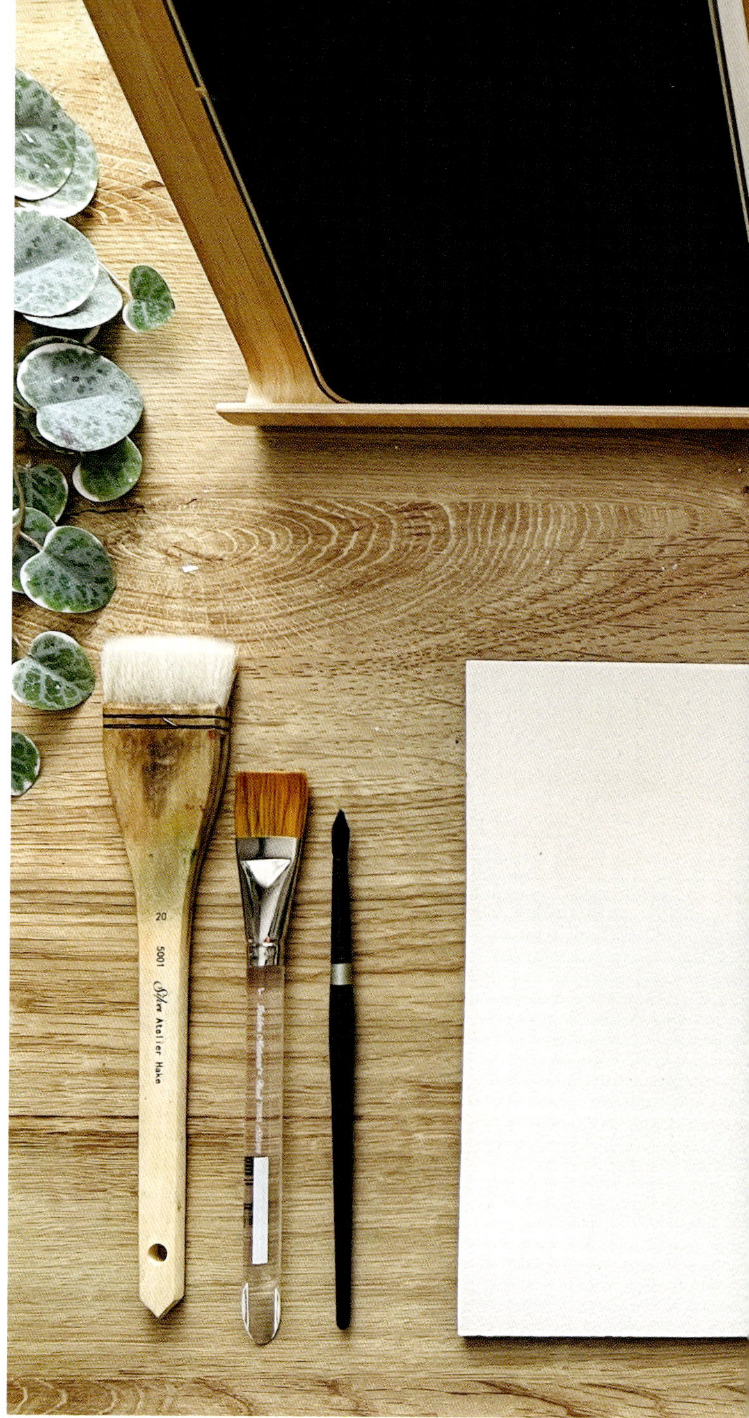

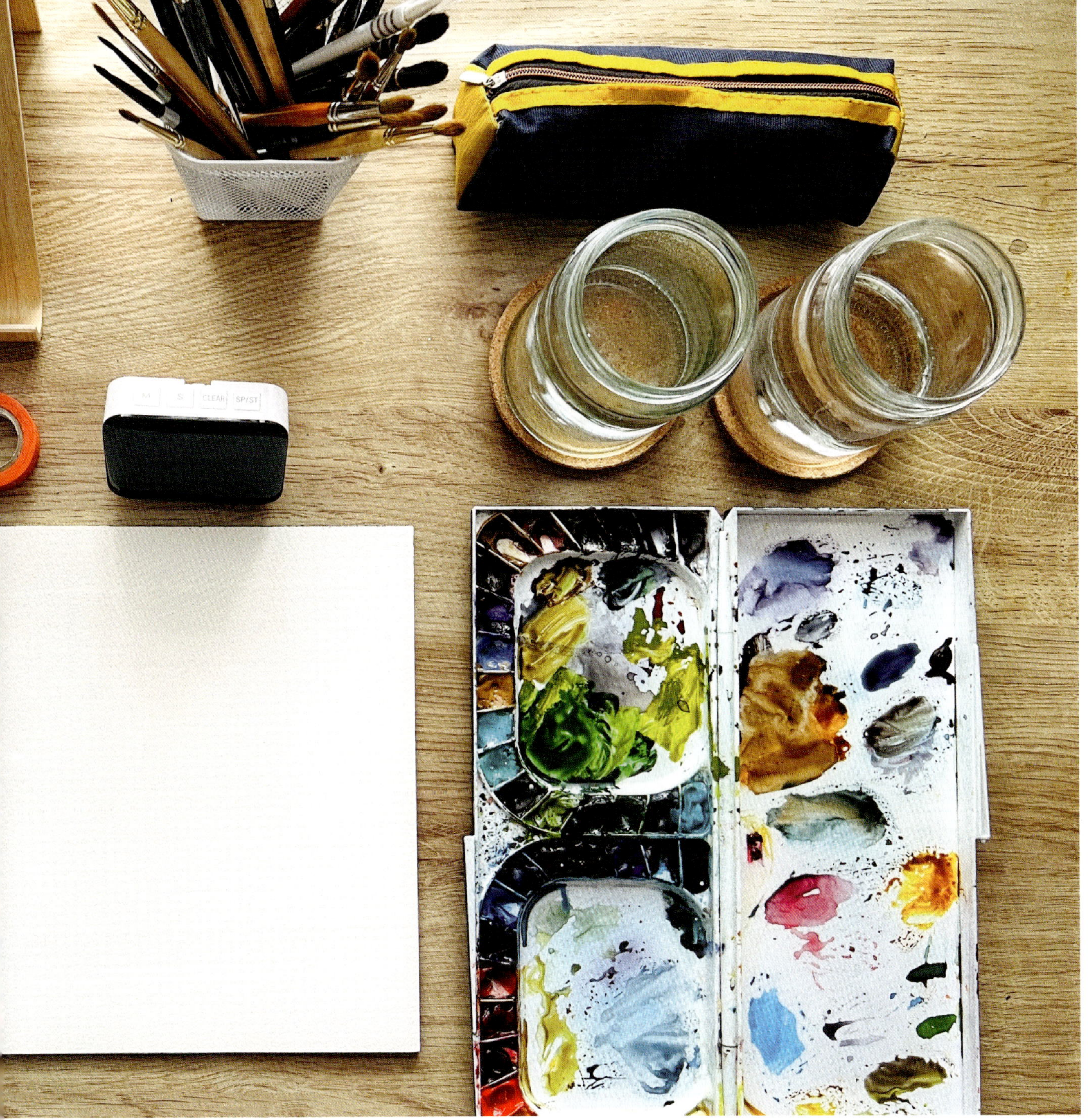

YOUR PAINTING WORKSPACE

It is important to have a workspace that makes your painting process easier. It could be a small table in your bedroom, your dining table, or a large studio worktable. It is ideal to have a designated workspace for your painting, as it eliminates the need for preparing your work surface every time you sit down to paint. This also increases your motivation, and you can easily get back to what you were doing without having to set it up all again.

It's best to work under natural lighting, as it reflects the true colors of the painting; however, getting your workspace right next to a natural light source is not an option for everyone.

Make sure to enhance your painting experience by positioning your materials for easy usage. Place the palette and water jars on your dominant hand side so that you don't have to cross over your paper to pick up paint or water; this prevents accidental spills.

UNDERSTANDING WATERCOLOR

It is of utmost importance that you understand the different properties of watercolor so that you can use this knowledge to your advantage while painting with various watercolor techniques. It will also help you understand why some watercolor pigments behave differently than others and why some pigments display unique characteristics.

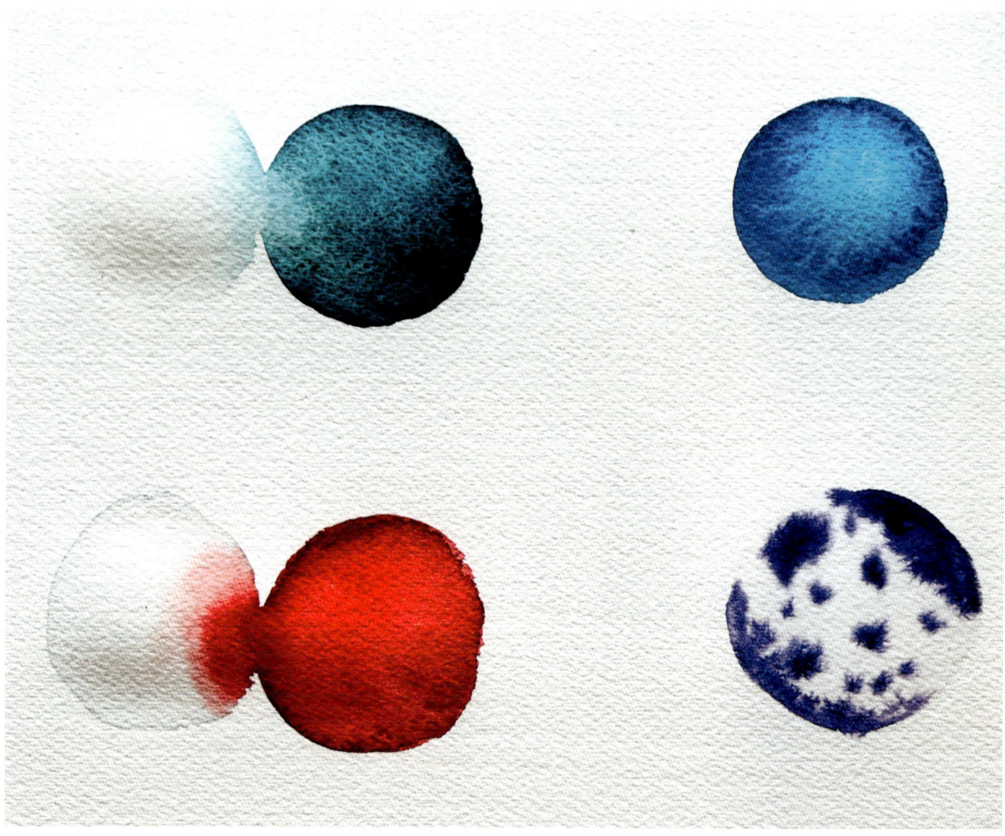

PROPERTIES OF WATERCOLORS

Transparency & Opacity

Watercolor pigments have different densities, which allows them to have different characteristics when mixed with the binder. Some of them are completely transparent, which means they allow light to pass through. Opaque colors, on the other hand, do not allow the light to pass through. This can be easily tested by drawing a thick black line on the paper using a permanent marker and painting over it. If the line can be seen through, then the color is transparent; if not, it is opaque.

Staining & Nonstaining

This property determines how much the color stains the paper. Staining watercolors penetrate the underlying fibers of the paper, whereas non-staining colors settle mostly on the surface of the paper. This property is helpful in determining the ability of your paint to be lifted off from the watercolor paper. If your pigment stains, it is very hard for you to apply the lifting technique and lift the color off from the paper to reveal the white of the paper underneath. Non-staining pigments, on the other hand, enable the paint to be lifted off and to mostly reveal the white of the paper underneath.

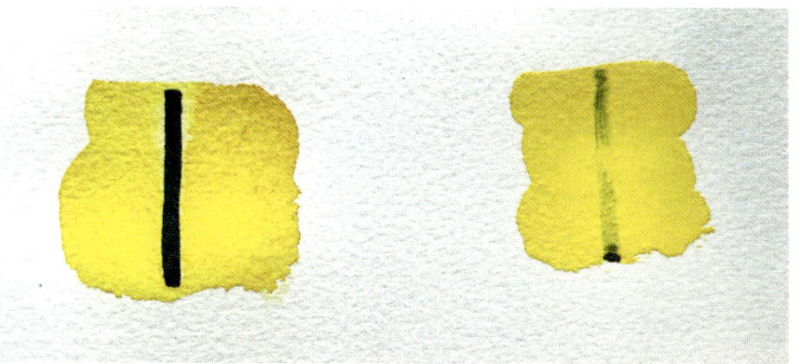

TRANSPARENCY AND OPACITY

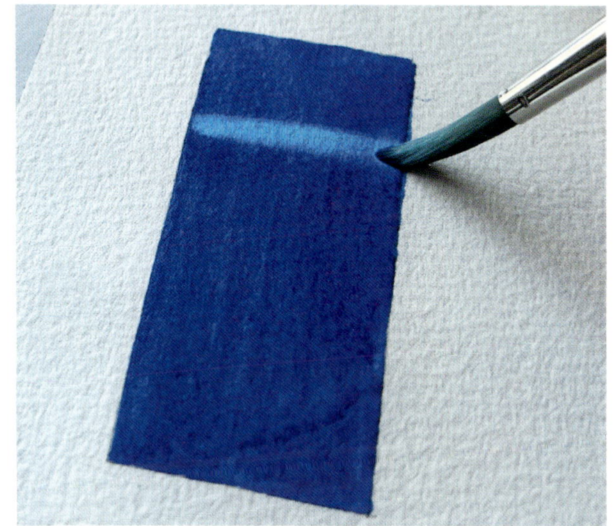

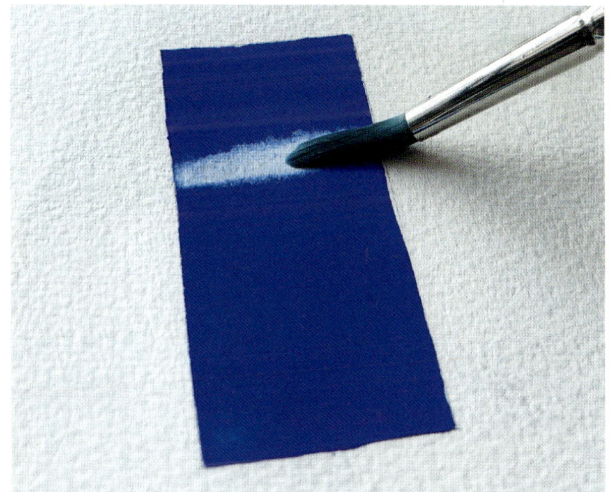

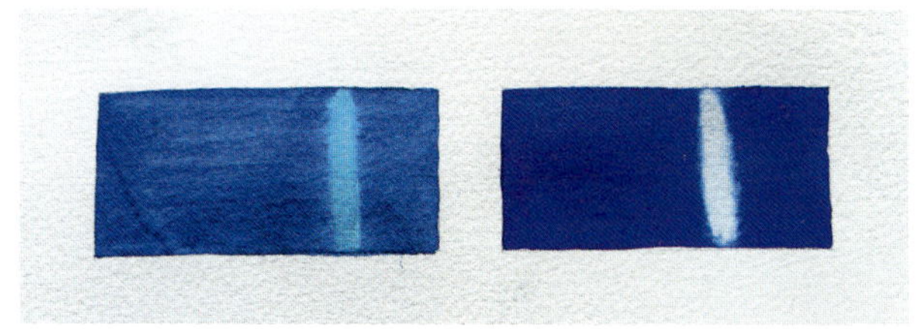

STAINING AND NONSTAINING

Granulating & Nongranulating

Depending on the pigment, the particles in the paint can be heavy and dense or thin and light; this affects the way they behave on the paper. Granulation refers to the property by which watercolor paints with heavier particles separate from the water and settle into the little hills and valleys of the paper. The heavier particles create a beautiful texture on the paper, also known as sedimentary property, because the pigment sediments itself on the troughs of the paper. To test for granulation, simply apply a wet wash of the pigment on the paper and observe. You will see whether the particles separate out and settle in sediments on the paper or not.

Fugitive & Non-fugitive

This property of watercolors refers to how fast colors fade over time when exposed to sunlight. This is also called lightfastness of a pigment. When it takes the pigment a long time to fade, it is known as extremely lightfast or non-fugitive. When it happens to fade quickly, it is referred to as a less lightfast pigment or a fugitive pigment. Unfortunately, this is one of the properties that is hard to test out; you would have to wait months or years to see the color gradually fading. Observe how the color alizarin crimson has faded after it was exposed to sunlight for a long time.

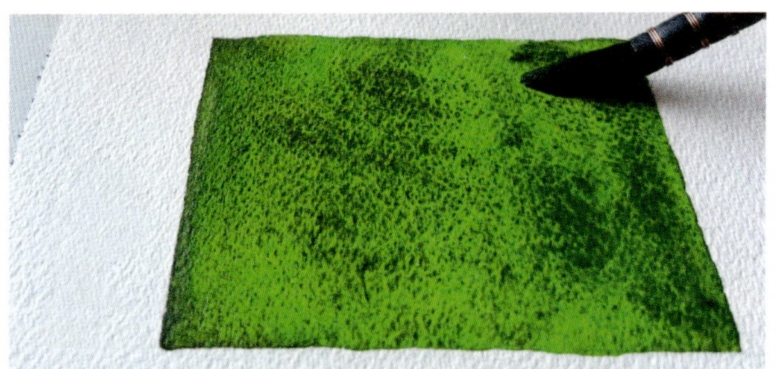

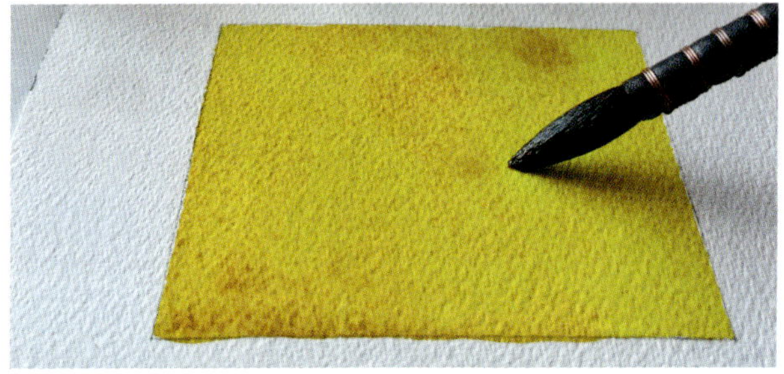

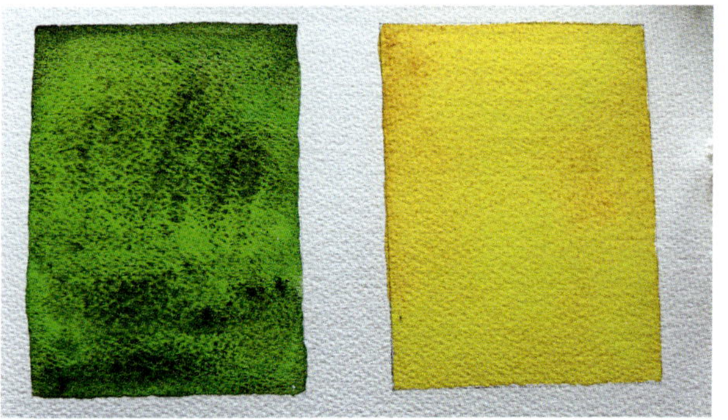

GRANULATING & NONGRANULATING

FUGITIVE & NON-FUGITIVE

WATERCOLOR LABELS

Professional watercolor brands usually describe the contents and properties of the shade on the label of the watercolor tube or pan so that the artist can use the color to its full potential.

Generic Name

This will usually be in bold, big letters on the tube compared to the other information. The name on a watercolor tube means nothing when it comes to understanding the colors. It is simply a generic name that the manufacturers use to make their color.

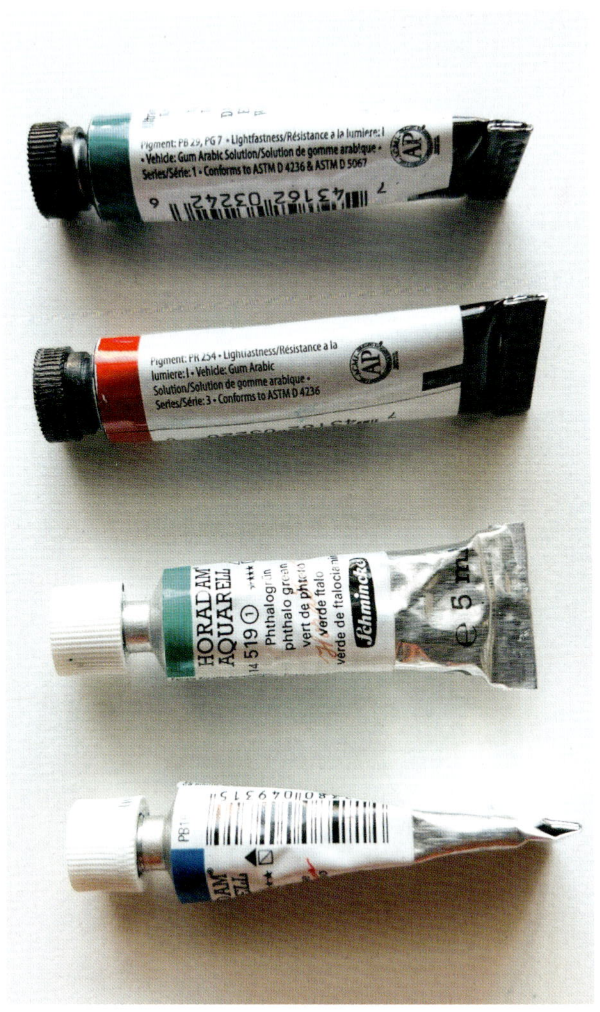

Pigment Number

Watercolor pigments are defined using a specific number known as the color index name or pigment number. Each pigment has a unique number, and knowing this pigment number can give you a lot of information about the paint that you're using. This is the main component of that watercolor shade, that is, the pigment that was used to manufacture that shade. Somewhere on the tube, you'll find the pigment number starting with P, followed by the color category. The color categories are Y for yellow, R for red, O for orange, B for blue, V for violet, G for green, Br for brown, Bk for black, and W for white. Some colors will be made of a single pigment and some with more than one pigment.

Transparency or Opacity

This is depicted by a square or circle on the label. An empty square or circle implies transparent pigment and a filled square or circle indicates an opaque pigment. Semi-transparent is usually a square or circle half-filled on the right side, while semi-opaque is half filled on the left side.

Lightfastness or Fugitive Rating

This is depicted either using stars or Roman numerals; I or five stars means extremely lightfast, and IV or 1 star means fugitive pigment.

Staining & Granulation

If this information is mentioned, then it would be Y for granulating, N for nongranulating, and a rating scale of 1–4 for staining pigments.

Series Rating

This depicts the price range of the pigment on a scale of 1 to 5, with 5 being the most expensive pigment.

UNDERSTANDING COLORS

Knowing the characteristics and properties of watercolor pigments will help us to create the perfect compositions and meaningful color mixes, as well as enable us to use those properties to our advantage in a painting. Colors can evoke a lot of emotions; hence, choosing the right colors and putting them together on paper can create a lot of visual attraction to your work and a harmonious painting.

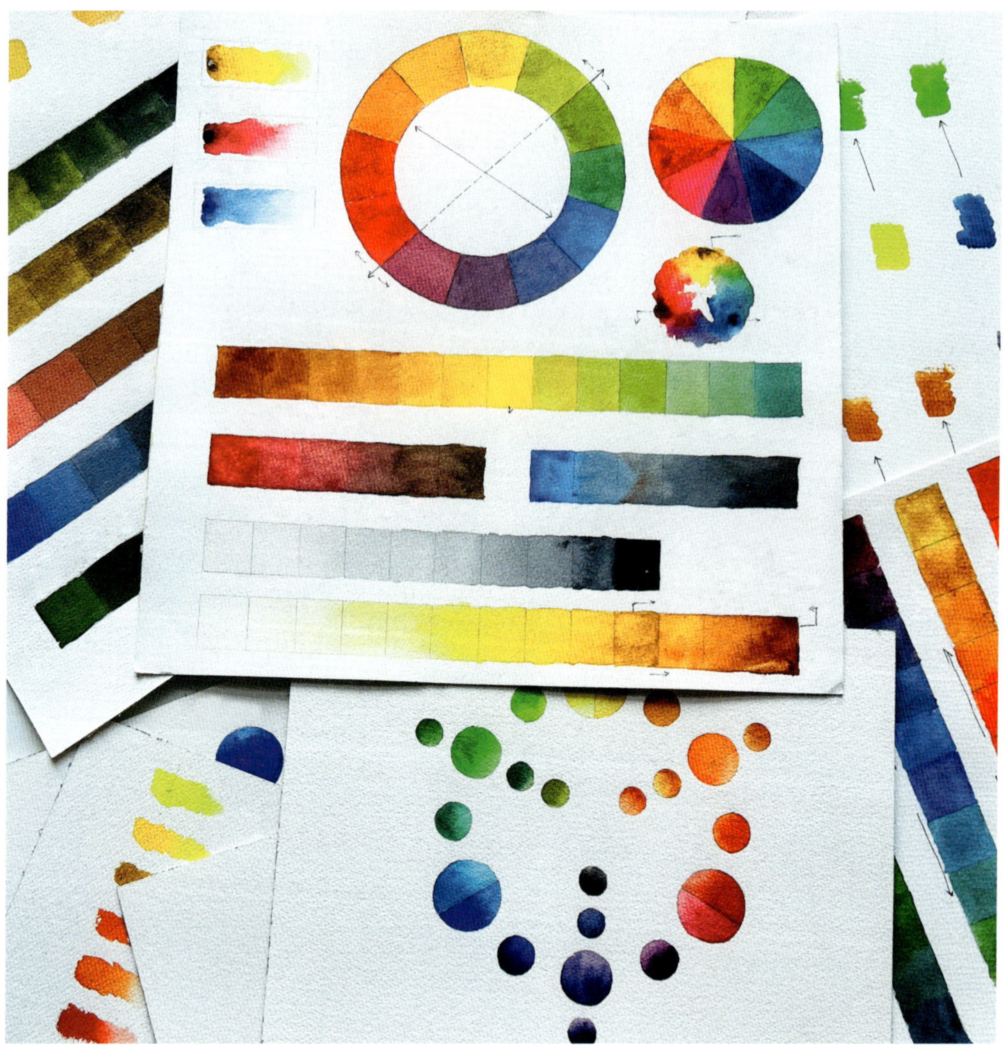

PRIMARY, SECONDARY & TERTIARY COLORS

Primary Colors

Yellow, blue, and red are the three primary colors. These are the basic building blocks needed to create a color wheel and cannot be made by mixing any other colors. All other colors on the color wheel are derivatives of these three colors.

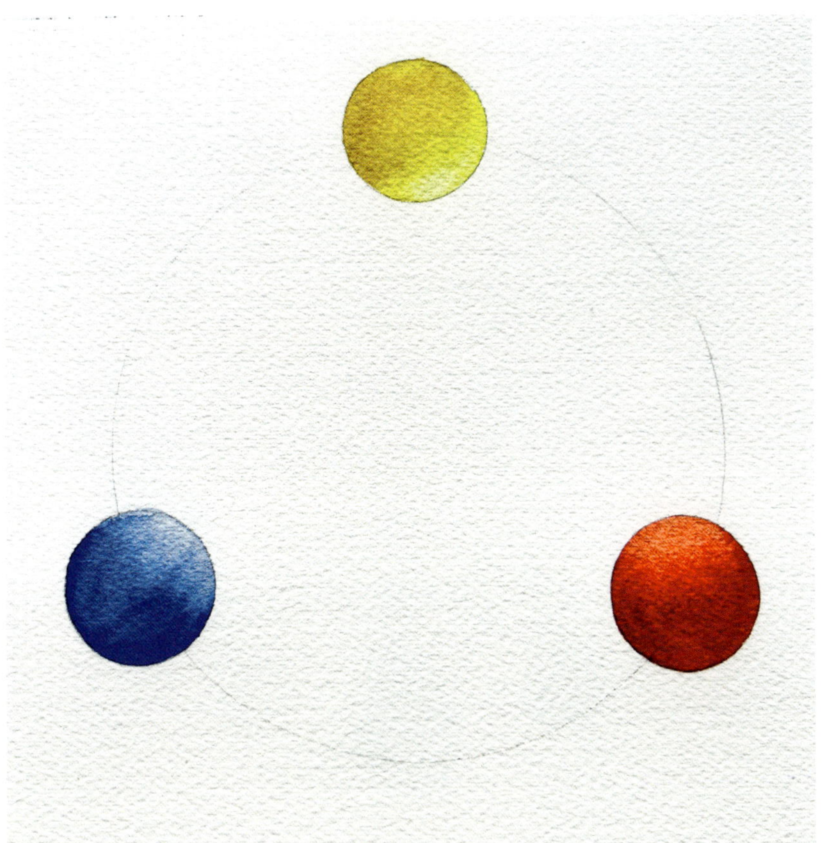

Secondary Colors

These colors are made by mixing two primary colors together. Orange, green, and violet are the three secondary colors.

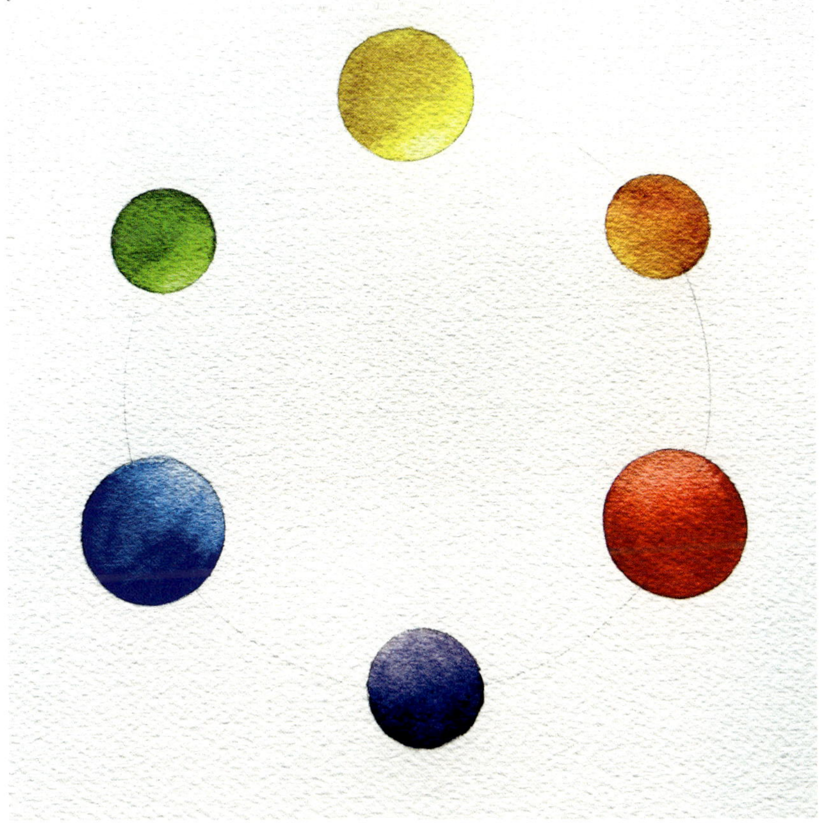

Tertiary Colors

These colors are formed when mixing a secondary color and a primary color together. Yellow-green, blue-green, blue-purple, red-purple, red-orange, and yellow-orange are the tertiary colors.

When you mix all three primary colors together in different ratios, you get different shades of grays and browns. Imagine the infinite number of colors you could mix if you had different shades of all three primaries!

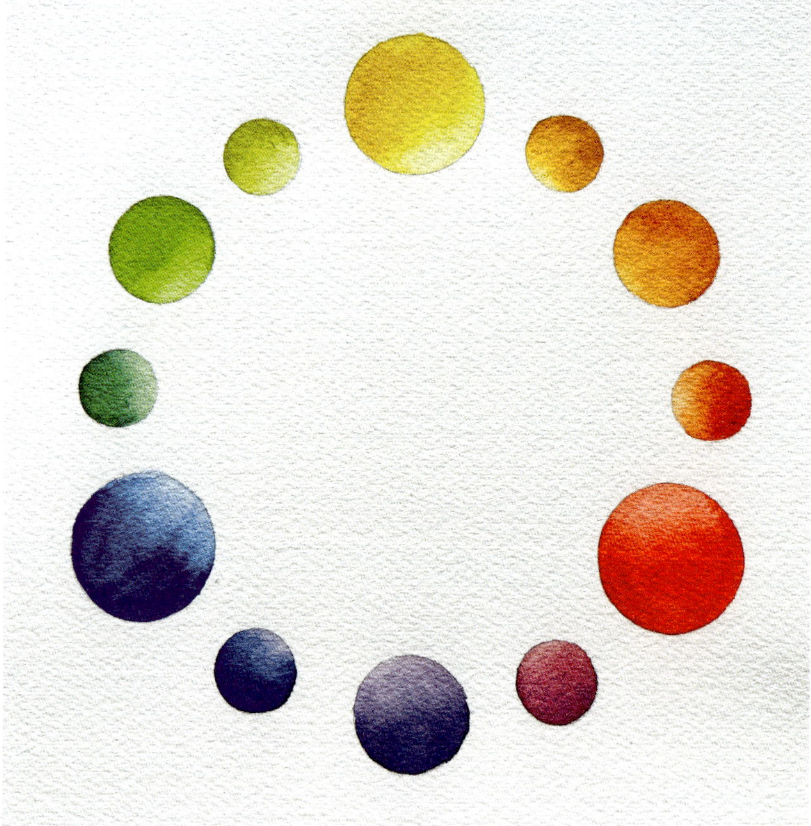

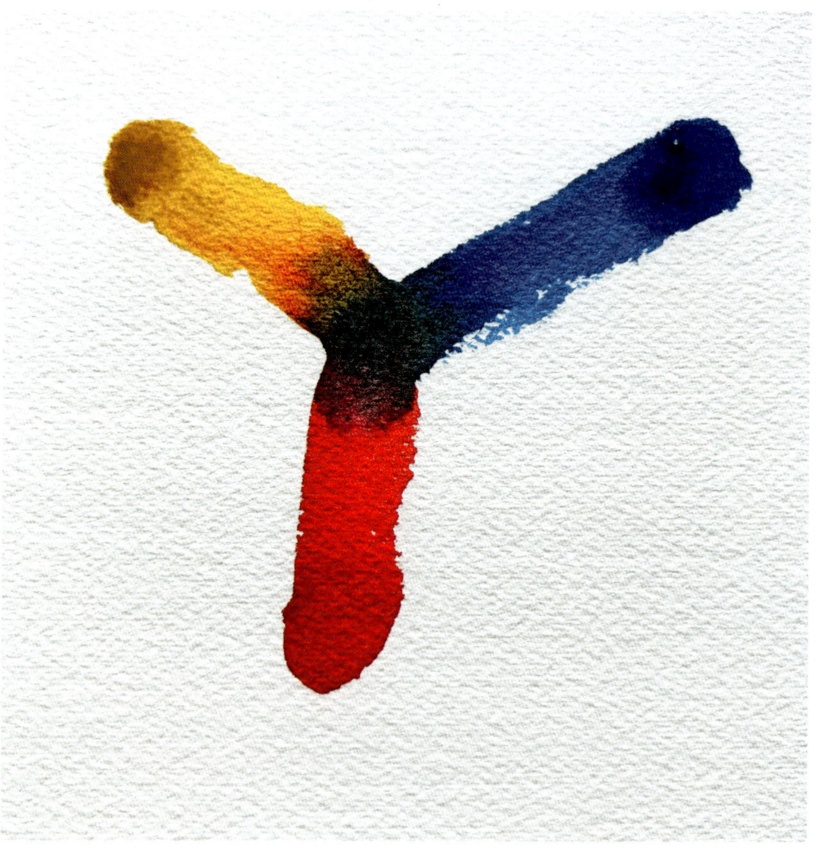

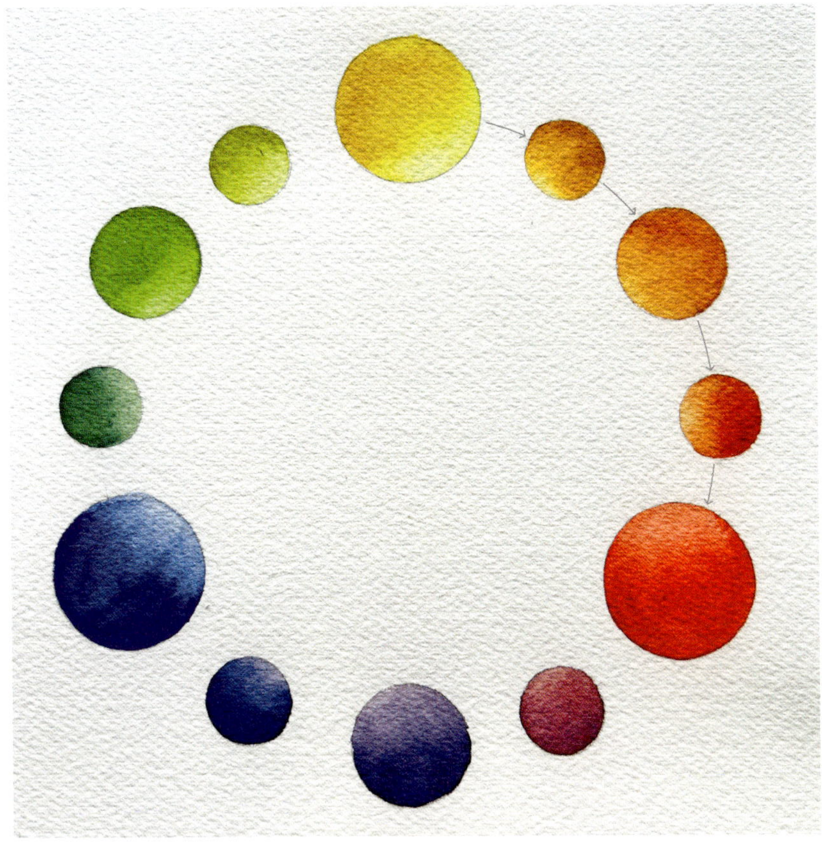

The colors next to each other on a color wheel are called analogous colors, and the colors opposite to each other are complementary colors. Hence, yellow and purple, red and green, and blue and orange are the complementary pairs. This is very important, because mixing two complementary colors creates grays and browns. For example, when mixing red and green, you are mixing red, yellow, and blue together—all three primaries. The practical use of this information in paintings comes when you want to desaturate or mute down a color. For example, you can simply add a green color to a red color to gradually mute it.

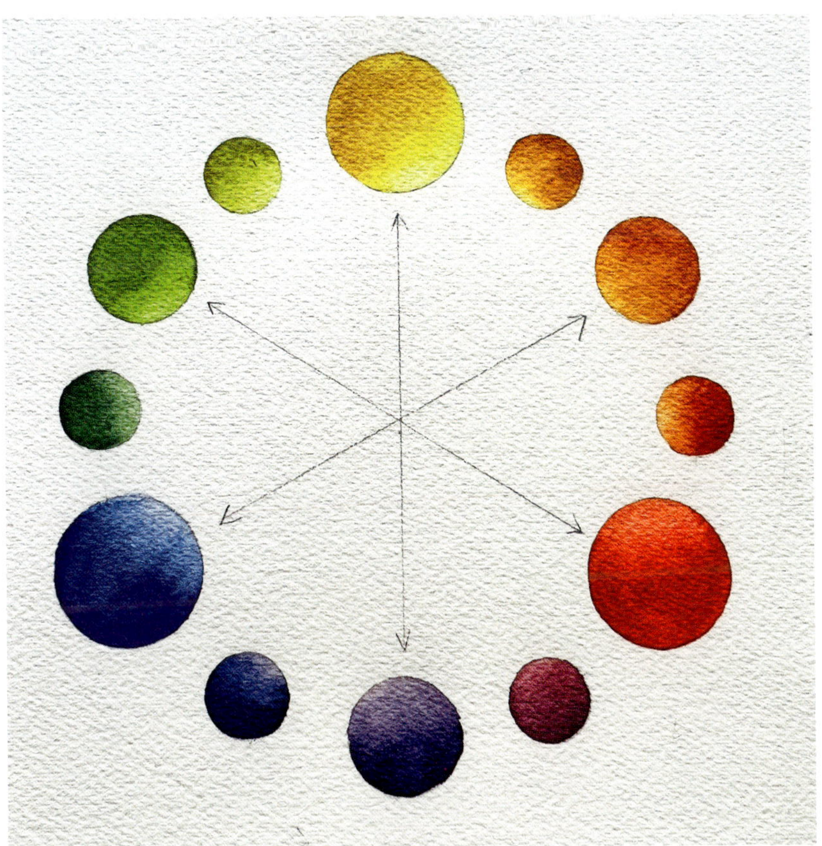

COLOR TEMPERATURE

The color wheel can be split in two based on temperature: warm and cool colors. Warm colors give a sense of warmth, like heat, fire, or the sun, whereas cool colors give the sensation of ice, snow, and ocean depths. Hence, the colors on the right side here (reds, yellows, and oranges) are the warm colors, whereas the blues and greens are the cool colors.

Knowing the color temperature helps to create the mood and depth in a painting. In general, warm colors tend to advance or come forward in a painting, whereas cool colors recede or go back in space. In the light spectrum, the wavelengths of warm colors are longer than the wavelengths of cool colors, so you see the warm colors before the cool colors, which creates the illusion of depth in a painting. Also, every color has a temperature bias of its own and can be categorized as a warm or cool shade.

Let us consider the case of the primary yellows. If you look at the lemon yellow on the left side, you can see it slightly tends toward a green shade; thus, it is a cool yellow with a blue bias (as green is mixture of yellow and blue). The yellow on the right side clearly is a warm yellow, as it tends toward orange; thus, it is said to have a red bias.

Now, let us look at reds. The cool red tends toward purple and hence has a blue bias. Similarly, the warm red tends toward orange and thus has a yellow bias.

With the blues, it is a bit tricky at first glance to see the bias. But if you try to mix a blue with a red shade, you will see that it gets darker and tends toward purple. Hence, the ultramarine blue on the right is a warm blue with a red bias and the phthalo blue is a cool blue with a yellow bias.

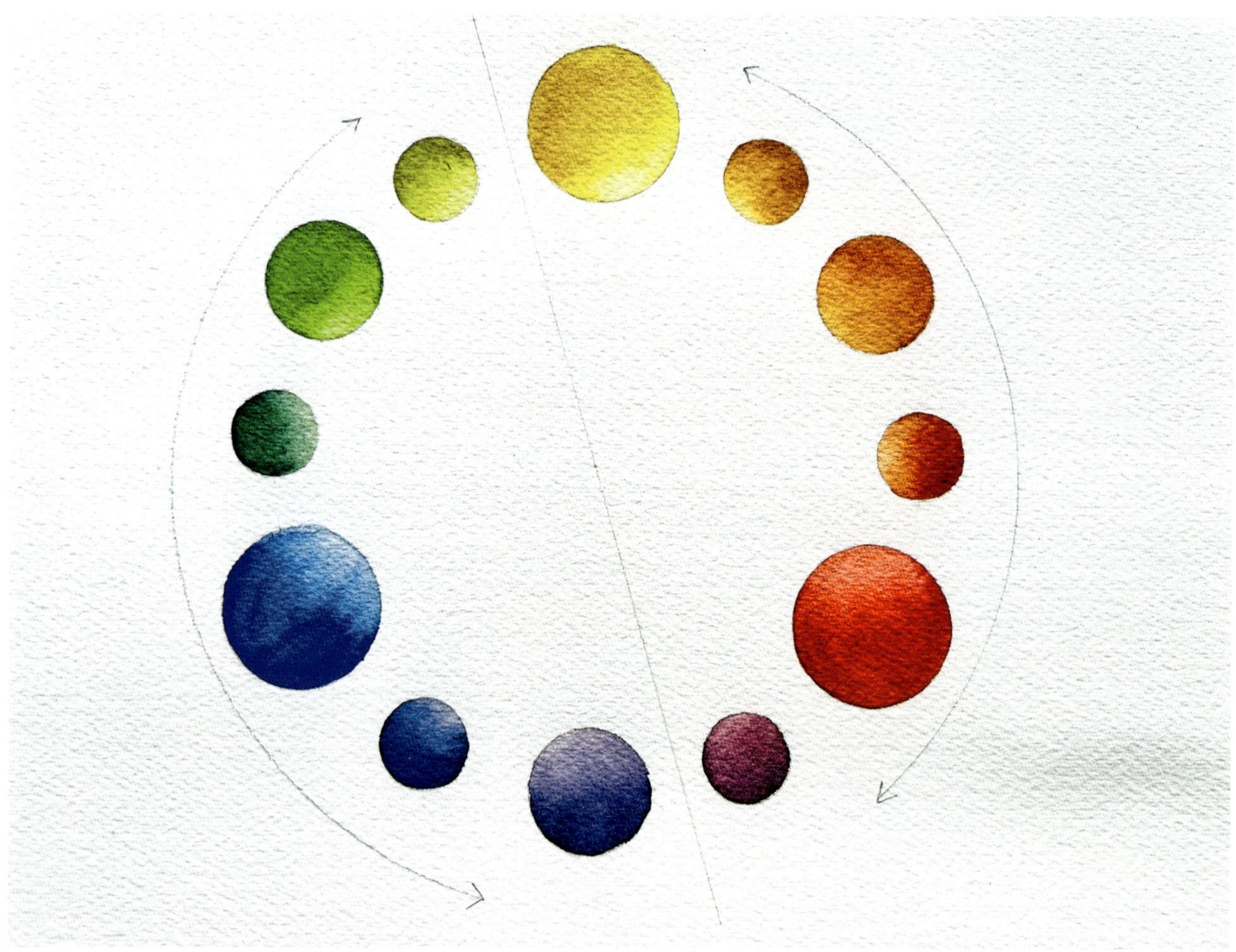

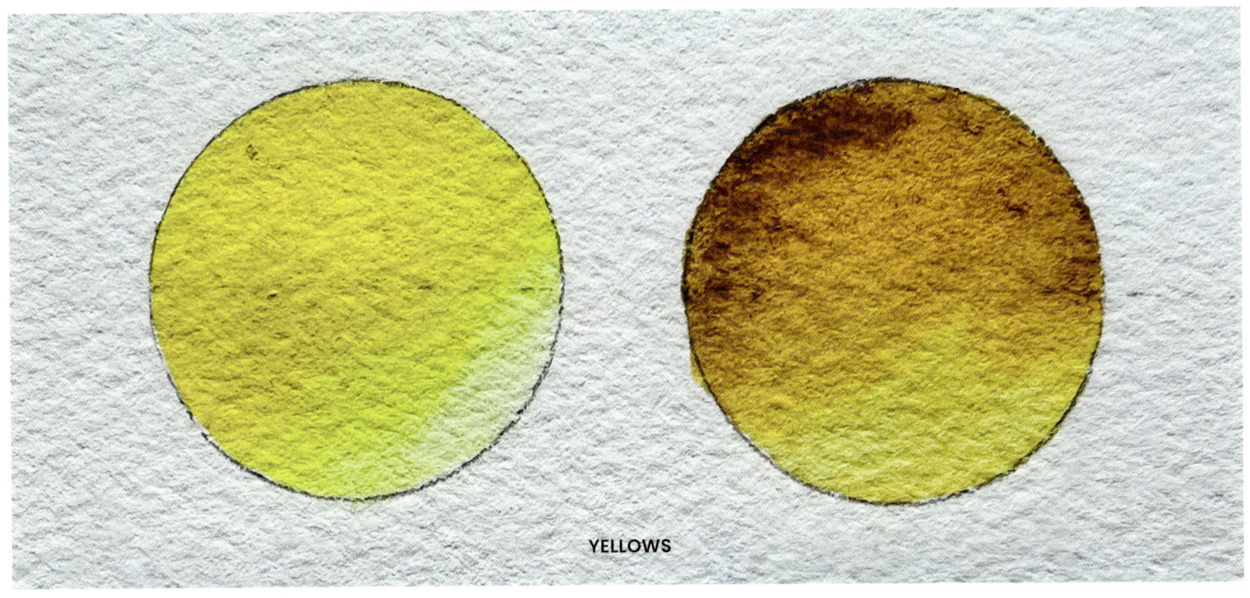

YELLOWS

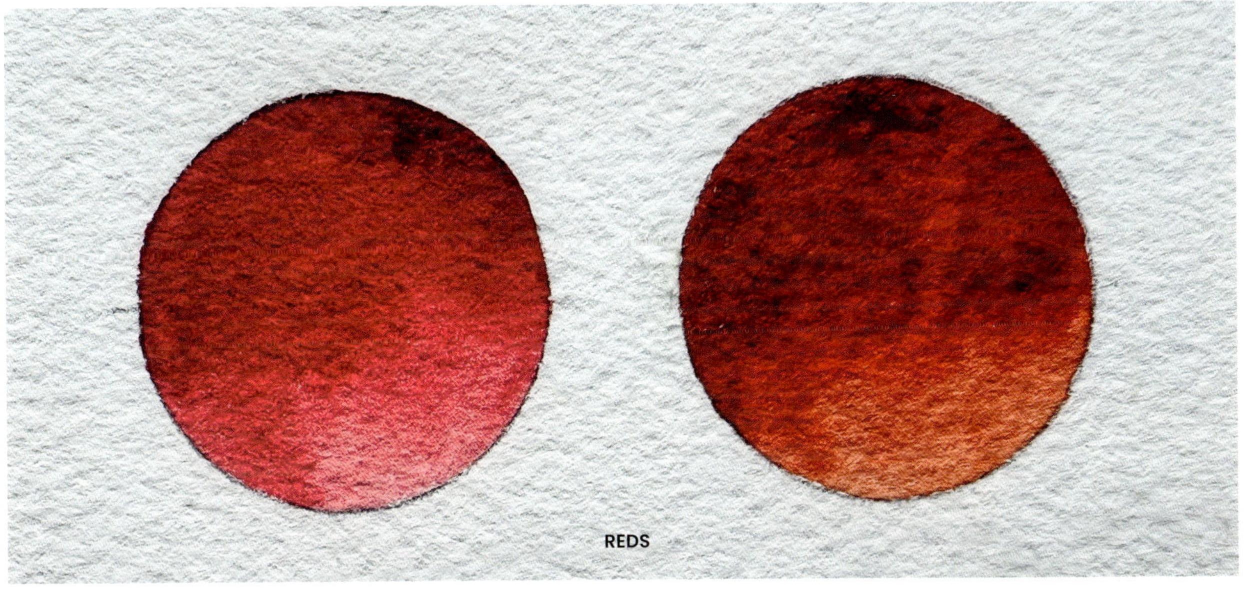

REDS

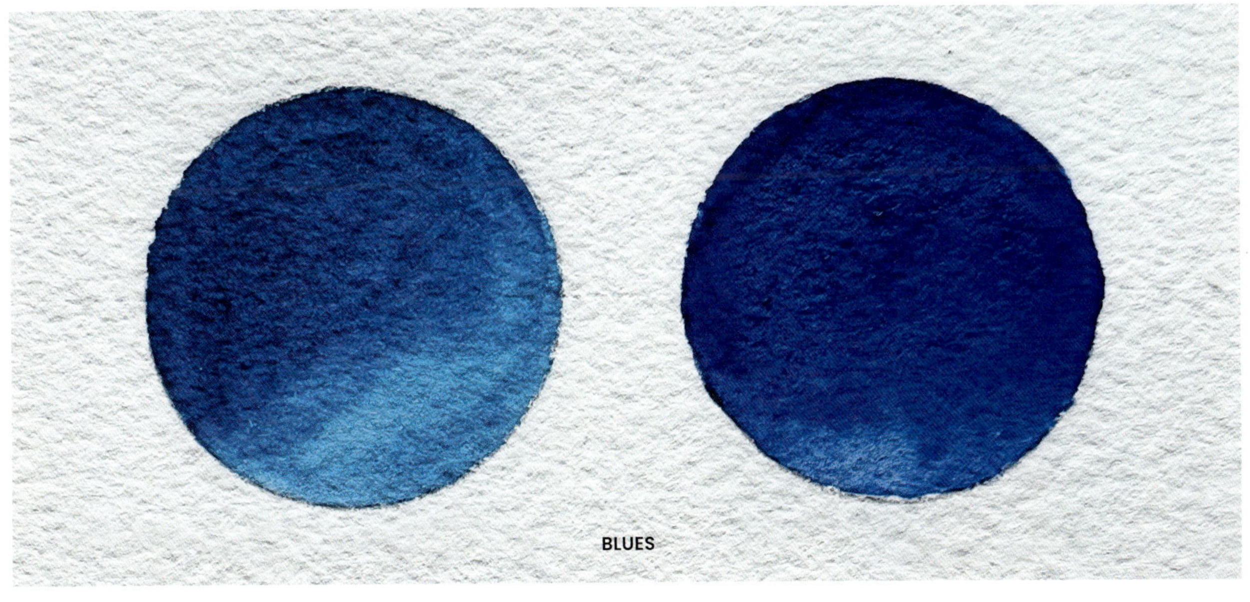

BLUES

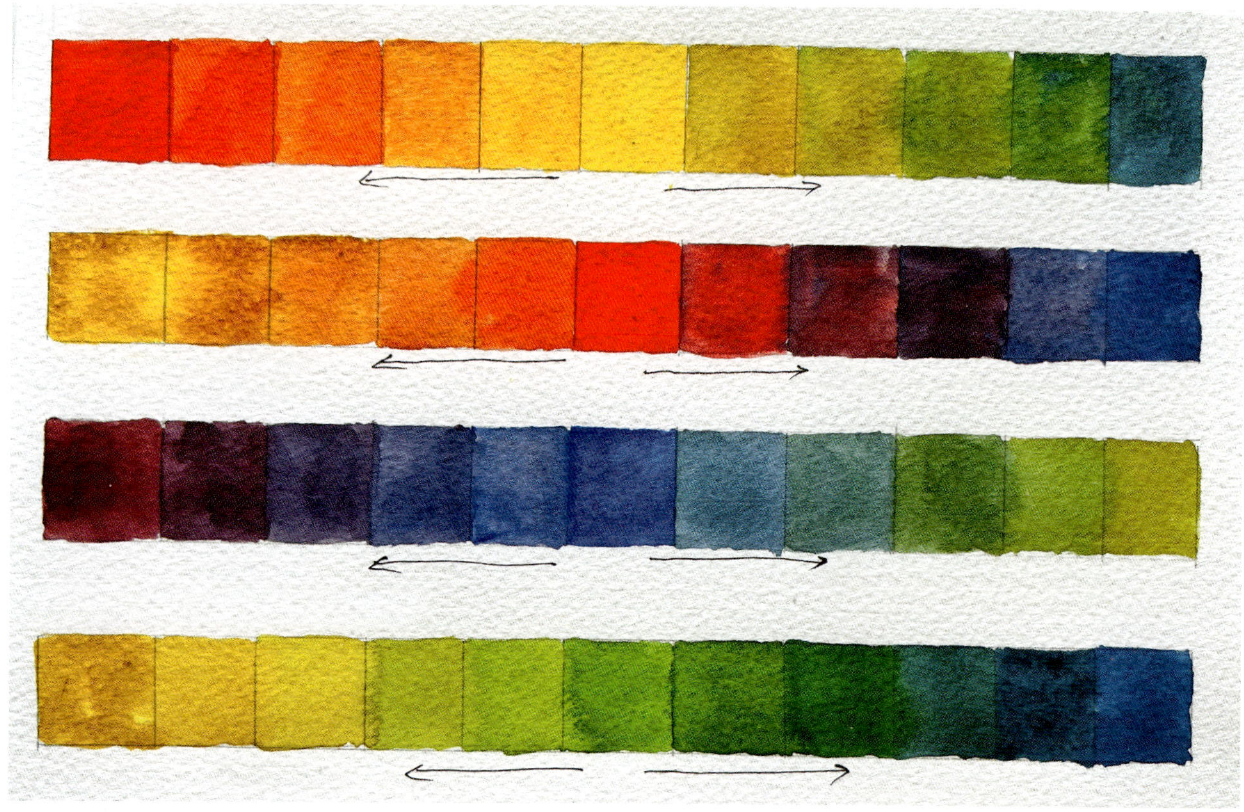

Creating cooler and warmer versions of yellow, red, blue, and green.

This information is very important to create beautiful color mixes and avoid muddy colors. This is because if you mix colors that are of the opposite bias, then you end up with colors that are less vibrant; that is, faded and possibly muddy.

We can easily make a color warm or cool. You can easily make a neutral red warm by adding more orange or yellow, or make it cool by adding purple or blue.

Blue is the most confusing color choice to create warm or cool versions. This is because you can either add a red or a yellow to the blue. Both are warm colors, so how do we decide which creates warm and which creates cool? It's simple. Out of red and yellow, the warmest is red; hence, adding red would make blue warmer, whereas adding yellow makes it more greenish and cooler.

Similarly, a yellow can be made warmer by adding warmer colors such as orange and red, or cooler by adding greens and eventually blues.

Split Primary Color Wheel

The split primary color wheel consists of the six warm and cool primaries, and the colors formed by them. The main circle consists of the most vibrant colors formed by the primaries of the same bias. For example, warm blue is biased toward red, and cool red is biased toward blue; the mix of these two colors creates the most beautiful purple color.

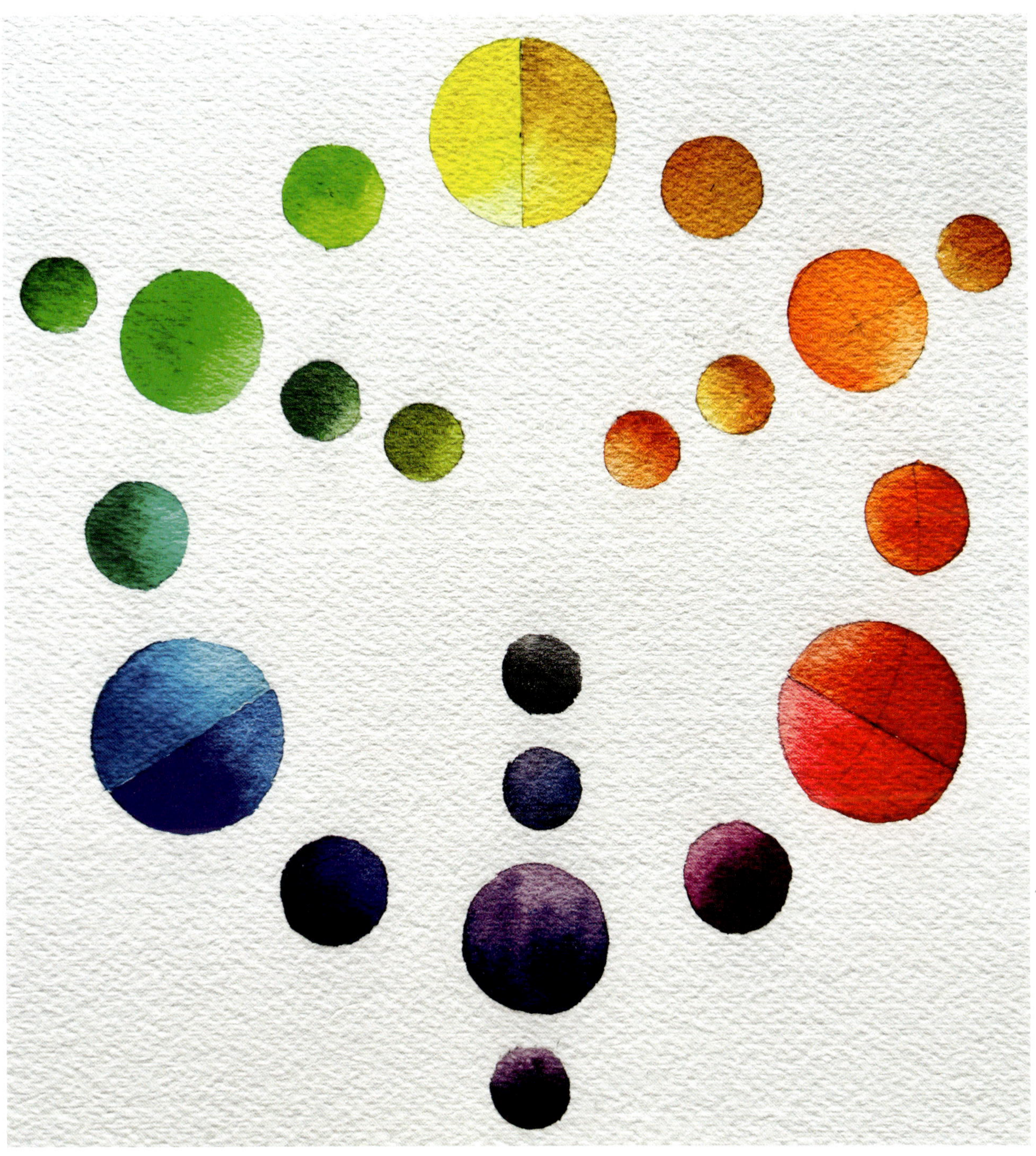

Dull and muted colors are formed when two primaries of opposite bias are mixed. The image shows the mix of a warm red and a cool blue. The cool blue is biased toward yellow, and the warm red is biased toward yellow; thus, you are essentially mixing all the three primaries together. This results in a muddy purple color.

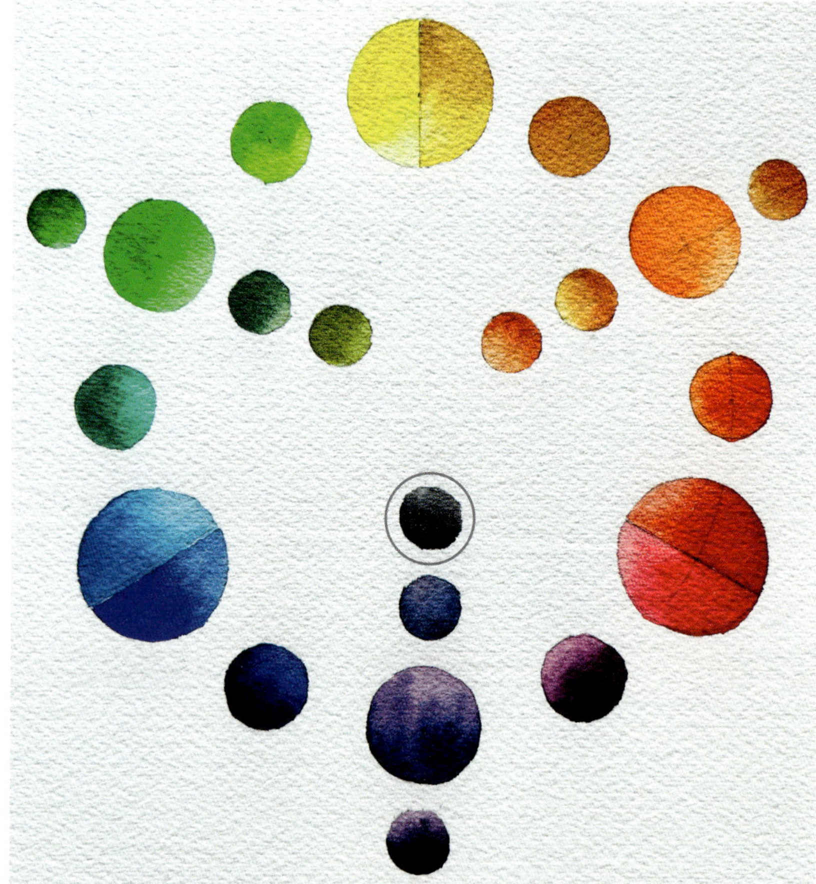

Have a look at the mixture of warm yellow and cool red. Warm yellow is biased toward red and the cool red toward blue; hence, the resulting orange looks dull.

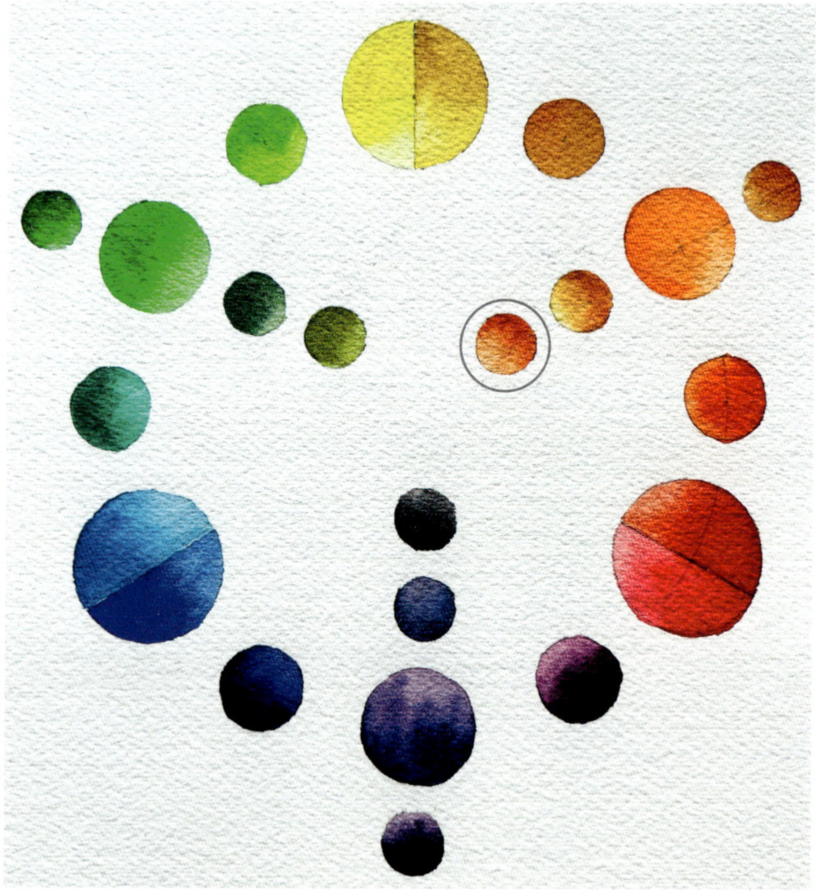

COLOR SATURATION

Saturation of a color is the intensity of the color. It refers to the brilliance or the richness of the color.

For example, cadmium orange is a high-saturation color and burnt sienna is a low-saturation color, but both colors are of the same hue, which is orange. Similarly, yellow ochre is less saturated than cadmium yellow, but both are a yellow hue.

It is useful to mute down a color when you're painting because you cannot find an object in a single-color saturation when you look with your naked eye. There will always be varying tones of it in different saturation levels. The easiest way to mute down a color is to add the complementary color to it. The second option is to add a gray or black tone to it. I prefer to use the complementary color method because when you add black to a color, it gets darker. On the other hand, when you add the complementary color, the saturation level of the color decreases, tending toward neutral and gray colors.

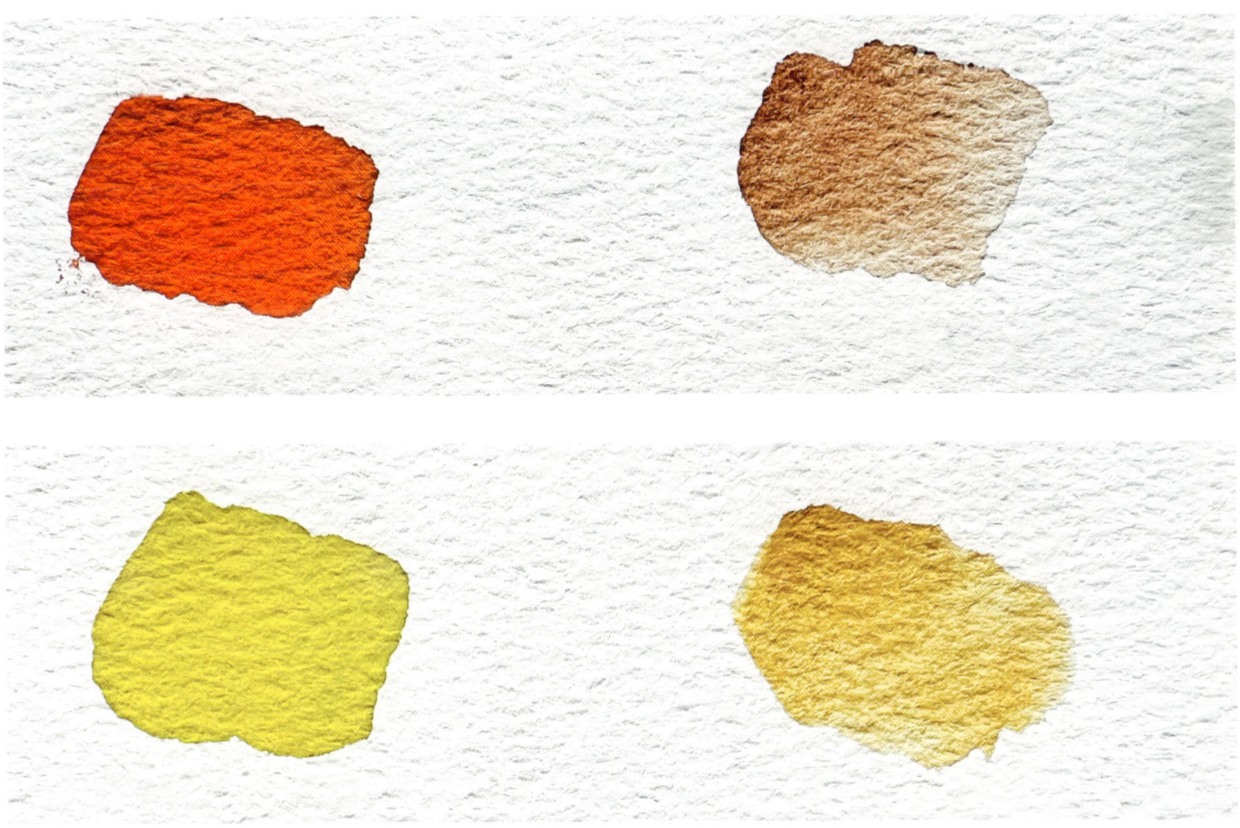

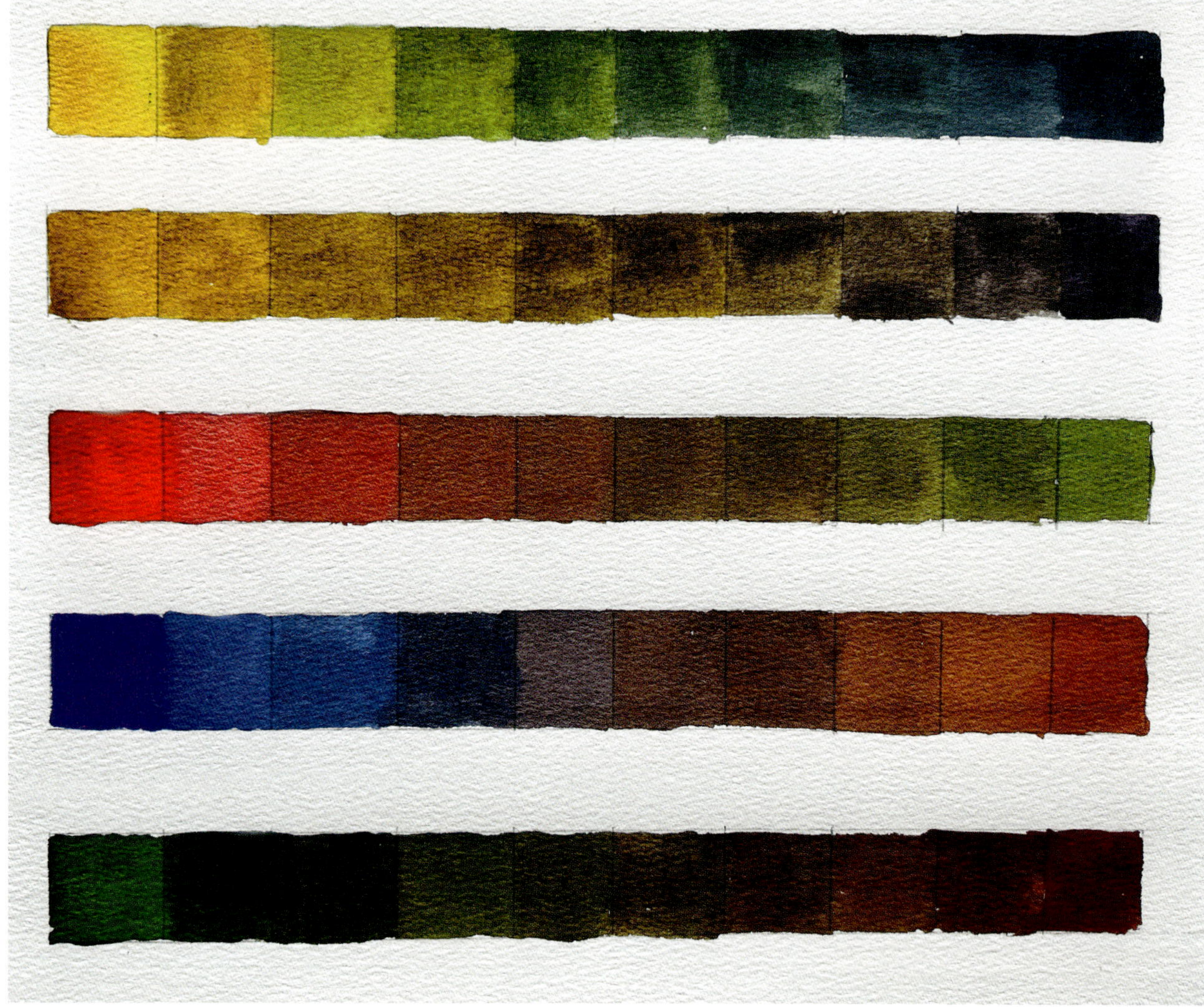

For example, here I've mixed green with ruby red gradually to decrease the saturation of the red. It decreases toward a neutral brown color, and as more green is added to it, the color gradually changes to muted green, then finally green.

Similarly, you can see that mixing orange with blue decreases the saturation of the blue.

Lastly, I've added red to green, and you can see a similar decrease in the saturation value until it reaches red. However, note that the green formed in the upper box and the green I started with is not the same, even though I have used the same green shade. This is because the green on the upper box is still contaminated with a little bit of red and hence is muted.

TONAL VALUE

Tonal value of a color shows the lightness and darkness of a color. The darkest value of a color is the color you get when it is used straight out of the tube. When you dilute the color with varying amounts of water, you get a tonal value scale.

There is a lot of importance to the tonal values of a color for a watercolor painting. The most important aspect is in depicting the subjects in a painting. The subjects that are far away from the viewer should be painted using lighter tones; as the subjects come closer to the viewer, they should get darker. Hence, the lightest tones of a color are used for background elements, while the darkest tone will be used for the foreground elements. This clarity in the use of the tones for a painting will give it depth and dimension.

Here, you can see the tonal value scale of Payne's gray, which has been created by adding more and more water to the darkest value until it becomes almost as transparent as the white of the paper.

With colors such as yellow, however, you can see that the darkest value is still bright and light. There is a way to darken this color or, in other words, increase the saturation of it. We can mix a dark color version with it, starting with orange, red, brown, and eventually black. This way we can create a darker value of the yellow shade.

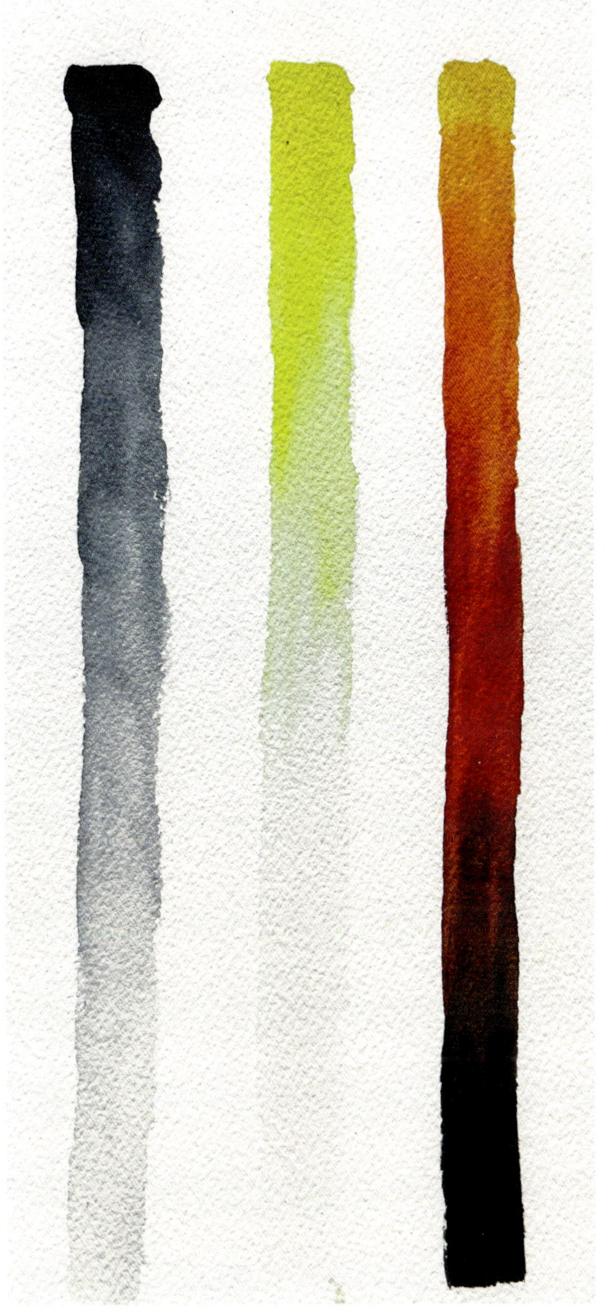

MY WATERCOLOR PALETTE

Below are the colors in my watercolor palette that I will be using for the step-by-step projects in this book.

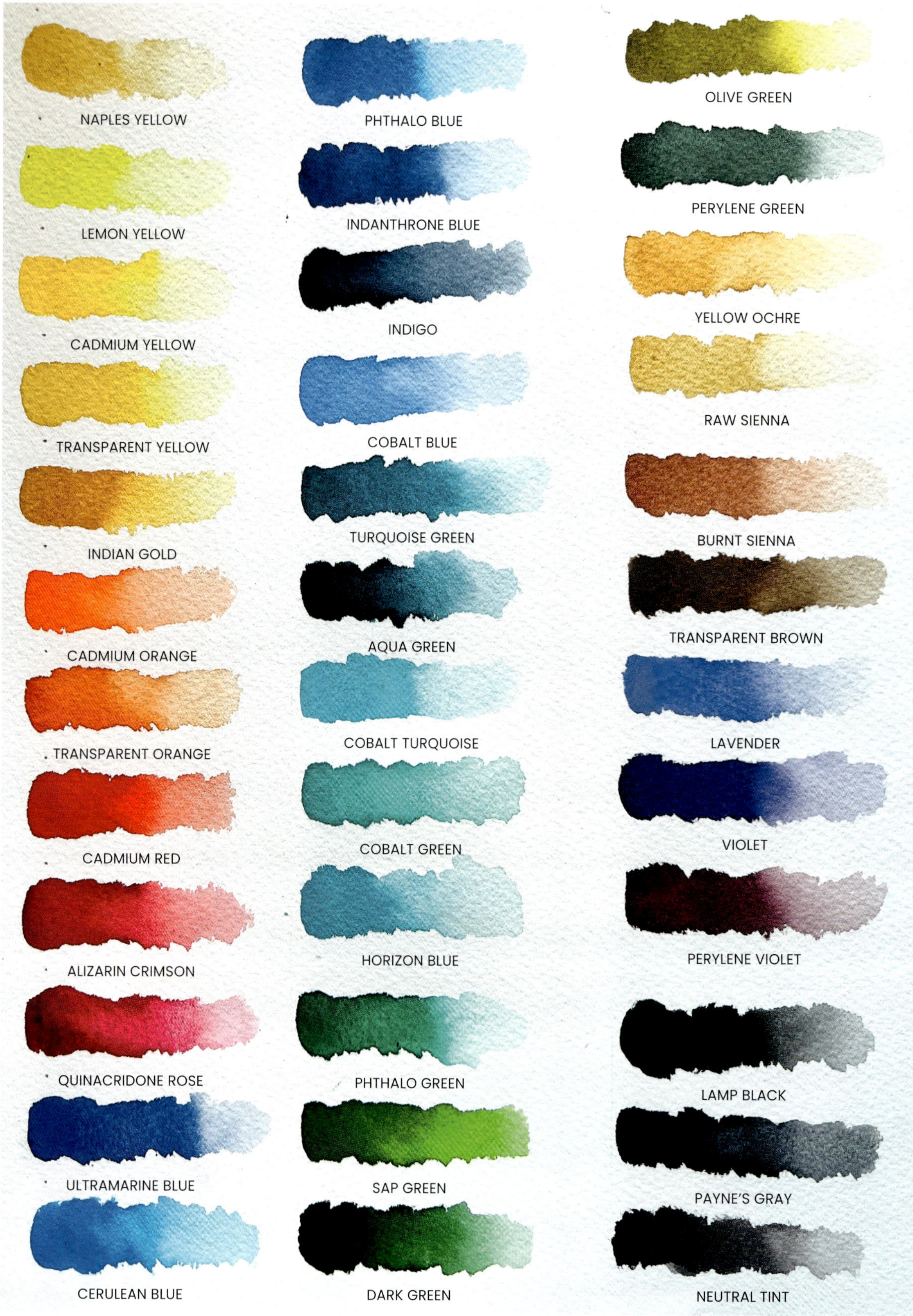

WATERCOLOR TECHNIQUES

There are several watercolor techniques that create beautiful effects on the paper. Understanding these techniques is the key to mastering watercolors. Make sure that you are thorough with learning the names of these different techniques as they will be useful for the step-by-step projects. I would also highly recommend practicing watercolor techniques on the paper with which you intend to paint the final projects because it is important that you understand how the paint behaves on that specific paper.

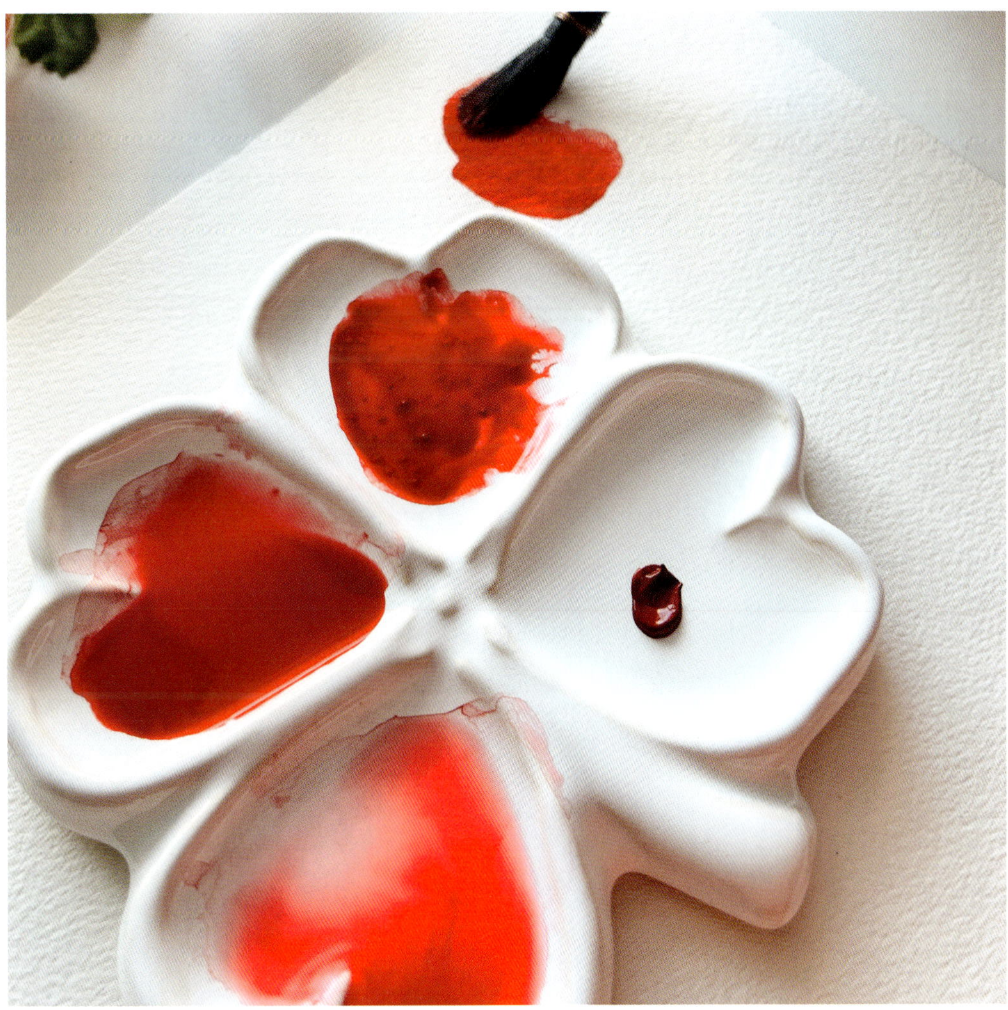

WATER CONTROL

Water is obviously the most essential component of watercolor painting. The movement of watercolor pigments on paper with the water is completely unpredictable, and this unpredictability is what makes this medium so interesting. The wetness of the watercolor pigments and the flow of water determines the outcome in a watercolor painting.

Here are some important concepts regarding water:

- We can use water to decrease the tonal value of a color.

- Different watercolor pigments behave differently when applied on wet paper. Some pigments disperse water, whereas some pigments are dispersed by water. You can see the two examples here.

- Use water to your advantage; it can carry pigment from one place to another.

- If there is more water on your brush than there is on the paper, it will create blooms or what is called the cauliflower effect.

- Paint spreads in water when applied on the top and it is impossible to predict its movement when the paper is laid flat on a surface.

- Water dries depending on the environment conditions. Apply more water multiple times if needed to keep the paper wet as desired. Always remember that hard lines are formed wherever the consistency of the water changes on the paper.

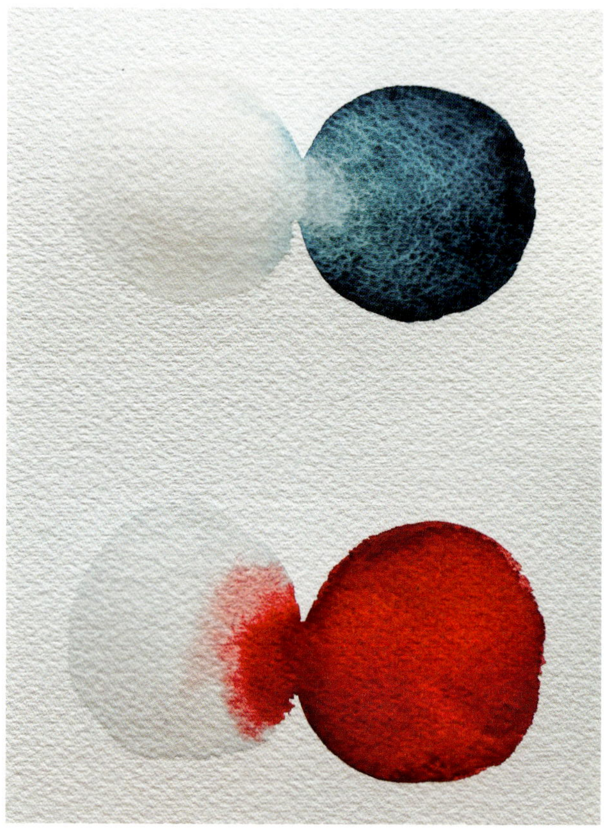

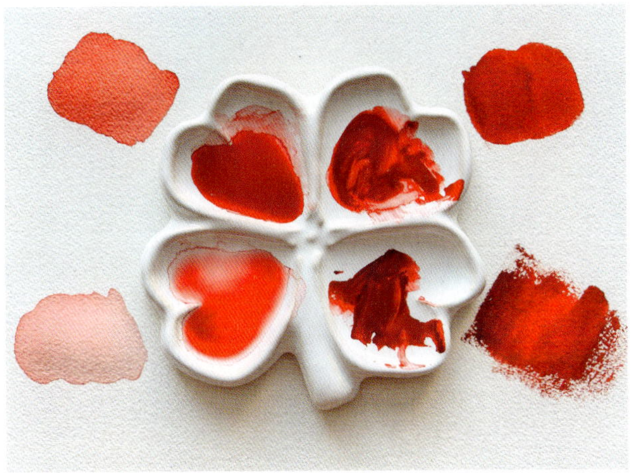

Water Consistency

It is important to understand the water to paint ratio that we need to use for different kinds of techniques. Hence, here are some consistencies that I will be discussing throughout this book.

Watery Consistency

This is mostly water (80%) with much less watercolor pigment (around 20%). This would be the lightest tone of the color that we are using.

Milky Consistency

This has a bit more pigment introduced to the watery consistency—around 40% pigment and 60% water. The mixture would be in the medium tonal range for the color used.

Creamy Consistency

This mixture is 60% pigment and 40% water. This is the best consistency for painting with the wet-on-wet technique. The mixture is smooth and almost feels like heavy cream.

Dry Consistency

You create this mixture by taking pigment directly out of the tube with a wet brush. The water to paint ratio is 1:4; that is, 20% water and 80% paint. It creates dry strokes when applied straight onto the paper and is the best consistency for dry-on-wet and dry-on-dry techniques.

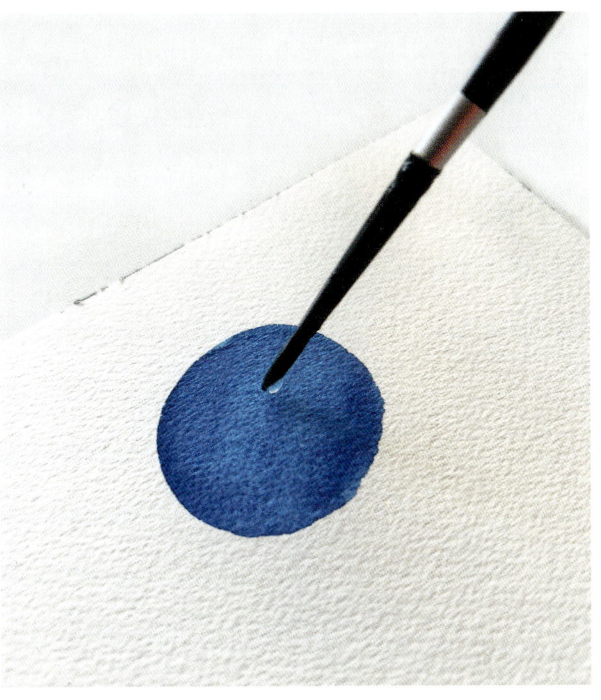

DROPPING WATER ONTO WET PAINT

THE DROP SPREADS PAINT, FORMING A BLOOM

PAINTING TECHNIQUES

When we refer to watercolor techniques such as wet-on-dry, the first word refers to the water consistency of the brush and the second to that of the paper.

Wet-on-Wet

As implied, this means applying wet paint to a wet surface. Apply an even coat of clear water to the paper, ensuring that there are no pools or uneven consistencies of water on the paper. A large, flat brush would be the best way to apply water for this purpose. You can repeat multiple times to ensure that this water does not get absorbed or dry up too fast. Then, using a round brush, pick up a creamy consistency of paint and apply it to the paper. You will see how the watercolor pigment spreads in the water.

To get the best wet-on-wet results, that is, for the paint to spread smoothly, make sure that the water consistency on your brush is lesser than the water consistency on the paper. I call this the **101 watercolor wet-on-wet rule.** Therefore, the creamy consistency is the best choice for the wet-on-wet technique.

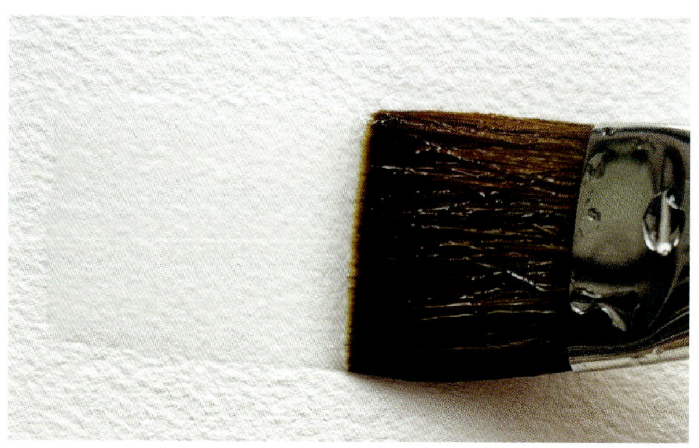

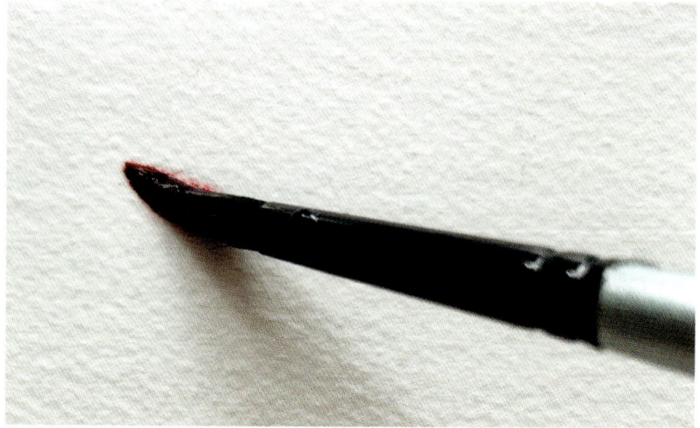

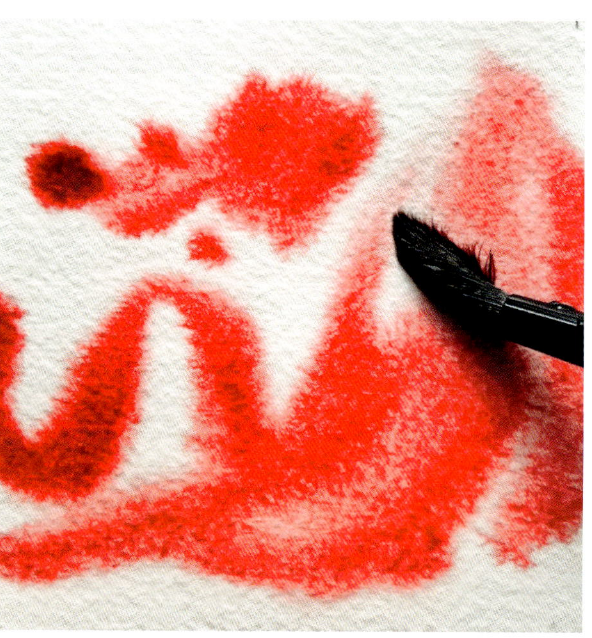

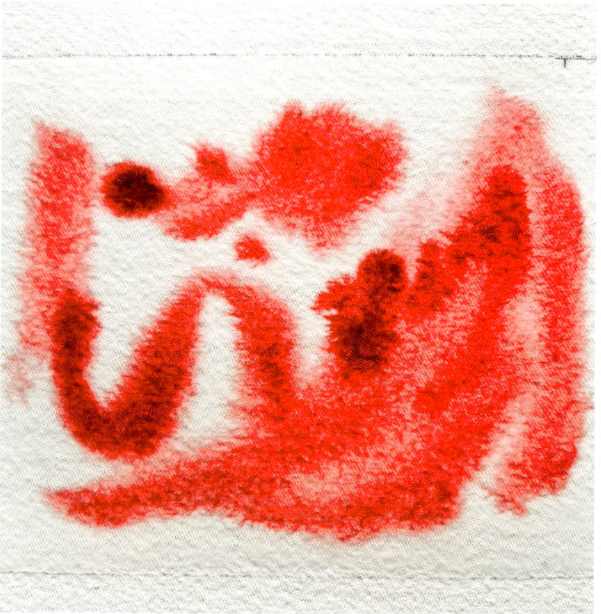

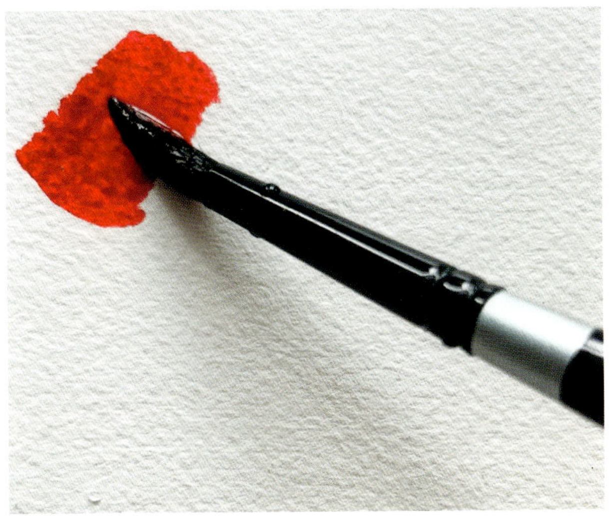
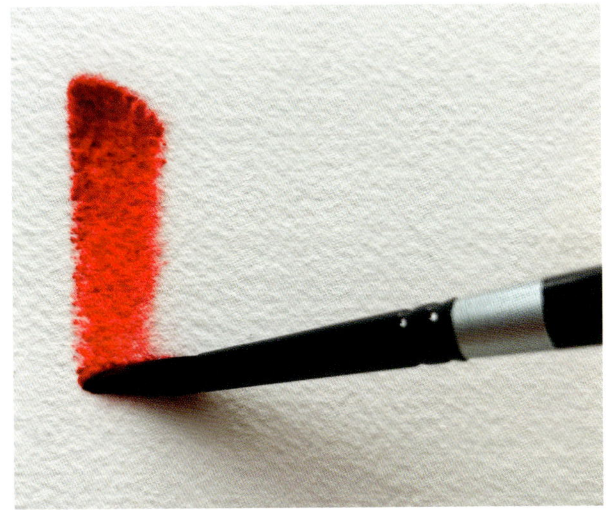
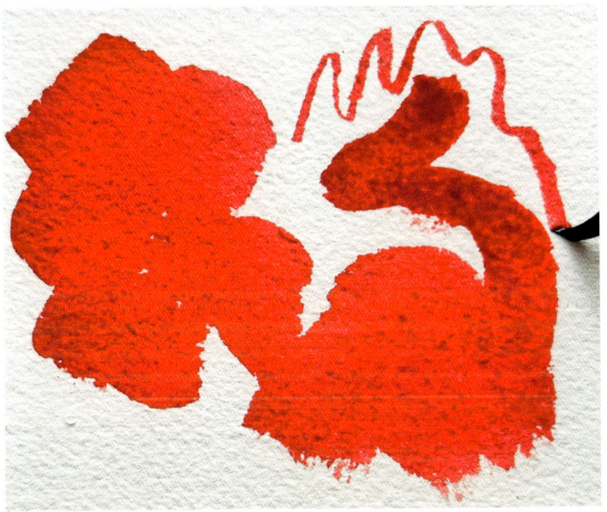
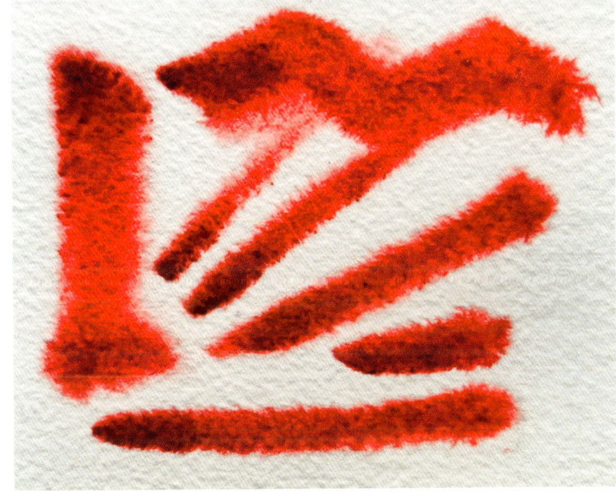

Wet-on-Dry

This means applying wet paint onto dry paper. The paper surface can be both clear as well as a surface with a dried layer of paint. You can create any shape with the brush when applying wet-on-dry strokes. However, when applying a wet-on-dry stroke on to an already existing dried paint layer, make sure that you do not rub a lot with the brush on the surface; the previous layer can get activated with water, causing undesired results. This technique can also be used for glazing, which involves painting over another layer with a second color so that the first layer is reflected underneath the second color.

Dry-on-Wet

This is an extension of the wet-on-wet technique, as it involves applying dry paint to a wet surface. Apply an even coat of water to the paper surface; the paint consistency on the brush should be dry. The paint stroke that you apply will not spread, but rather will stay at the same place and create a smoother edge to your stroke. This is ideal for creating shapes in the background or to create objects and elements under the misty effect.

Dry-on-Dry

Also known as the drybrush technique, this involves applying a dry consistency of paint onto dry paper. This is most useful when the paper has a texture because the dry stroke that you apply stays on the top surface of the texture without allowing the pigments to move into the troughs of the paper. Hence, a cold-pressed or rough-surfaced paper is ideal for this technique. Use a paper towel or cloth to absorb the excess water from the brush if there is any.

It creates a random dotted textured appearance to the strokes that you apply. It can be used to create the glistening sun beam effects when painting waves, or the texture on mountains, and so on.

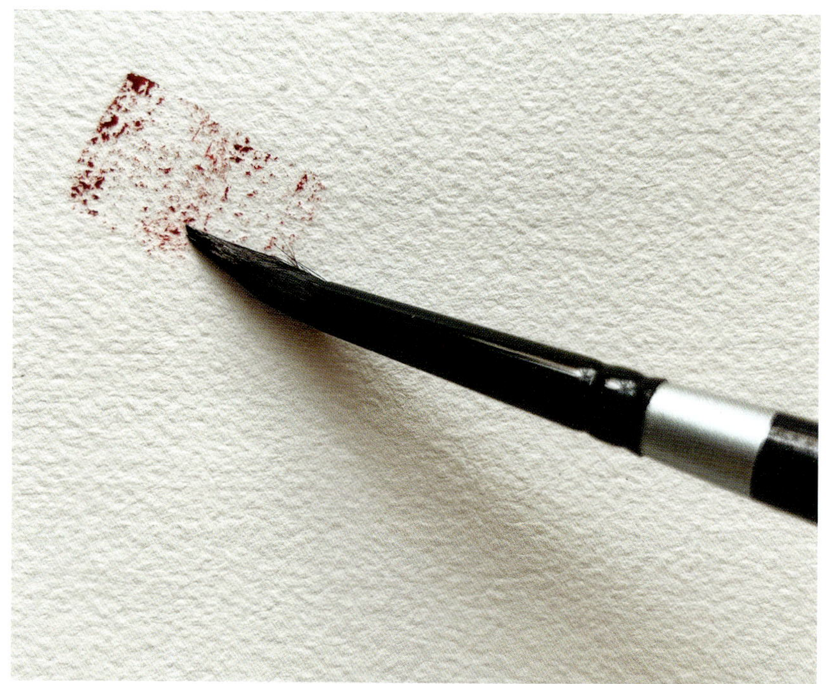

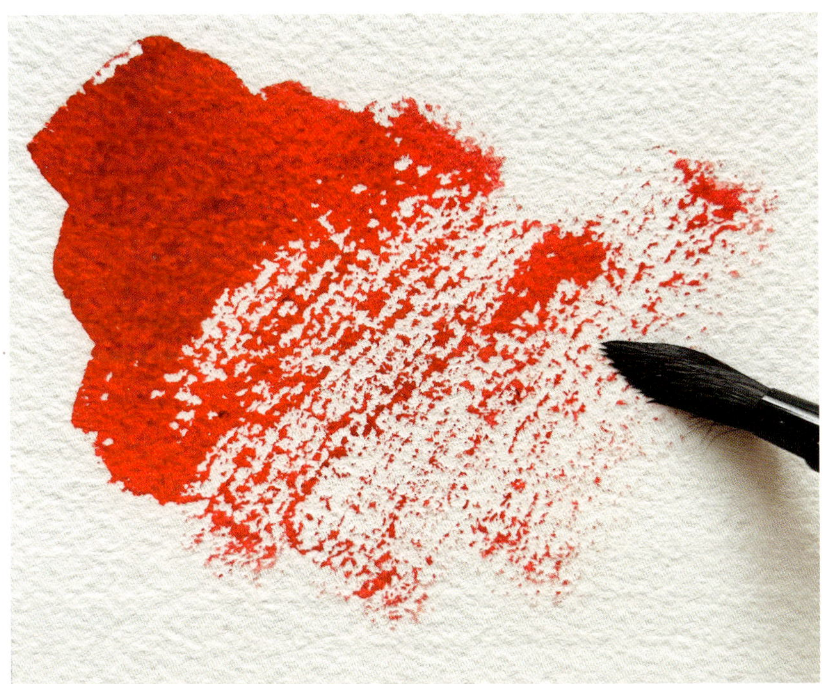

Mixed Wet & Dry

This is a combination of the wet-into-dry and the dry-on-dry methods. Start with a creamy consistency of paint on the brush and apply some strokes. As you keep applying, you will notice that the water in the brush decreases and the paint starts to come out dry. Sometimes you can use this effect to create beautiful textures like the waterfall effect in paintings.

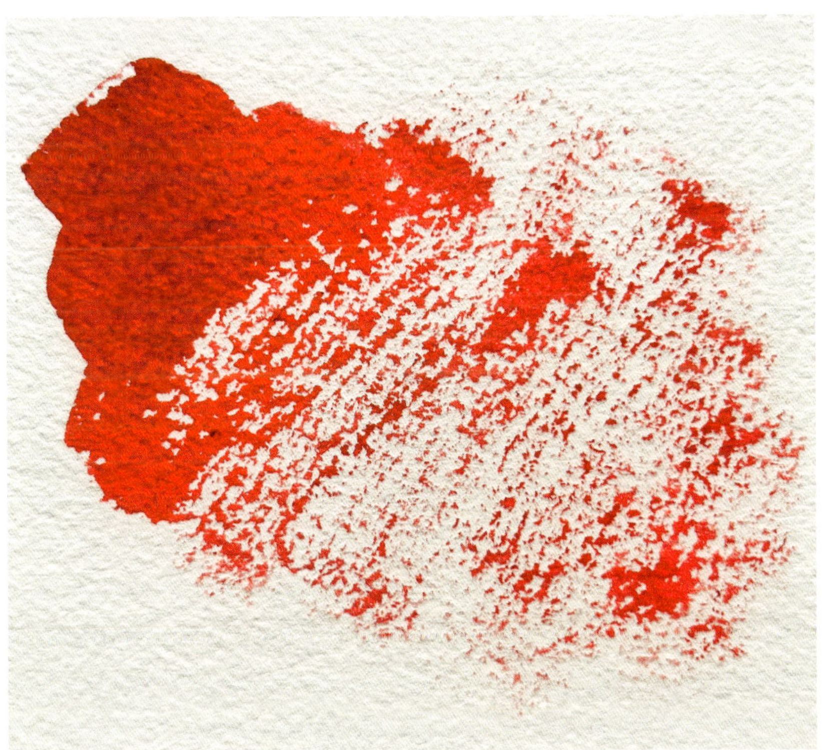

PAINTING TIME

Time is an important factor when it comes to watercolor paintings, especially when painting with the wet-on-wet technique. The water always dries up fast and you will eventually learn that time is always against you. Hence, we must learn to keep the paper wet when painting wet-on-wet strokes.

When there is a lot of work to be done on the wet paper, use a watery consistency of paint in the beginning, as the brush also absorbs some extra water from the surface of the paper as you paint. Decrease the water consistency gradually as you finish up the wet-on-wet technique—but always keep in mind the 101 watercolor wet-on-wet rule.

If the paint on the paper has started to dry, then do not work on the same area again; you may cause the water to create hard edges and blooms on the paper. The best method is to wait for the paper to dry out completely and then to reapply the water on the top, softly, without disturbing the underlying layer.

You can use time to your advantage in a watercolor painting. You can time yourself in such a manner that while you are applying your wet-on-wet stroke on one part of the paper, the other part of the paper is ready for you to start with the wet-on-dry strokes.

Similarly, the wet-on-dry strokes can be converted into dry-on-dry strokes by using the right consistency of paint in the brush and timing your strokes correctly on the paper.

While applying water on the paper, time is very important, as the longer you wait, the quicker the paper will dry. Make sure to understand the paper you are working on and to see the signs of the paper drying off. You can hold the paper at an angle to see the glaze of the water applied on it.

When working with multiple layers on the paper, make sure that the first layer is completely dry before proceeding. You can check the dryness of the paper by using the back of your hand and touching the paper. If it feels cool, then it is not completely dried yet.

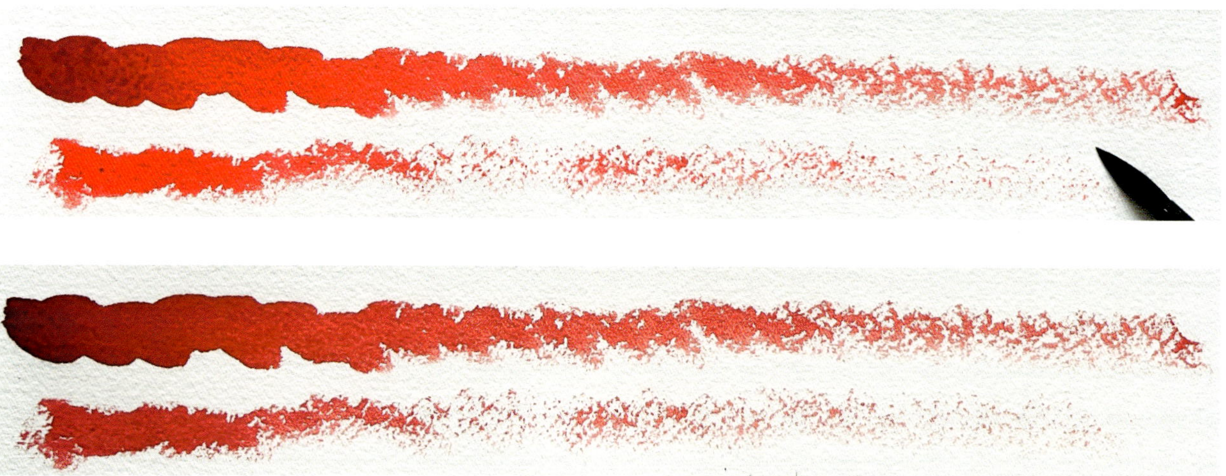

BLENDING METHODS

Flat Wash

Flat wash, as its name suggests, involves applying a flat layer of paint to the surface of the paper. The best way to create washes on the paper is to use an angle on the paper. For this purpose, I usually tilt the surface of the paper by keeping some object underneath so that gravity aids in moving the paint and the water. Remember to have your paper taped onto a board or some surface that can be lifted, or use the whole paper block without removing the sheet from it.

Start by applying a large stroke with your brush. Use a milky consistency of paint and observe the water accumulating at the bottom of the stroke area. This is known as "the drop." The drop, or puddle of water, at the bottom will help to create the next strokes on the paper without forming a hard edge at the end of your previous stroke. Use this to your advantage as you gradually move down while applying the flat wash.

You can also use a flat brush to apply the flat wash. Another alternative to the wet-on-dry application using the drop method would be to use the wet-on-wet method to apply the wash of paint on the surface of the paper.

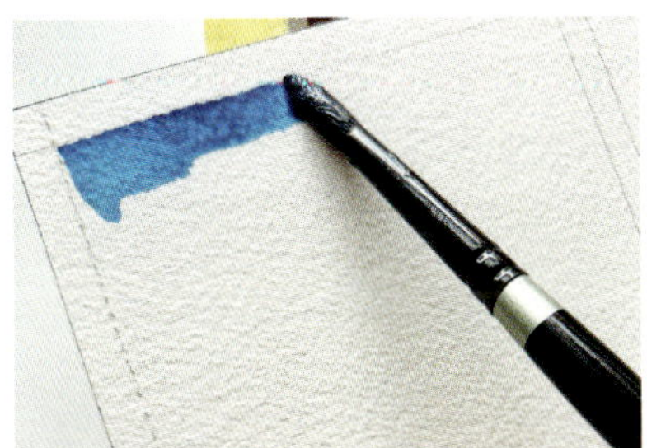

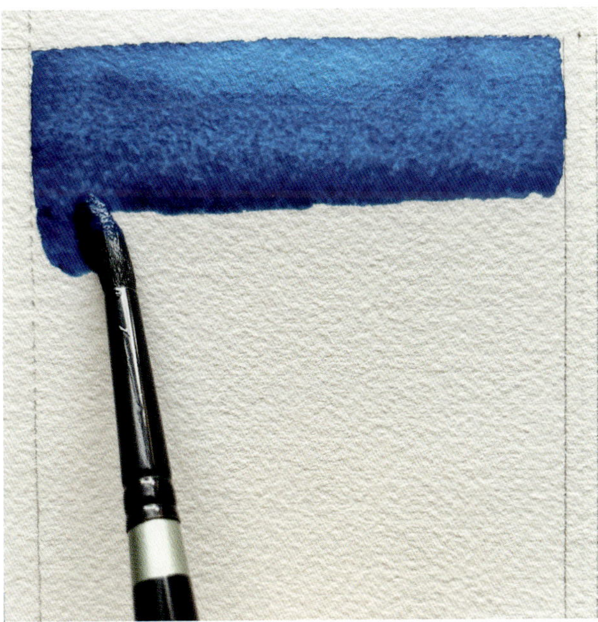

Gradient Wash

The gradient wash is similar to flat wash, except that the tone of the paint decreases as you move down the paper. The best method to apply a gradient wash is to use the wet-on-wet method. Apply an even consistency of water on the area in which you want to create a gradient, and then start with a creamy consistency of paint. The idea is to gradually fade out the color on the paper as you move your brush swiftly toward the bottom. If you have picked up a good, creamy consistency of paint at the beginning, you may not need to pick up the paint again.

If, while reaching toward the bottom of the paper, you find that the paint is still not transparent enough, you can wash off the remaining pigment from the brush and just use water to tone down the transparency of the color toward the bottom.

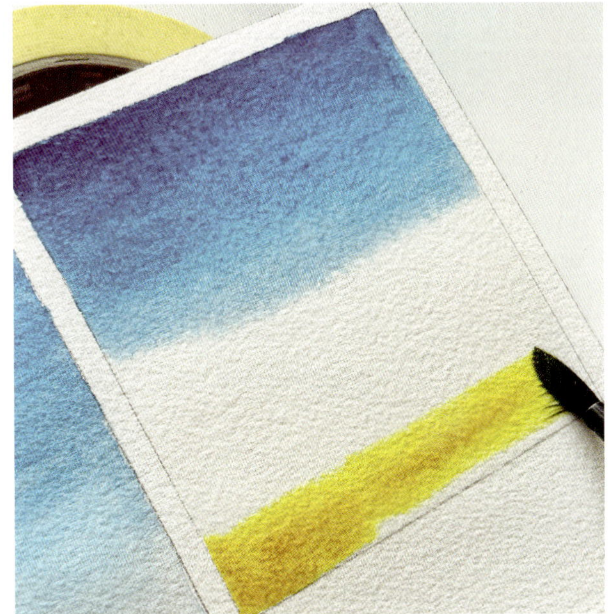

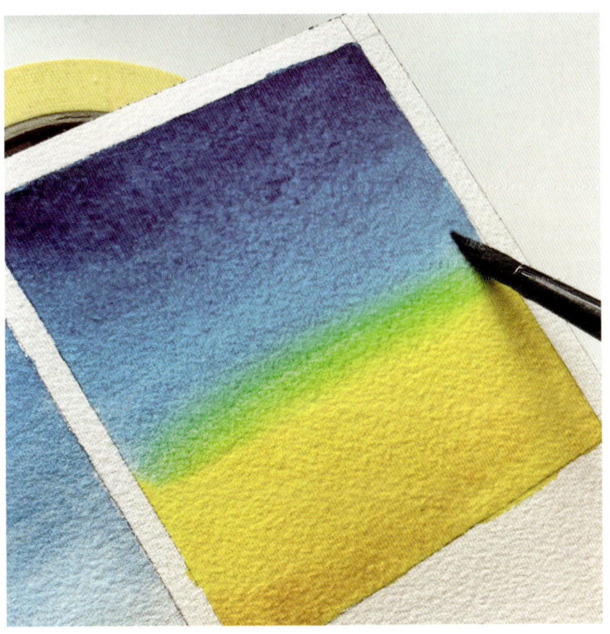

Variegated Wash

A variegated wash is a mix of two or more colors blended such that the colors used are visible as flat washes, and the place where they blend has a mix of those colors. The wet-on-wet method is the best technique to evenly blend colors on the paper.

Apply an event coat of water on the paper, then start with one color at the top and apply a flat wash. Stop around the middle and then start with the second color, moving from the bottom toward the top in a similar manner. As you reach the middle, start moving your brush swiftly from the left to the right and vice versa to create an even blend of the two colors in the middle. Always remember to wash excess paint from your brushes, especially when using a light and dark color. For example, here I have used a yellow and a blue color, and since blue is very dominant compared to the yellow, I make sure to always blend from the bottom toward the top and to get rid of excess blue pigment from my brush.

ADDITIONAL WATERCOLOR TECHNIQUES

Wet-on-Wet Splatters

Splatters are created by tapping a brush loaded with a creamy consistency of paint with your finger or another brush while holding it closer to the surface of the paper. Wet-on-wet splatters, as its name suggests, implies that you will be splattering onto a wet surface. You can see how the yellow splatters have turned out on the wet blue paint. Splatters are completely random; you can't predict where they will be on the surface of the paper. If you intend the splatters to be only on a certain area of your painting, you can cover the rest of the paper with something so that the splatters fall only to desired place. However, when the surface is wet, this is difficult; you may not be able to place something on the surface. I have observed that using my index finger to tap on the brush while holding it with the other fingers of the same hand yields a bit more control over the splattering process.

Wet-on-Dry Splatters

This involves splattering paint onto a dry surface. Although the splattering is still random, the paint will not spread, creating an effect more like tiny dots on the surface. This is ideal to paint snow, stars, or random details on a painting.

Toothbrush Splatters

These splatters involve loading up a toothbrush with paint and then running your finger across the bristles while holding it near the paper. This creates tiny, concentrated splatters—quite different in look to the splatters with the brush. You can do this with both the wet-on-wet and wet-on-dry method.

Blooms or Cauliflower Effect

This effect is created when the water pushes the pigment away on the paper and creates small shapes like cauliflower or blooms. To create this effect, simply use a brush loaded with water and splatter it on the wet paint.

Using a Sea Sponge

A sea sponge can be used to create certain textures on the paper. You can dip the sea sponge in wet paint and then dab it onto the paper. It can be dabbed to create any shape you want.

Using Melamine Sponge

Melamine sponge, otherwise known as magic eraser in the artist's world, is a very useful tool that can be used to remove dried-up pigment from the paper. When the paint has already dried, you can wet a small melamine sponge and run it across the surface where you want to lift the paint. The lifting process is smooth and creates soft edges. This is highly useful to lift off sunlight reflection drops when painting water.

Using Salt

Adding salt to wet paint creates a different kind of bloom effect. Salt absorbs water and can be used to create textures in watercolor. Sprinkle some normal table salt on wet paint and you will see the magic. I have used fine salt here, but if you have larger crystals, you will observe that they create different sized blooms depending upon the size of the crystal.

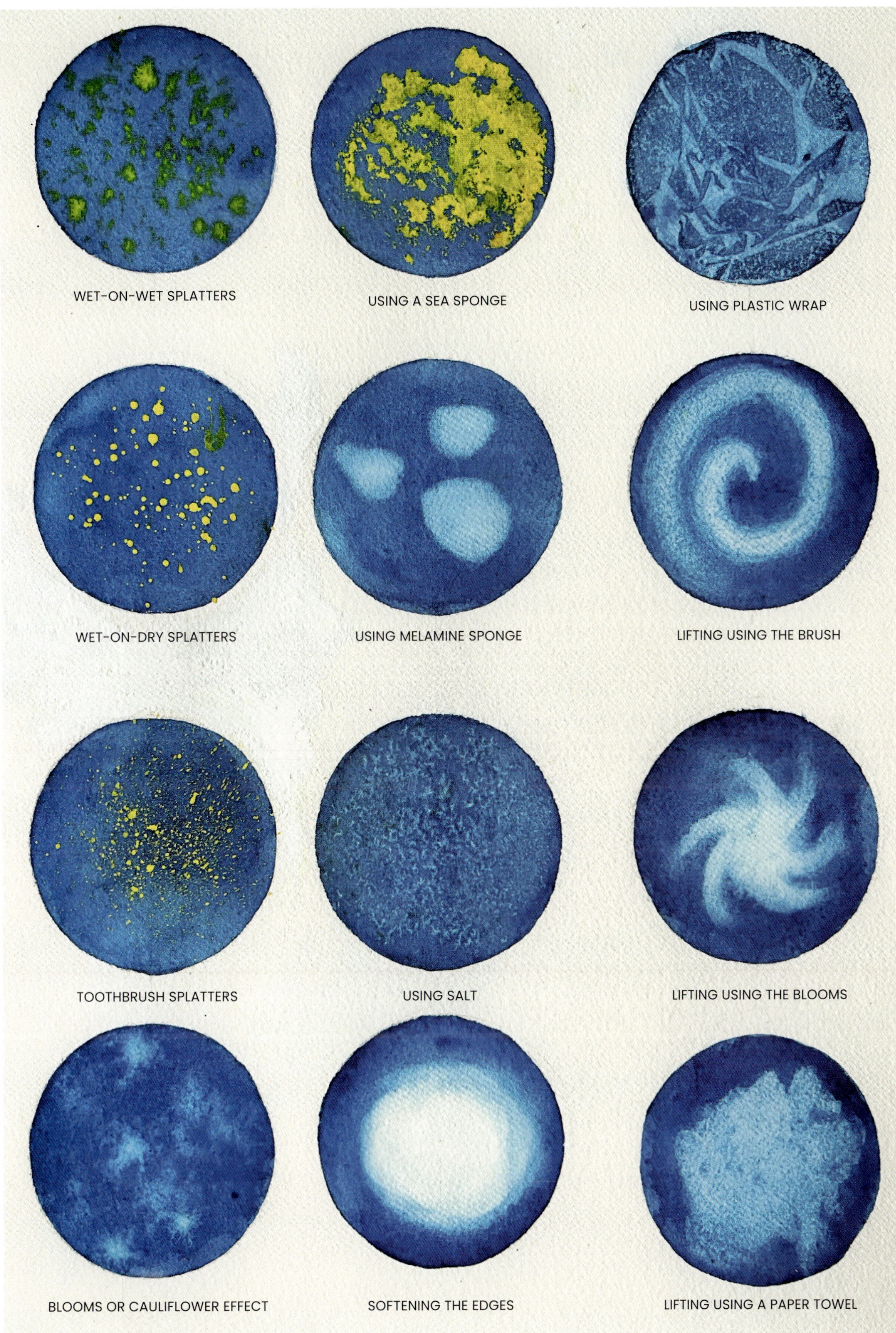

WET-ON-WET SPLATTERS
USING A SEA SPONGE
USING PLASTIC WRAP
WET-ON-DRY SPLATTERS
USING MELAMINE SPONGE
LIFTING USING THE BRUSH
TOOTHBRUSH SPLATTERS
USING SALT
LIFTING USING THE BLOOMS
BLOOMS OR CAULIFLOWER EFFECT
SOFTENING THE EDGES
LIFTING USING A PAPER TOWEL

Softening the Edges

This is one of the best methods to get softer edge to your objects when painting with watercolors. Do a wet-on-dry application and then run a wet brush repeatedly across the edge where the wet-on-dry stroke ended. You will see that the brush pulls the pigment and creates a softer look to the edge of that stroke. Here, I have applied paint just to the outer area of the circle and then used this edge-softening method to soften the area toward the inside of the circle.

Using Plastic Wrap

Normal household kitchen plastic wrap creates a very interesting effect in watercolors. Start by applying a wet stroke on the paper, then cut a piece of plastic wrap and stick it on the top of this application so that there are a lot of folds and creases. Wait for the paint to completely dry before removing the plastic wrap. You will see a very beautiful and amazing texture on the areas where the creases and folds were. This is because these folds allowed the paint to settle in different consistencies on the paper, creating crisscross lines.

Lifting Using the Brush

This is the basic lifting method to lift off paint from the paper while it is still wet. Repeatedly glide a damp brush across the area where you would like to lift off the paint. Make sure you wash the brush after each pass so that the paint you removed from the paper is washed off from the brush and not accidentally applied back on the paper. Also make sure that your brush is damp and not wet, because adding extra water to the paper through your brush can create blooms. Use a paper towel to absorb extra moisture from the brush. Here, I lifted off in a spiral shape.

Lifting Using the Blooms

This method is a combination of the blooms and the lifting using the brush method. Use your brush to drop water droplets on the area where you want to lift off the paint. Remember that water displaces the pigment. Then, immediately use the brush to lift off paint and this excess water in any desired shape.

Lifting Using a Paper Towel

This involves using a paper towel to absorb the pigment from the paper. You can use the paper towel to dab onto the wet paint; it absorbs paint from the paper, creating white areas. This is highly useful for creating cloudy shapes in the sky.

PERSPECTIVE

To give the viewer a sense of depth and space in our painting, it is absolutely essential that we capture perspective. If the painting lacks perspective, then it will not make any sense and it will look unreal. The two major types of perspective are linear perspective and aerial perspective.

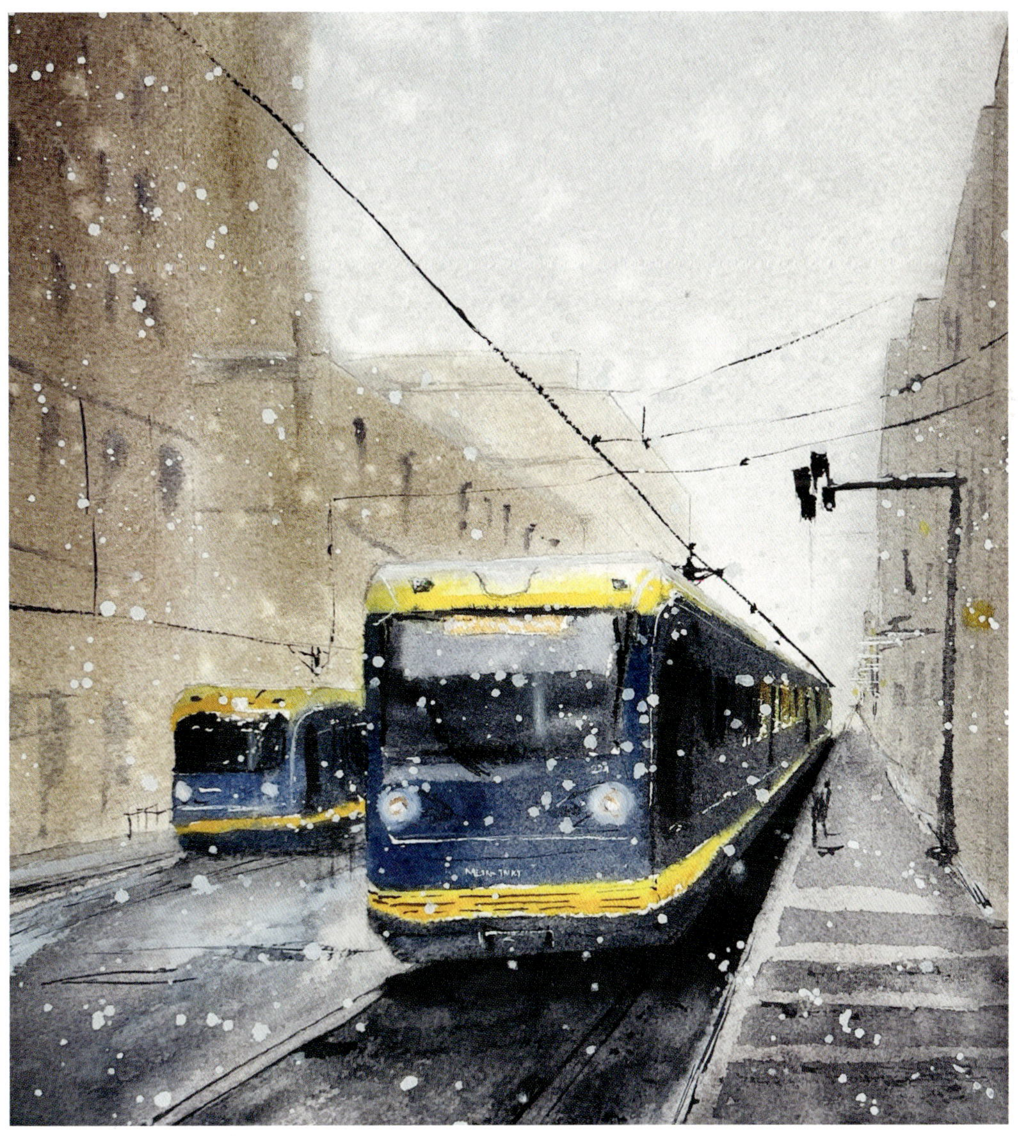

LINEAR PERSPECTIVE

Linear perspective is the concept of creating an illusion of depth in the painting using converging lines. All the parallel lines in the painting's composition converge to a vanishing point that is fixed at the horizon level in the painting.

- Determine the horizon level in the composition of your painting. This would always be your eye level or the eye level of people in the painting when standing on a noninclined surface.

- The vanishing points are always on the horizon line. This is the point where all the parallel lines in the painting converge to, creating depth by giving the illusion of objects getting smaller toward the horizon.

- Sometimes the vanishing points may be outside the paper on the level of the horizon line itself and you may have to use your imagination to draw the converging lines.

- The horizon line typically divides the sky from the ground. The objects at the horizon line are the furthest in a painting; as we go further away from the horizon line toward the top or bottom of the paper, we get closer to the viewer in the painting.

We will discuss the two basic forms of linear perspective here, namely one-point and two-point perspective.

One-Point Perspective

This implies that there is only one vanishing point on the horizon. This is useful for straight roads and mostly for objects that are directly facing you. Note that all the parallel lines converge to that single point. Even if the heights of the buildings or other objects in the painting may differ, you will note that adding the parallel lines converging to the vanishing point gives a sense of realism to the drawing.

Two-Point Perspective

This is the case where there are two vanishing points on the horizon line. It is usually used when standing at a crossroads and you can see the two sides of the objects fading further away. Here you will have to use both the vanishing points to draw the converging lines of the sides of objects, such as buildings and roads.

Make sure that both of the vanishing points are placed reasonably apart to prevent the distortion of the image. They can also be well outside the paper on the horizon line.

A third point of convergence can also be established if the object we are trying to draw is very tall and hence needs to depict the illusion of depth along its height.

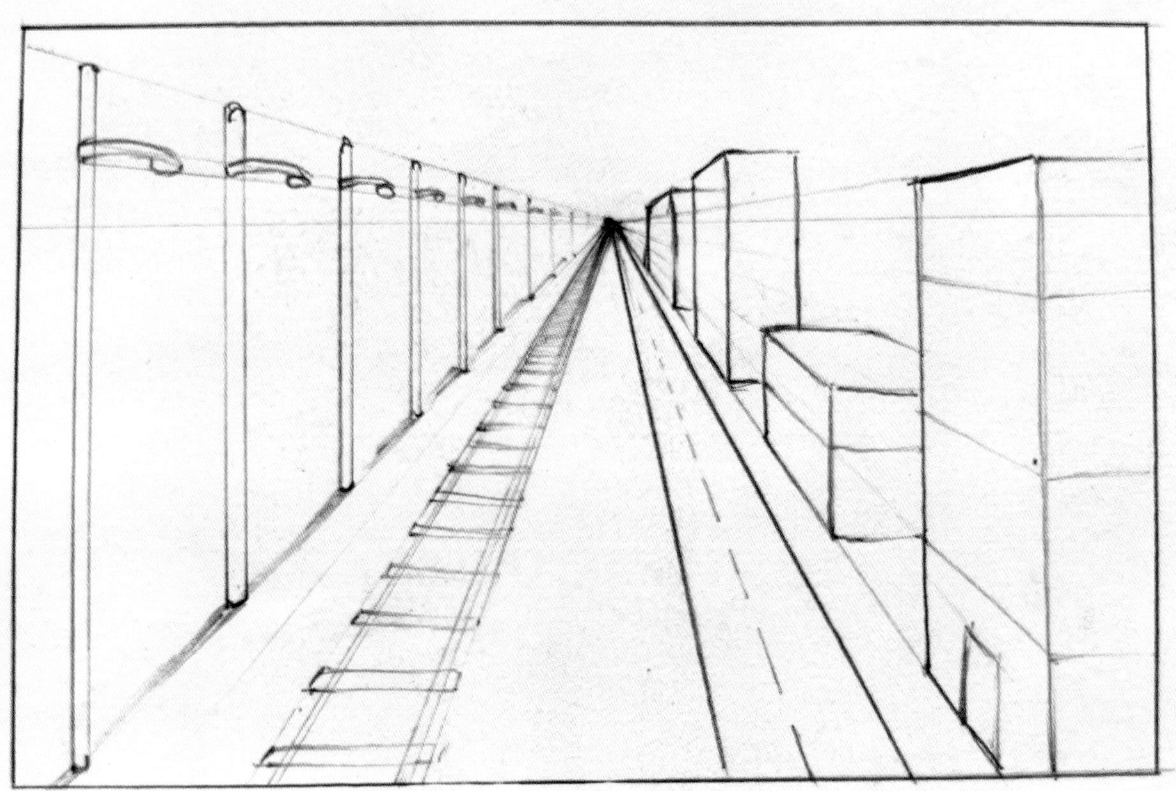

One-Point Perspective

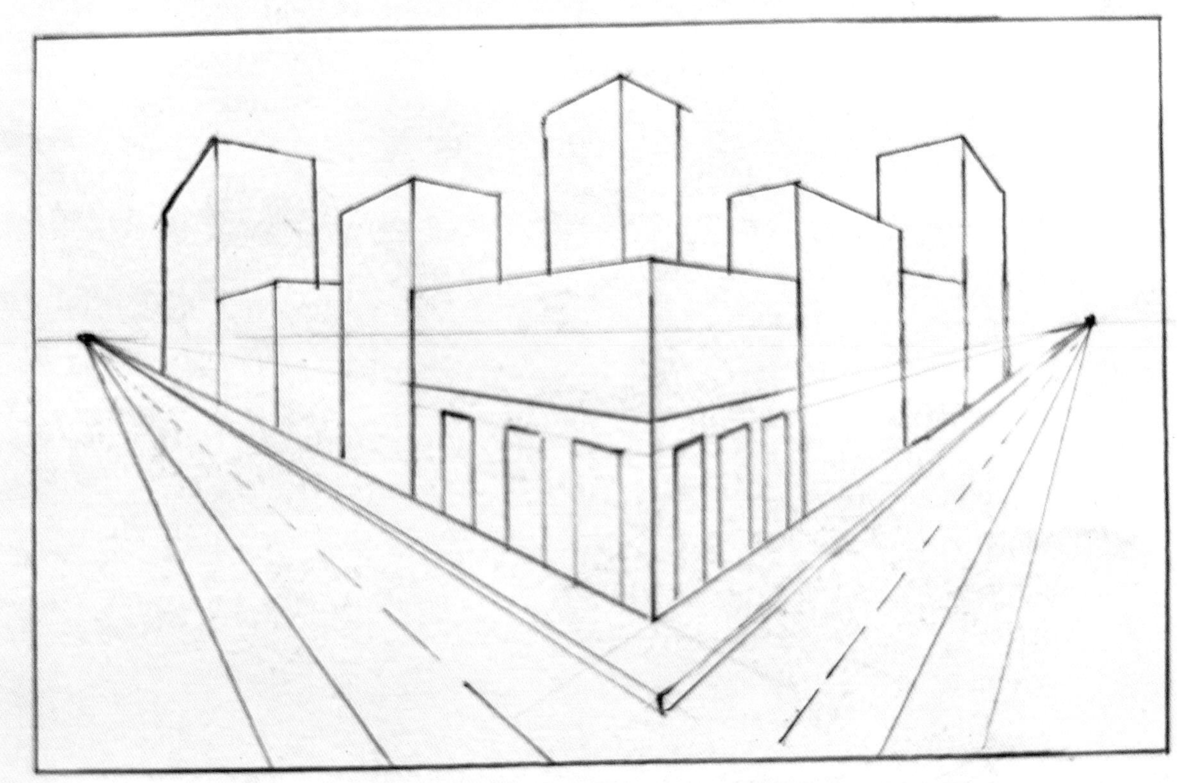

Two-Point Perspective

AERIAL PERSPECTIVE

Aerial perspective, also known as atmospheric perspective, is the art of creating the illusion of depth and spatial awareness in a painting by using several techniques to depict the furthest and closest objects. It can be done in various ways, such as by modulating the colors of things seen at a distance, making softer edges on the furthest objects, and creating crisp and fine details on objects that are closer to the viewer.

As you can see in the first image, there isn't much illusion of depth; the mountains, which are further away in the painting, are made with clear, detailed edges. This is purely for illustrative purposes; however, if you wish to divert the focus of the viewer to the mountains, then it is okay to do so.

In the second image, the mountains have been painted using a dry-on-wet method that makes a softer edge; this pushes the mountains further back, giving an atmospheric effect. The third image depicts the mountains painted in a cooler tone in a wet-on-wet manner, which further pushes it backward and has a misty effect.

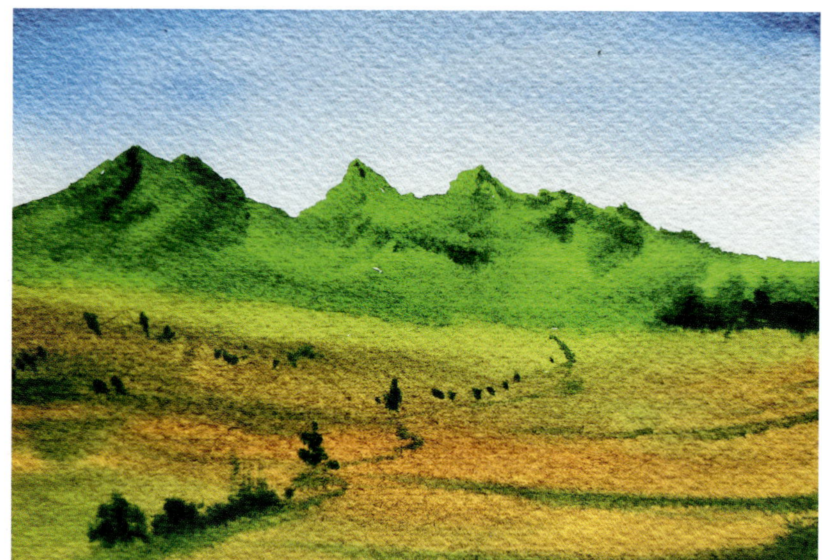

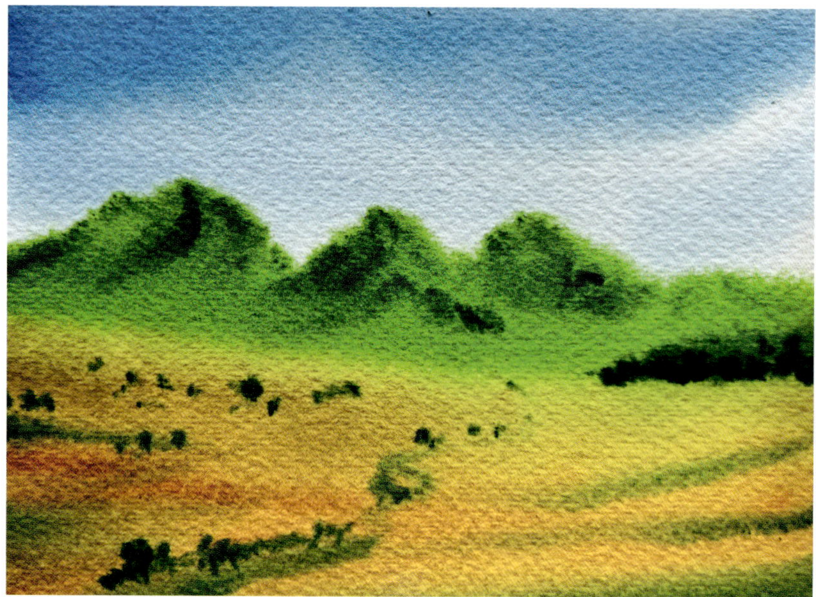

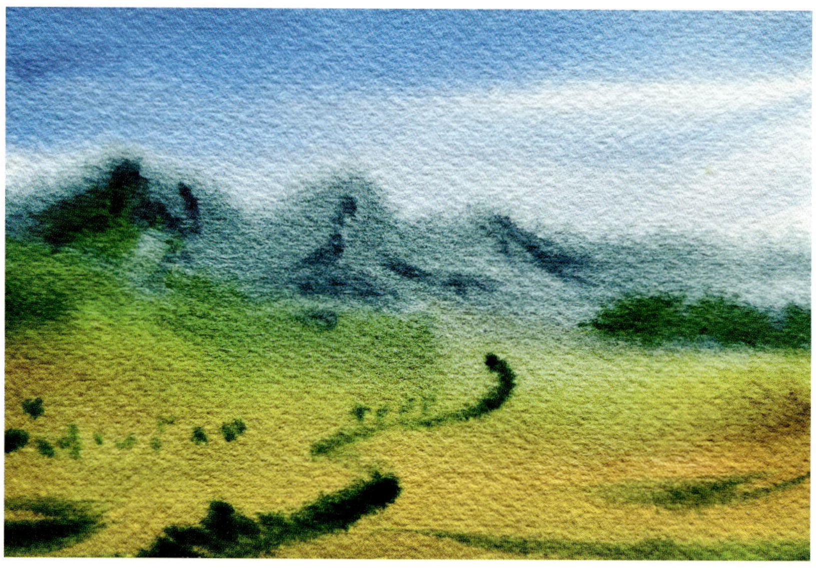

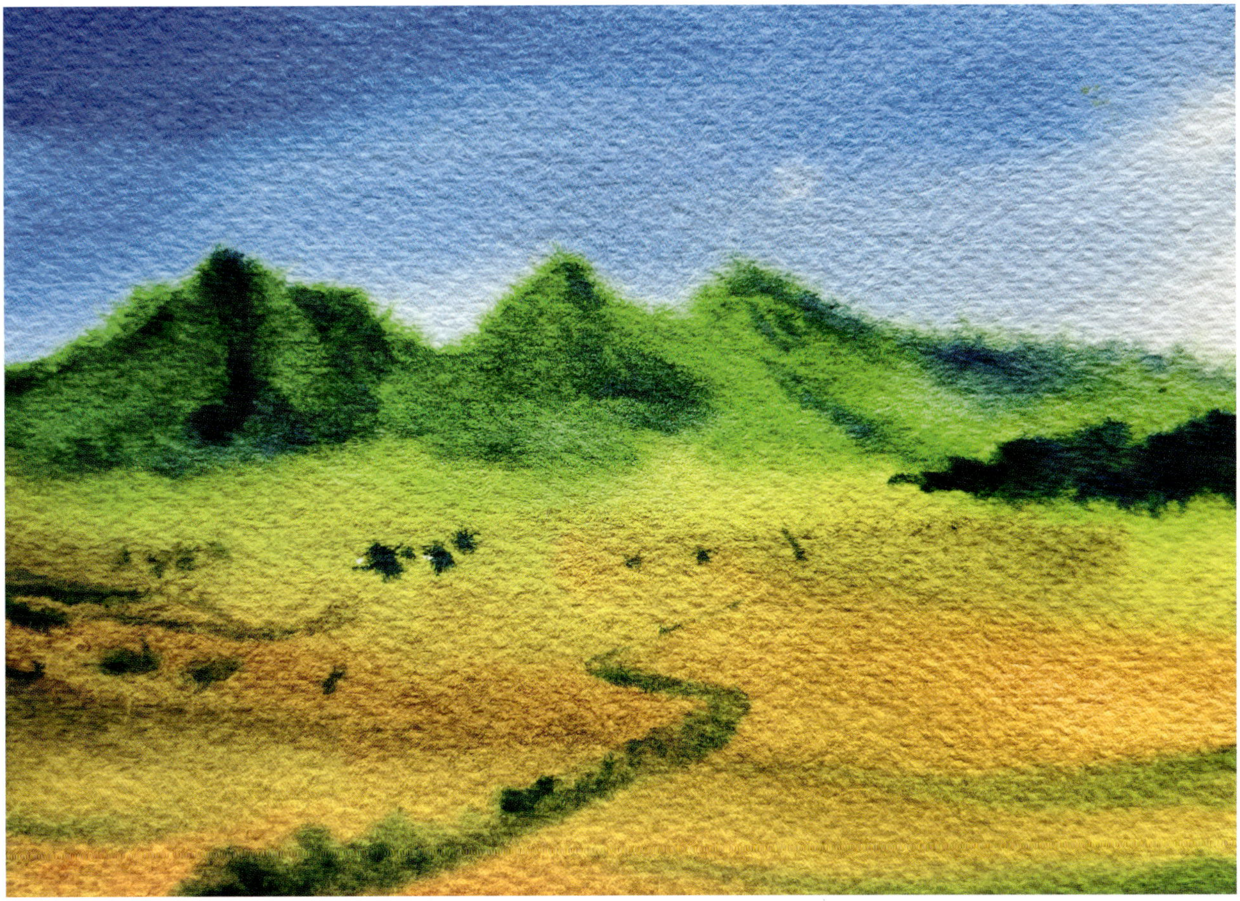

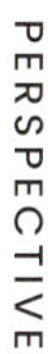

The last image depicts a combination of the dry-on-wet mountains with some cooler tones in it. This is the atmospheric effect that I personally would use; however, every artist has their own personal choices and realistic looks that they intend to create with their paintings.

In general, to create the best atmospheric aerial perspective, here are some useful tips:

- Use wet-on-wet or dry-on-wet techniques for painting objects that are further away so that they are blurred and toward the horizon. As you come closer to the viewer (further from the horizon), use wet-on-dry strokes so that these strokes are perceived in detail.

- Paint background strokes with lighter monochromatic tones and foreground strokes with darker multicolored tones.

- Minimize the details and refined strokes for the background; paint the foreground with crisp details and clear, defined strokes.

- Reduce the size of things toward the horizon. For example, birds in the sky at the horizon should be smaller than those in the sky at the top.

- Use cooler tones toward the back and warmer tones toward the front, except in the case of sunset, when it is quite the opposite.

- Increase the contrast of light and shadow toward the foreground while the background can be painted with minimal contrast effect.

COMPOSITION

Without a successful composition, your painting can lack integrity or lose its visual appeal. Hence, it is very important to plan your composition before you start and decide on how to place down different objects in your painting so that it doesn't look monotonous.

For example, the lack of a focal point in your painting can cause the viewer to misinterpret the emotion connected to the painting and get distracted with the other elements irrelevant to that painting. The first step involved is to find the focal point in your reference image or the scene that you intend to paint.

The general rule of composition is known as the **Rule of Thirds**. Divide your paper into three, both vertically and horizontally. If you place the key elements in your painting along the intersection of these lines, then the composition becomes much more pleasing and interesting to the eyes.

Here are some tips to get better compositions:

- Don't try to replicate the reference exactly as it is; you are not a camera.

- You are free to remove any object from the scene or reference that you feel does not convey the emotion behind the painting or is completely avoidable.

- Do not overcrowd the painting with unnecessary objects.

- Feel free to replicate similar objects of interest to your painting even if they don't exist in your reference.

- You can add more details, figures, or objects to enhance your composition, especially when painting cityscapes from a reference image that does not have any people in it.

- Do multiple thumbnail sketches if needed to decide on your ideal composition.

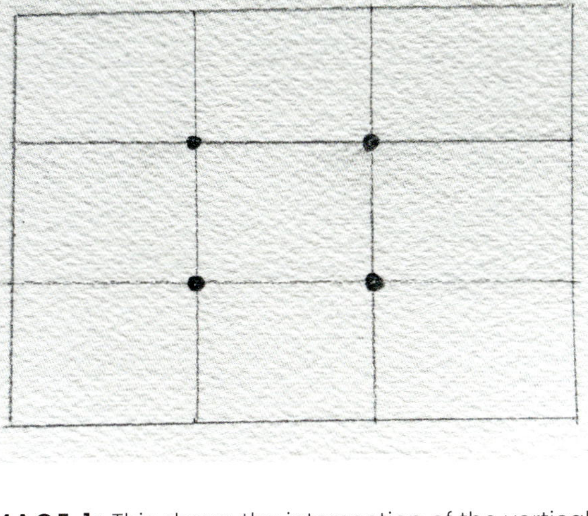

IMAGE 1: This shows the intersection of the vertical and horizontal lines where it is ideal to place the focal point of your composition.

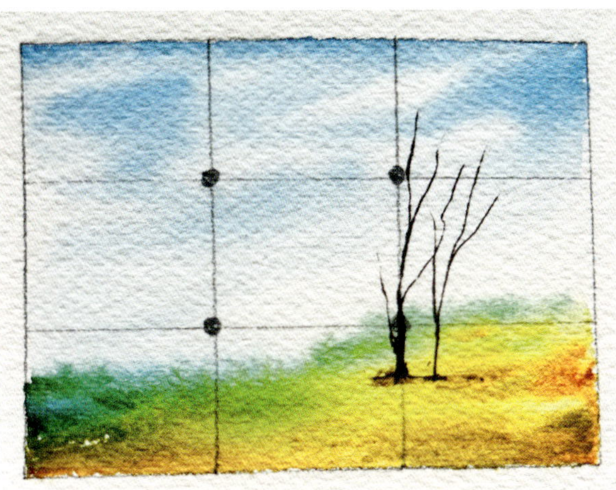

IMAGE 2: This is the most ideal composition for painting this scene. The horizon line is near the top third horizontal level and the trees are placed at the intersection.

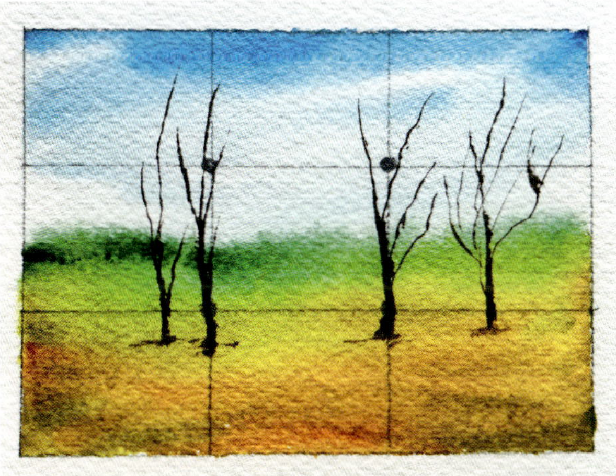

IMAGE 3: The placement of the trees is somewhat ideal, as they have been placed along the intersection; however, the horizon line of the composition is exactly at the middle, which makes it less interesting.

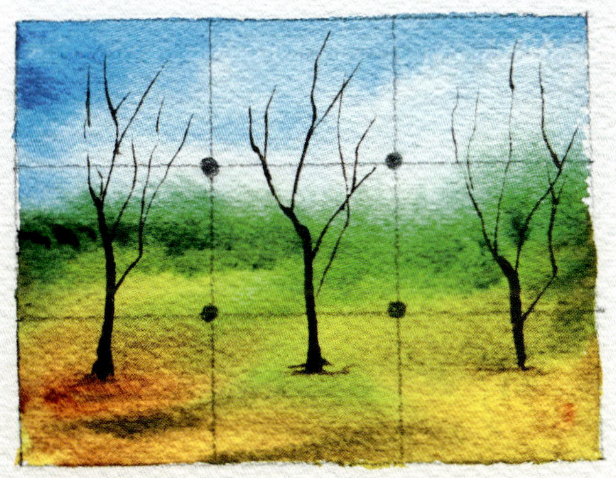

IMAGE 4: The trees are placed in a symmetrical manner and the horizon level is exactly in the middle. This is the most displeasing effect when it comes to things that do not need to be symmetrical.

LIGHT & SHADOW

Light and shadow are the most important things to consider when painting with any medium. Shadows and the light that casts those shadows are what essentially creates the world we see around us; it is essential that we capture them in our painting. They give the depth and form to the objects in our painting.

Shadows are always in the opposite direction from where the light falls on the object. There are two main types of shadows on an object: a cast shadow and a form shadow. A cast shadow is the shadow cast by the object onto another surface, and a form shadow is the shadow on the object itself on areas where the light does not reach.

I have demonstrated some general shapes here where you can see both the cast shadow and the form shadow for each. The part where the light falls on the object is depicted in white and is known as highlights. For all of these objects, I have assumed that the light is falling on it from the top left.

Notice how the cast shadow and form shadow is depicted for each of these forms. The cast shadow is opposite to the source of light and decreases further away from the object.

However, notice how each of the objects has a lighter tone on the side completely opposite to the light source. This is the reflected light. This lighter part is created because of the light bouncing off the surface and hitting back on the object.

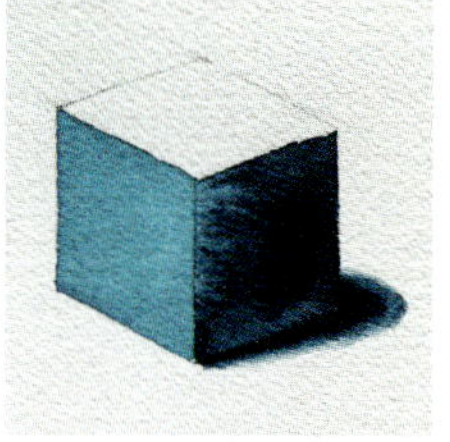 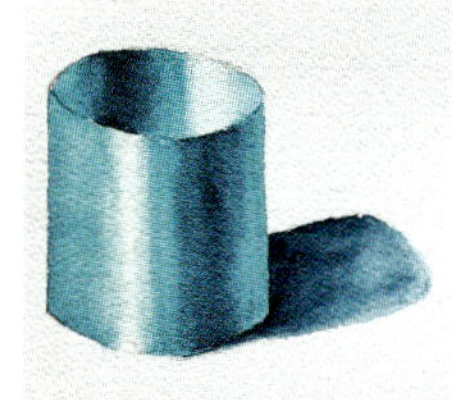 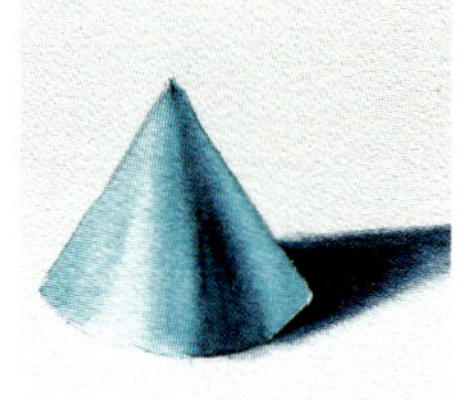 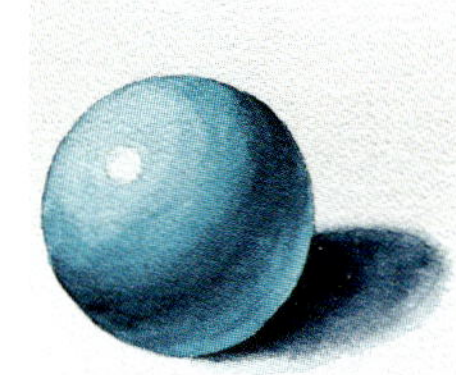

ELEMENTS OF A LANDSCAPE PAINTING

Things to note before you start into the projects:

- Cut your paper into your desired size. I have painted the projects in A4 (8.3" × 11.7" [210 × 297 mm]) and 10" × 7" (25.4 × 17.8 cm) sizes, which will be mentioned alongside each project.

- I prefer to squeeze my paints from tubes onto my palette, as this makes the paint thicker and easier to use for larger formats and to achieve a vibrant look.

- You can either use masking tape to tape the edges of your paper or the method known as two-side water application. You apply the water on both sides of the paper and use this wetness to stick it to a nonabsorbent board, such as a plastic board or an acrylic board. Don't use a wooden board, as it can absorb the water, and the paper will dry quickly. This method gives us a lot of time to use the wet-on-wet technique and gives a softer look to our blends.

Various elements go into a landscape painting. These could be skies, mountains, trees and foliage, water bodies, pathways, and so on.

Just because a painting is called a landscape does not mean that you must paint a reference in the landscape format; it could be in the portrait format too. Landscape is a generic name referring to paintings inspired by nature in general.

When painting landscapes, keep in mind the general rules regarding composition, light and shadow, and perspective, and you will see that everything falls into place.

SKIES

Skies are an integral part of every landscape, as there will be some part of the sky involved. It could be a clear sky, a rainy day, or even during sunset time.

Clear Sky

STEP 1: Start by evenly applying clear water on the paper, preparing it for a wet-on-wet application.

STEP 2: Start applying a flat wash of blue color. I have used phthalo blue (PB15:3) here. I like to create some gaps in my flat wash, even though it is a clear sky, to create an atmospheric effect to my painting.

STEP 3: Intensify the color at the top to implement the aerial perspective. I have added some ultramarine blue over the top area to further enhance the color.

STEP 4: Create some kind of ground area to add a visual boundary to the sky area you've painted. Here, I have used some dark green mixed with transparent yellow to create a sap green color to start with, and then toward the bottom added a bit of olive green and burnt sienna to the foreground to bring some warm colors into the composition. Finally, add some details with an intense dark green.

Cloudy Sky

STEP 1: Apply an even coat of water onto the paper for a wet-on-wet application. Add a very light tone of raw sienna or yellow ochre to the areas where you want to add the clouds. This yellow light is the area where the sunlight is reflected off the clouds; adding this warmer tone gives the maximum contrast with the darker shadows, thus enhancing our picture.

STEP 2: While the paper is still wet, add in some darker shadows to the clouds with a lighter tone of Payne's gray (use milky consistency of paint but absorb extra water from the brush using a tissue) or a gray mixed from primary colors. When painting clouds like these, I prefer to mix the shadow color from the primaries, as I can vary the coolness of the color by adding more blue to the paint mixture.

STEP 3: Apply phthalo blue to the other areas of the sky using wet-on-wet technique. Keep in mind to make it brighter toward the top, decreasing the tone as you move down and leaving sufficient white gaps near the clouds.

STEP 4: Finish off the foreground with a mixture of cool and warm green tones. Adding burnt sienna to the foreground lends a naturistic look.

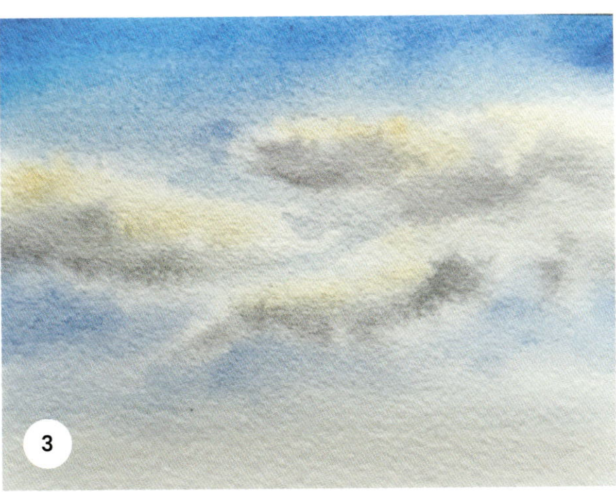

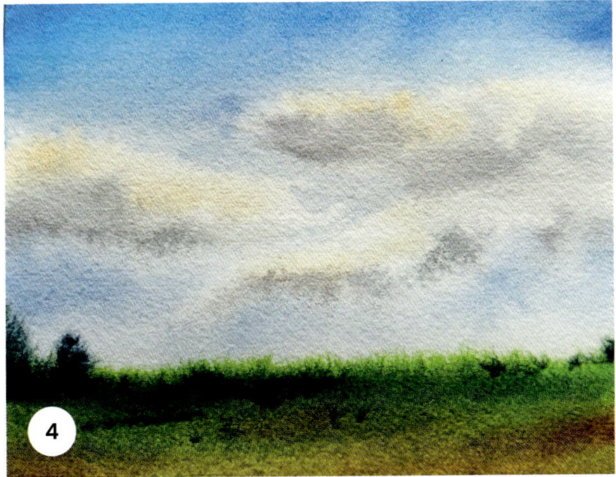

Rainy Sky

STEP 1: Start with a wet-on-wet application of Payne's gray to the sky region at random places; be sure to leave sufficient white spaces. Tilt the paper to let the color bleed down and create those hairlike structures on the paper. This adds a misty effect to the dense rainy clouds in the sky, giving the painting a natural atmospheric look.

STEP 2: Finish off with any kind of foreground. Here, I have mixed cobalt blue with dark green to create a cool green color to depict the cool rainy day. I added some yellow strokes to the very bottom, which blended with the cool green tones to create a subtle warm tone. Finish with some details with the dark green.

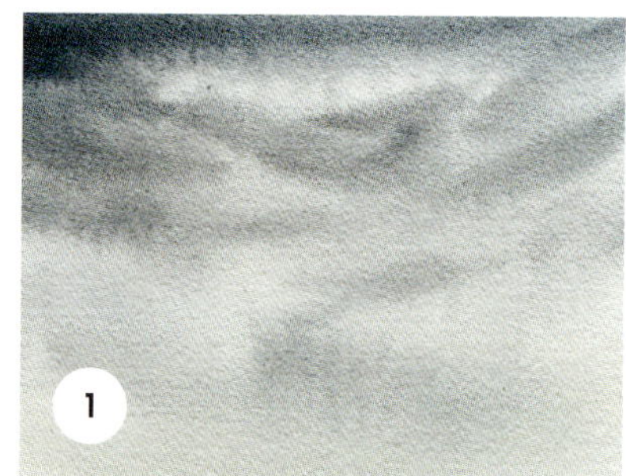

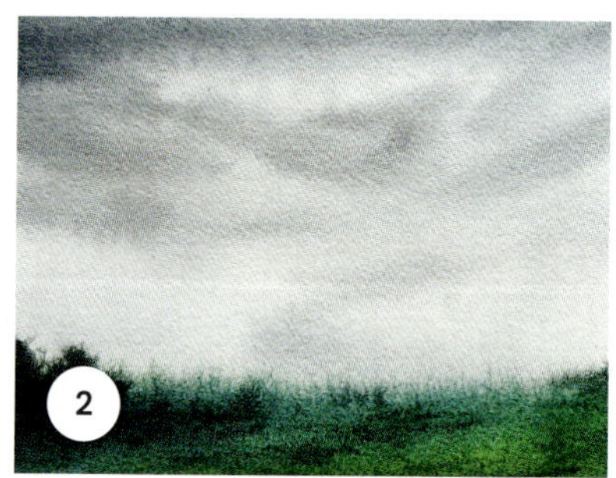

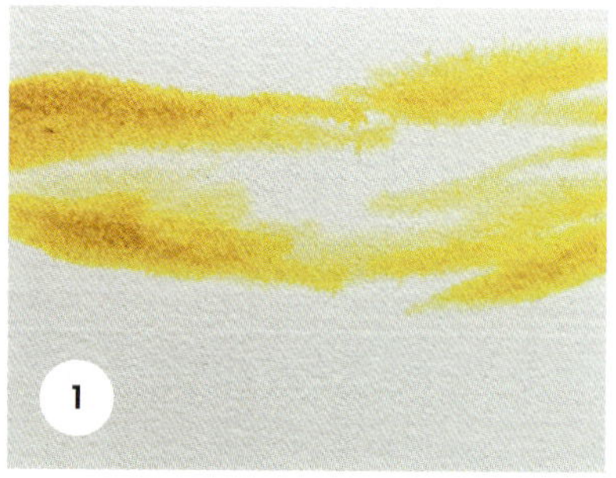

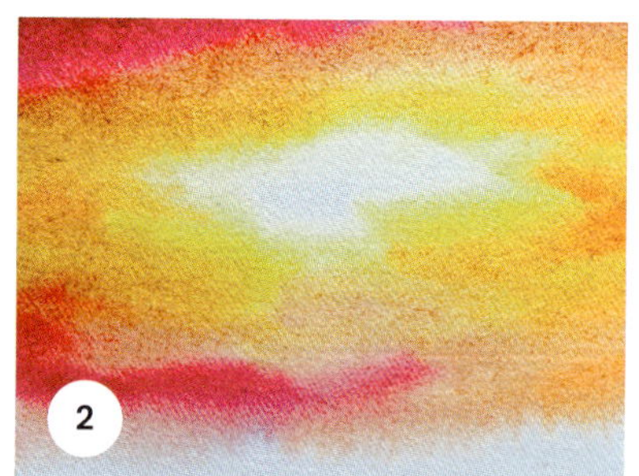

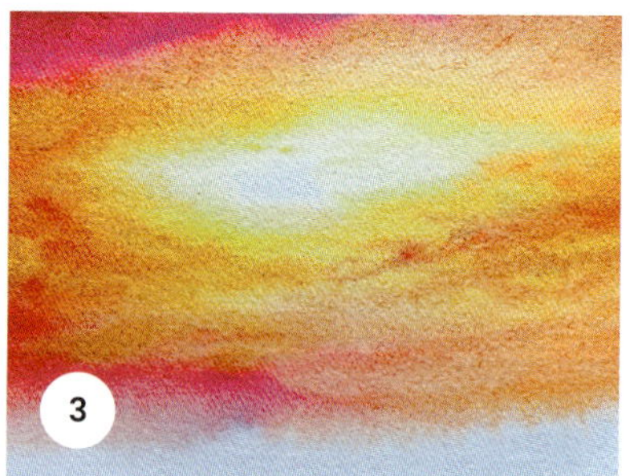

Sunset Sky

STEP 1: Start with a wet-on-wet application of yellow to some random areas in the sky, leaving a large chunk of white area for the sunlight.

STEP 2: Using a pink shade (here, quinacridone violet rose), add some clouds to the sky. The areas where the pink mixes with the yellow will create red shades.

STEP 3: Add some additional cloudy forms using orange and pink shades as you like. Remember to preserve the white of the sky.

STEP 4: Finish off the ground with a dark brown color. Remember to drop in some lighter orange or burnt sienna to the top areas of the foreground to depict the areas lit by the setting sun.

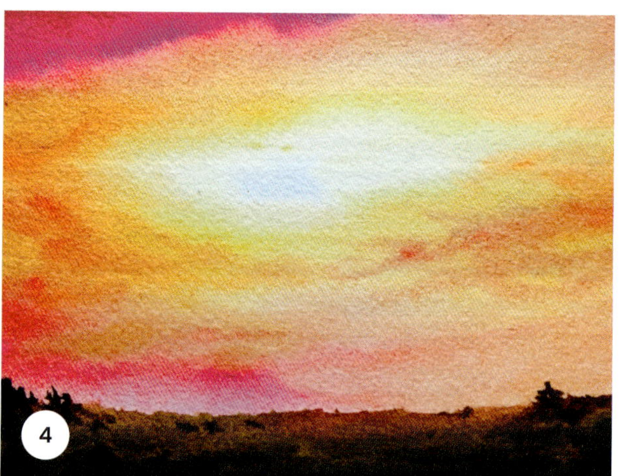

MOUNTAINS

Mountains may not be part of every landscape, but painting them is a good exercise. There are several ways that they can be painted. I will share some of my favorite methods here. Bear in mind that these methods can be interchanged for any kind of mountain.

Winter Mountains

STEP 1: Start by sketching the outline of the mountain. Using the wet-on-wet method, apply a random sky using phthalo blue and ultramarine blue while keeping in mind to leave a lot of white spaces and decreasing the tone toward the bottom.

STEP 2: Apply some random strokes of Payne's gray to the mountain area after the sky has dried. You can use the edge-softening technique to soften certain areas of the mountain so they look like a mixed wet-on-wet and wet-on-dry application.

STEP 3: Now use a darker tone of Payne's gray to start adding random streaks to the mountain. You don't have to wait for the step 2 application to dry out. Some strokes will be wet-on-wet and some wet-on-dry, making it completely irregular.

STEP 4: Using a brown paint, apply some more random strokes and make sure you use the edge-softening method again to let some of the brown bleed into the gray and white areas.

STEP 5: Now, add some dry-on-dry strokes with Payne's gray irregularly to the mountain.

STEP 6: Finish off with some ultramarine blue strokes. This depicts the shadows on the mountain.

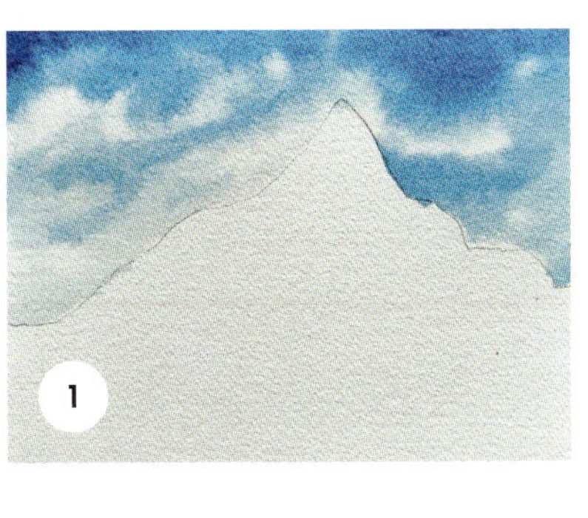

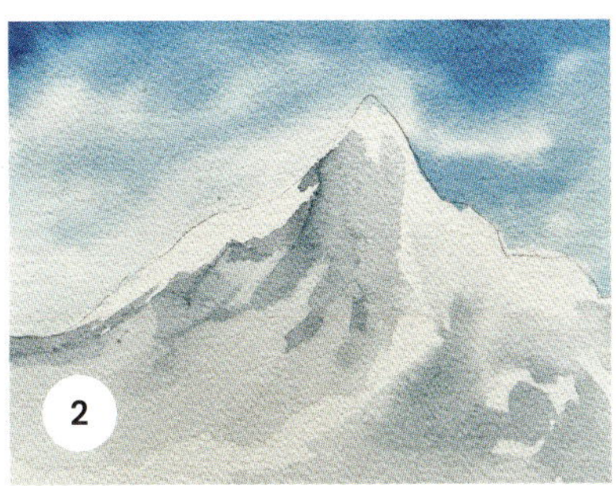

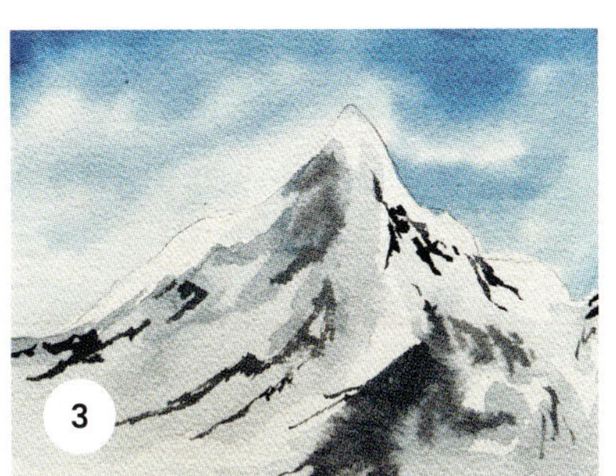

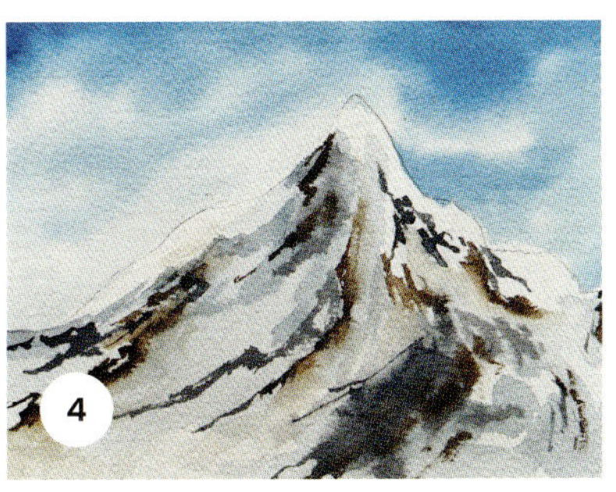

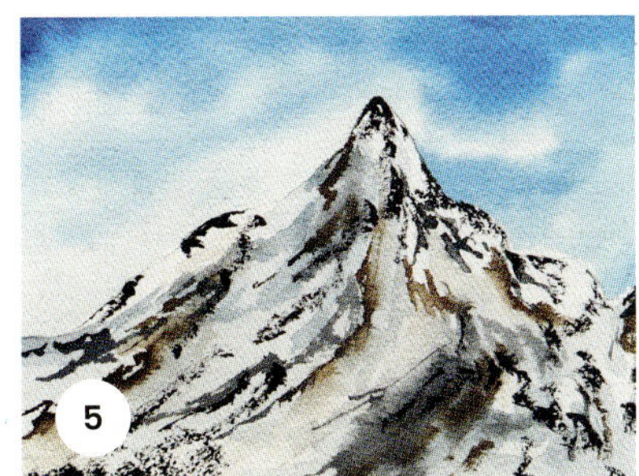

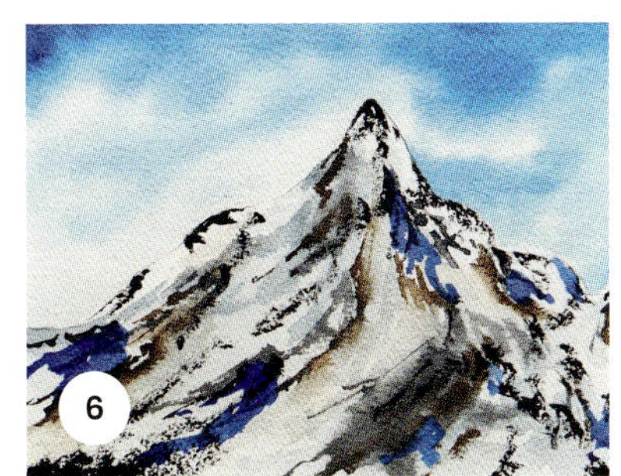

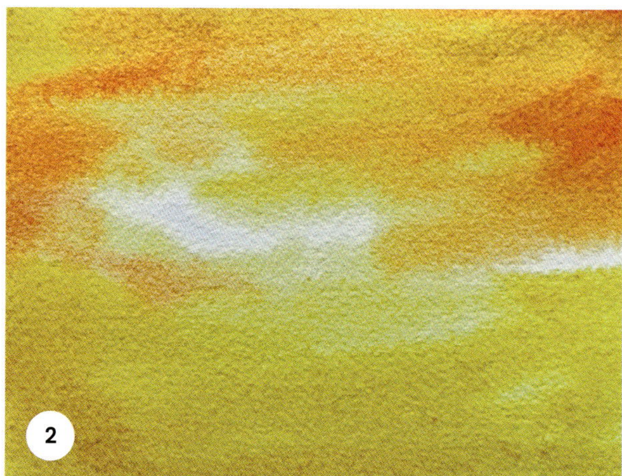

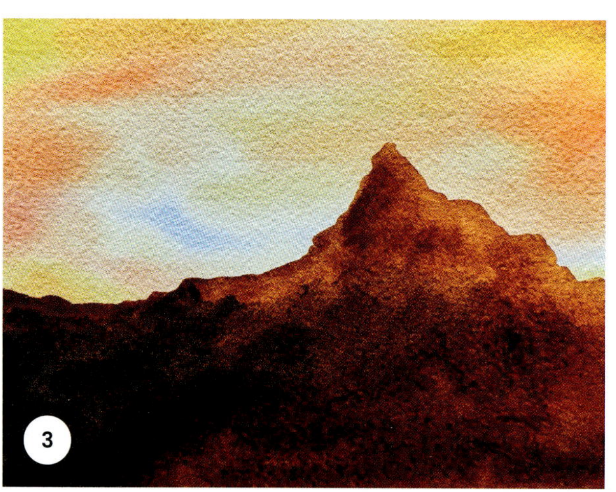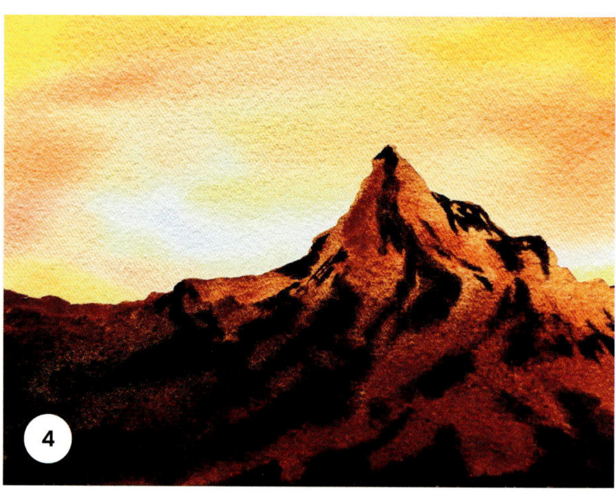

Sunset Mountain

STEP 1: Paint a random sky with yellow and orange, leaving some white gaps to depict the sunlight using wet-on-wet application.

STEP 2: It is okay to paint the whole paper with yellow, as the mountain is painted using darker colors on the top.

STEP 3: Once the sky has dried, start with a mix of orange and brown to paint a mountain peak, keeping in mind to vary the mix of orange and brown at random depending upon the lighter areas.

STEP 4: Then, using some darker brown, add in random details to the mountain using wet-on-wet technique.

TREES

There will always be a tree or some foliage when painting a landscape scene, and it is very important that the greenery we paint does not look like a whole mass of green on the paper.

STEP 1: Apply water to the area where you wish to paint the tree foliage, but in a random manner so that there are gaps without water.

STEP 2: Using olive green, start making strokes into the area. Some strokes will be wet-on-wet, some wet-on-dry, and of course, lot of white gaps because of the way we applied water in step 1.

STEP 3: Add dark shadows using green, and even darker shadows by taking a darker tone, or you can mix green with Payne's gray.

STEP 4: Finish off by adding the tree trunk and random branches with a brown color. Remember to apply shadow to the trunk area away from the light. I have assumed the light to be from the top right side here.

The trees during autumn can also be painted in a similar manner using yellow, orange, red, and brown shades.

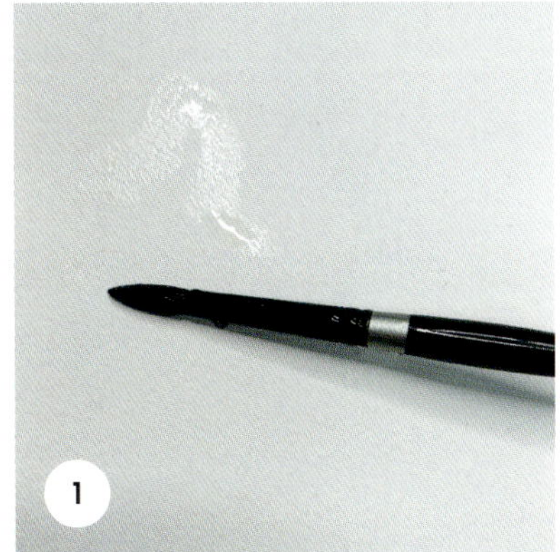

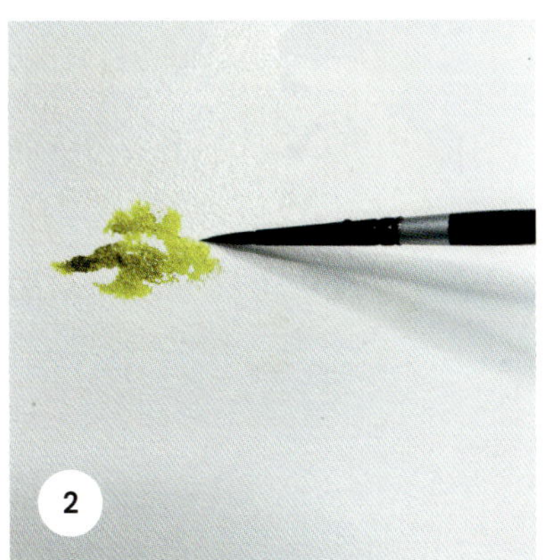

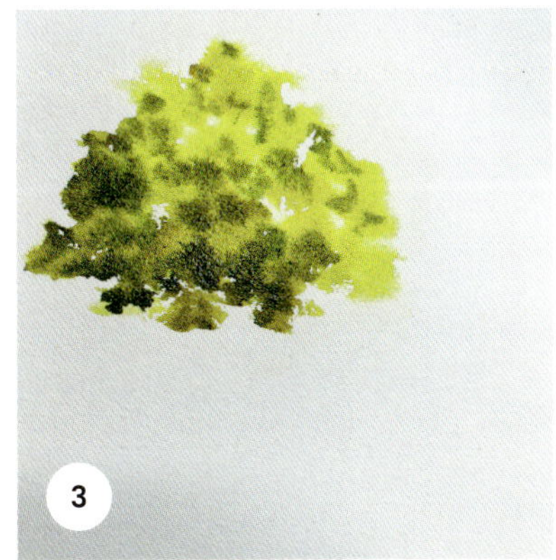

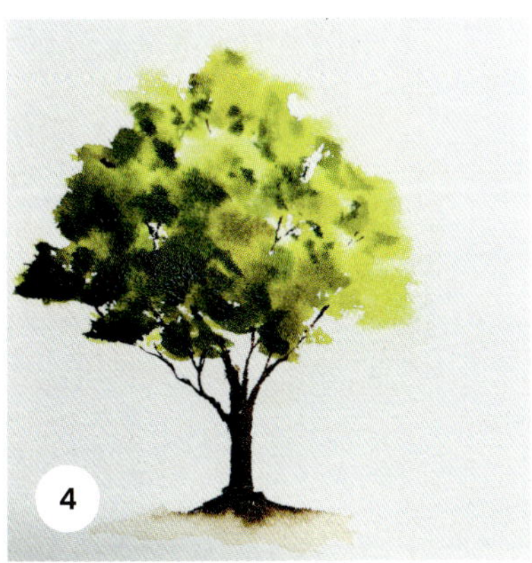

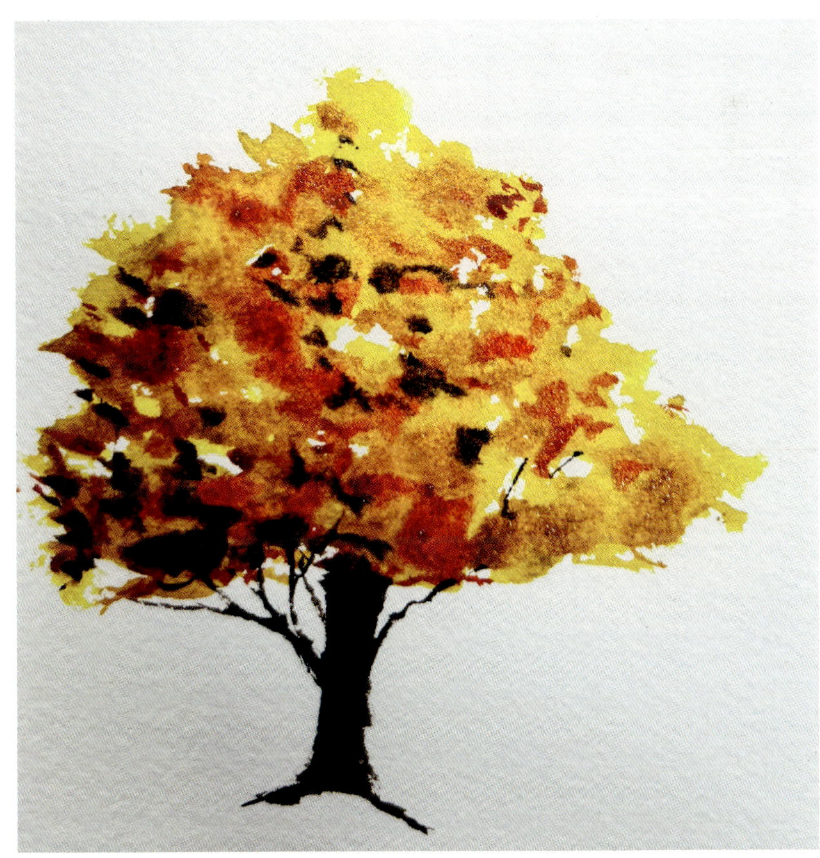

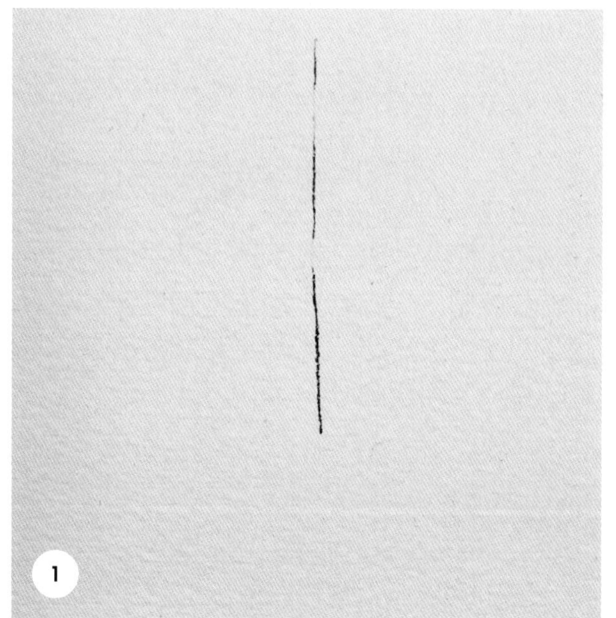

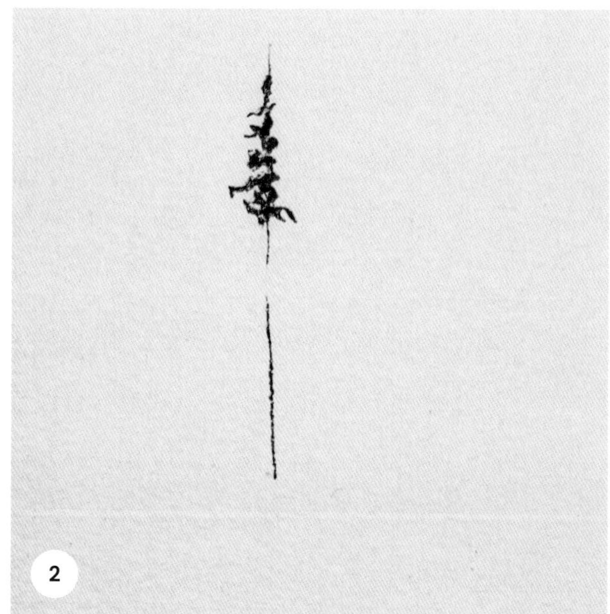

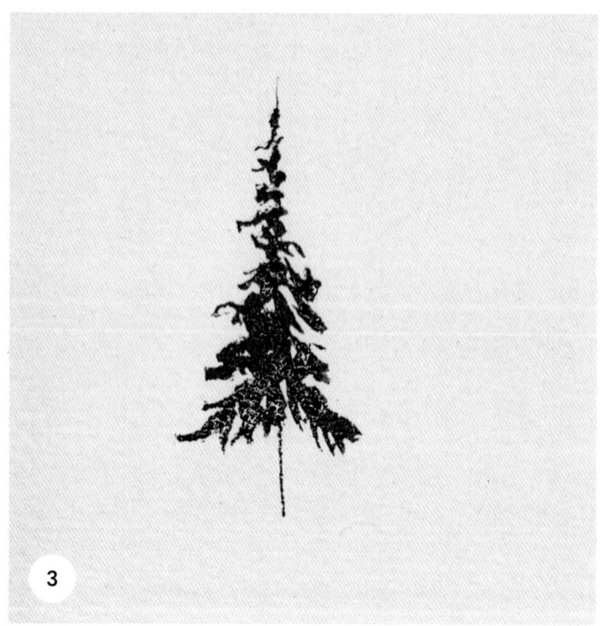

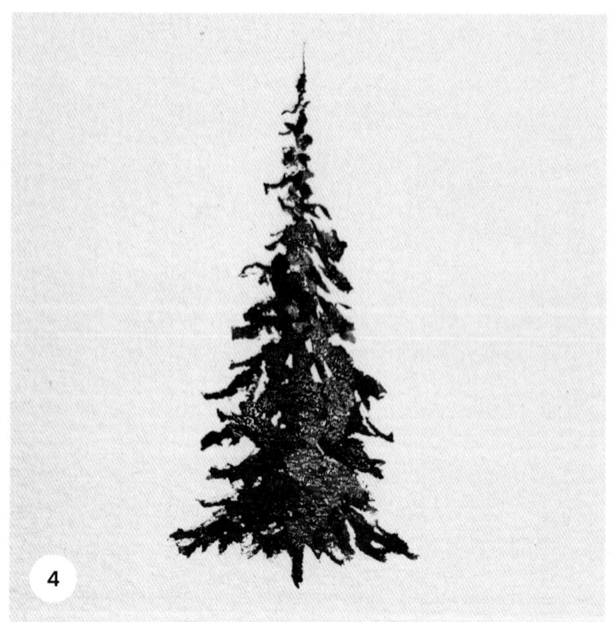

Pine Tree

Pines trees are beautiful elements to add to landscapes; however, getting the shape correct can be quite difficult.

STEP 1: Start with the center line, which will the basis for the foliage of the pine tree.

STEP 2: Start from the top using a dark green to slowly make small branchlike shapes.

STEP 3: Increase the depth and the thickness of the branches toward the bottom.

STEP 4: Add an opaque color, such as cadmium yellow or olive green, to create highlights at the top of the pine tree.

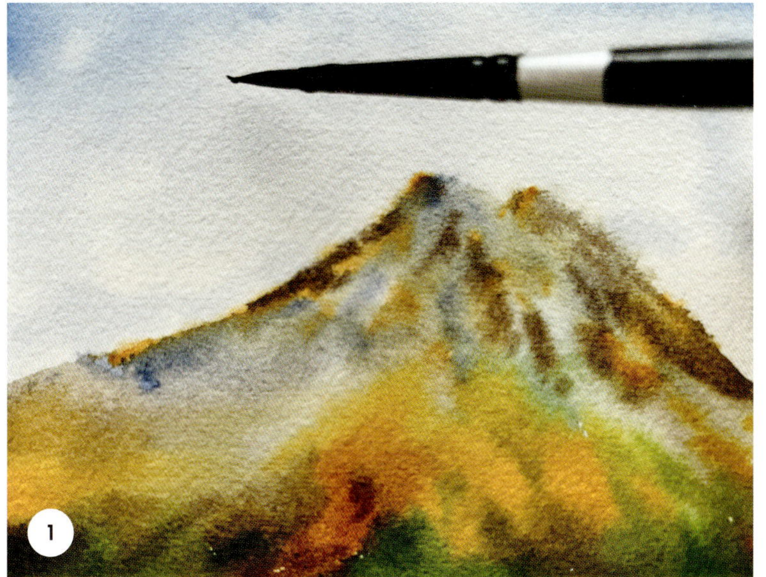

OTHER SMALL DETAILS & TIPS

Other small details can be added with a size 2, 1, or 0 brush.

STEP 1: These steps demonstrate how tiny birds can be added to your painting. I have used a small size 2 brush here.

STEP 2: With Payne's gray, make a tiny 'V' shape in different directions so that the two ends of the V, which are the wings, taper toward the edges.

STEP 3: Continue adding more tiny bird shapes, keeping in mind to make them smaller in the distance.

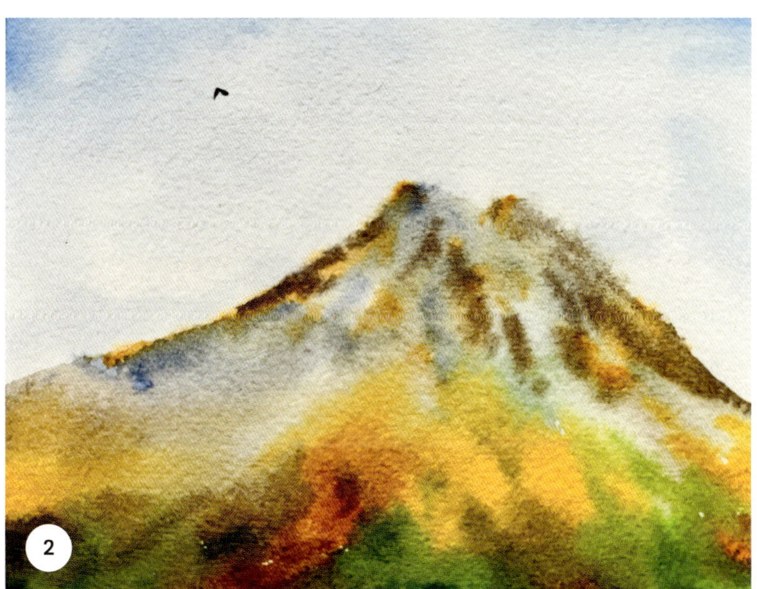

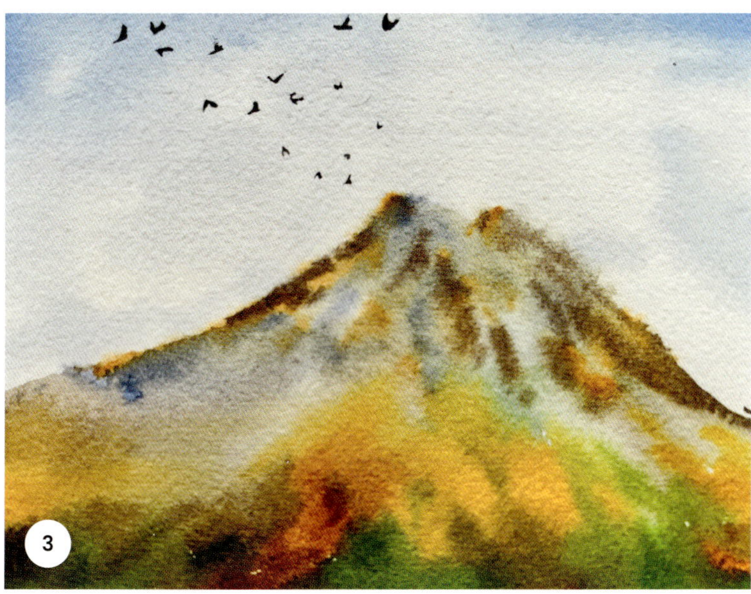

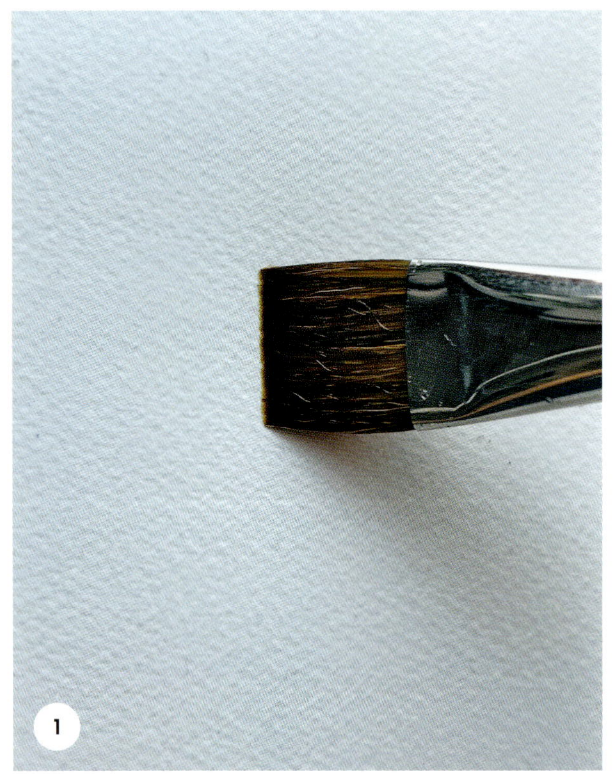 

WATER

Let us discuss the basic method of painting water and adding some waves to it.

STEP 1: Start by applying water to the whole surface of the paper.

STEP 2: Paint a gradient using phthalo blue, with the darkest part at the bottom and the lightest at the top. To depict water with aerial perspective, the areas toward the top will be lighter and have lesser details.

QUICK TIP

The best colors to paint water are phthalo blue and phthalo green. You can try the same process with phthalo green or a mixture of both. Experiment by creating a variegated wash with both the colors and see the magic of watercolors on your paper!

STEP 3: Using the entire length of a small pointed rounded brush and a darker tone of phthalo blue, add waves by pressing down with the brush and turning it as you move in a wavy manner. Use a creamy or dry consistency of paint over the wet blue paint for best results.

STEP 4: Add multiple waves in a similar way, but keep in mind to reduce the tonal value, the thickness, and the waviness of the stroke as you move toward the top.

STEP 5: Darken the waves toward the bottom using indigo. Create a change in value gradually from the bottom toward the top with the waves that you add. Remember that the top should have subtle waves and less curvy strokes.

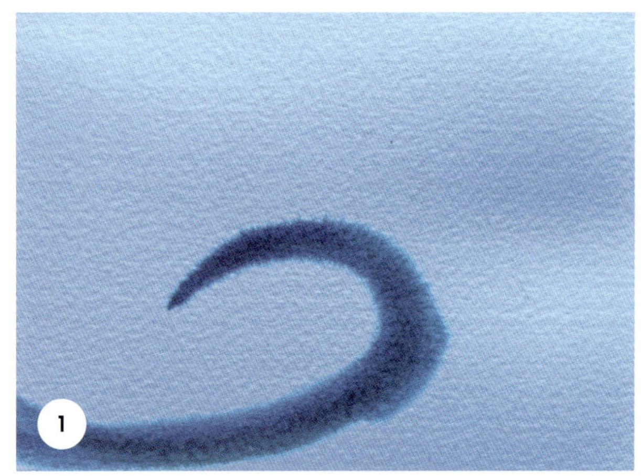

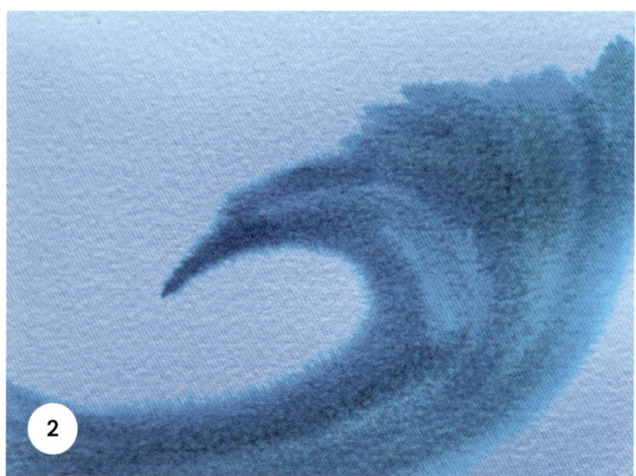

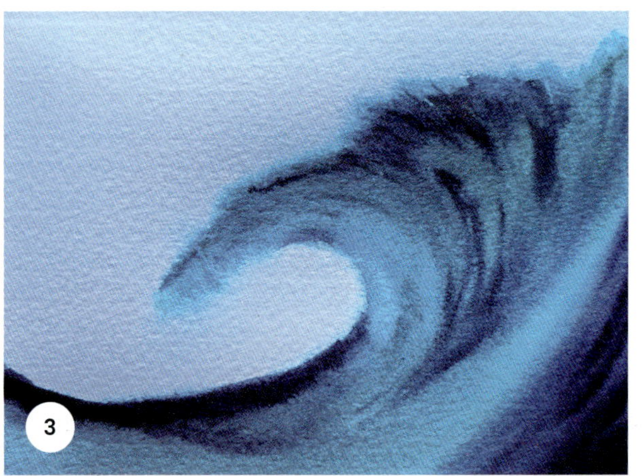

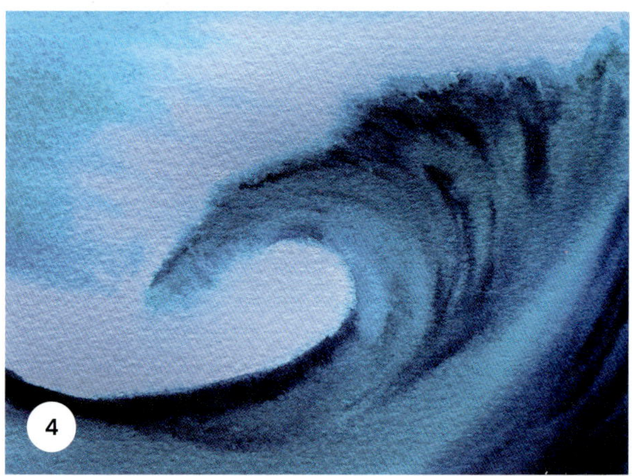

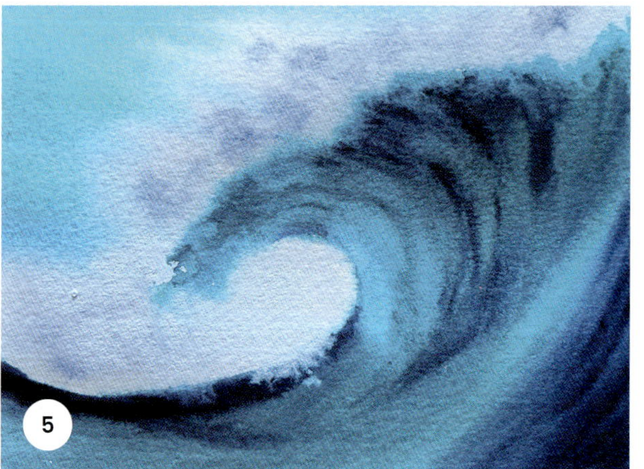

Waves

STEP 1: Apply water to the paper and create a wavy structure using a round brush. I have used a mixture of phthalo blue and phthalo green here to get a turquoise shade.

STEP 2: Continue adding to the wave, making it larger.

STEP 3: Add in some darker areas with indigo. Keep in mind to add the strokes following the shape of the wave.

STEP 4: Add the background part of the ocean behind the wave with phthalo blue, but remember to leave sufficient white areas to capture the foam in the water.

STEP 5: While the paper is still wet, use lavender to add some drops of shadow to the white areas.

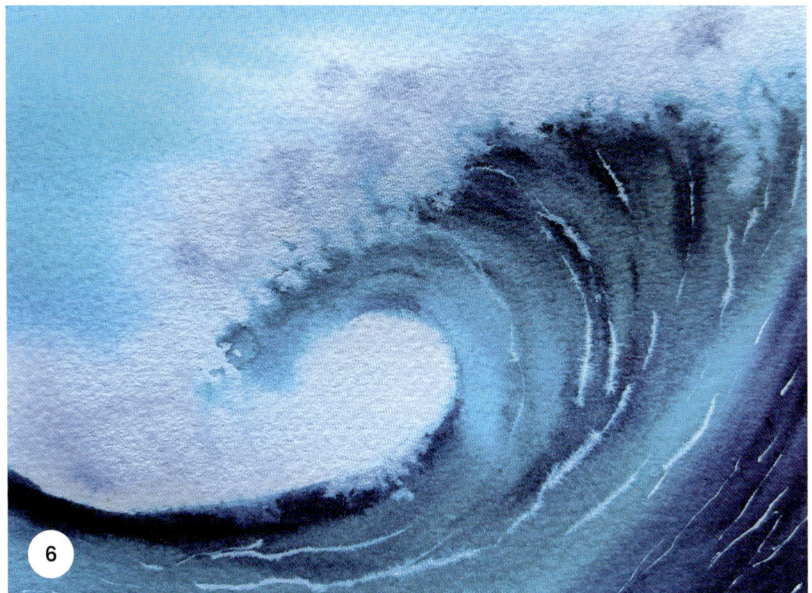

STEP 6: With white gouache paint or opaque white watercolor paint, add on several drops to the wet paper using the pointed tip of your brush. Also add in some lines following the curve of the wave.

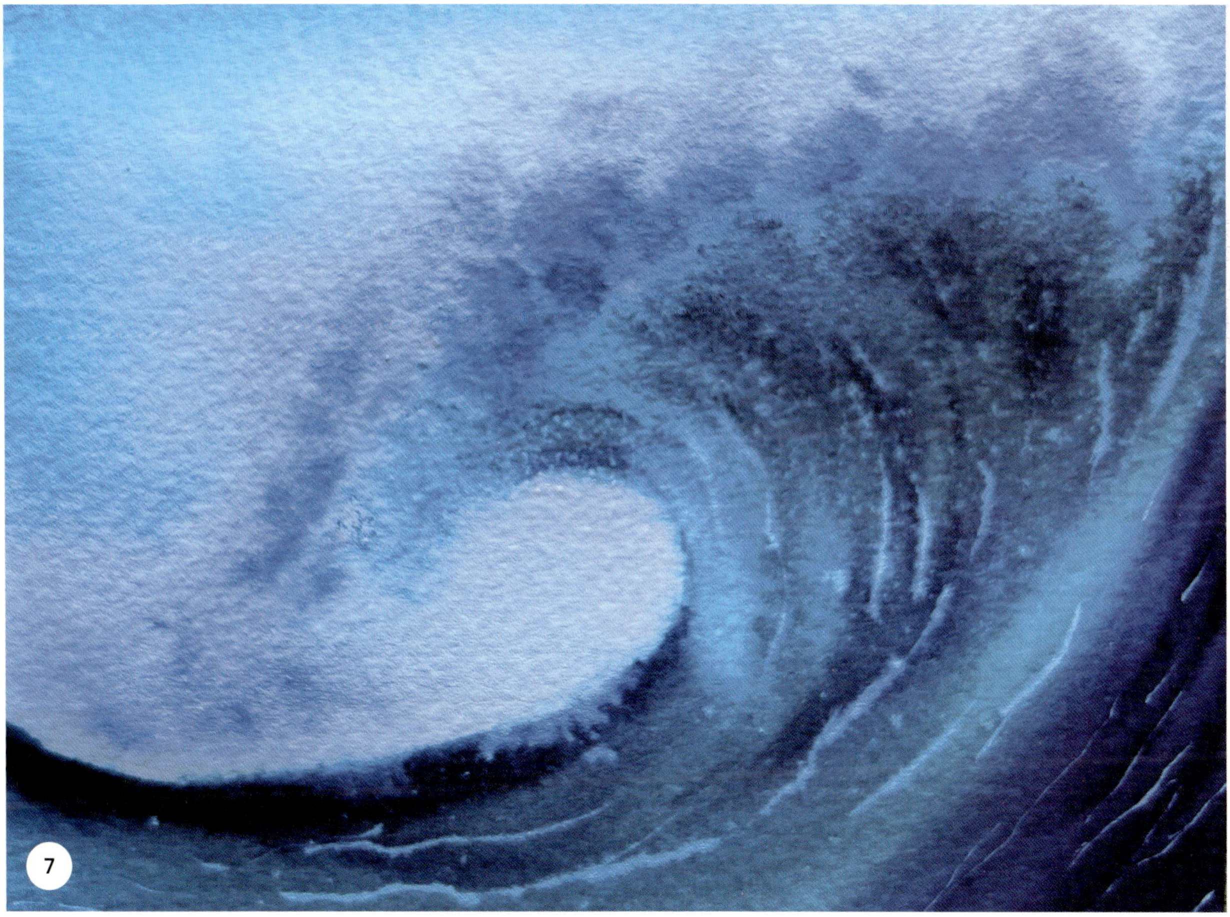

STEP 7: Use a toothbrush to make tiny splatters of white paint to depict the splash of water and the foam in the ocean wave.

Beach Top View

The aerial drone shot view of the beach is a fascinating view of the ocean, and you will find yourself with tons of reference pictures when looking for ocean pictures.

STEP 1: Start by applying water on to the whole of the paper. Mix phthalo blue and phthalo green together to create a turquoise blue color and use this in wet-on-wet to create the first layer of the water area.

STEP 2: Using phthalo green only, blend into the first turquoise stroke to create the lightest areas on the beach.

STEP 3: Add in more turquoise blue and create a good contrast toward the top regions.

STEP 4: Add in indigo to create the darkest shadows and dense areas in the ocean. Most of it can be toward the top of the paper, with some drops in random areas. These could represent many things, like shadows, underwater reefs, water discoloration, and so on.

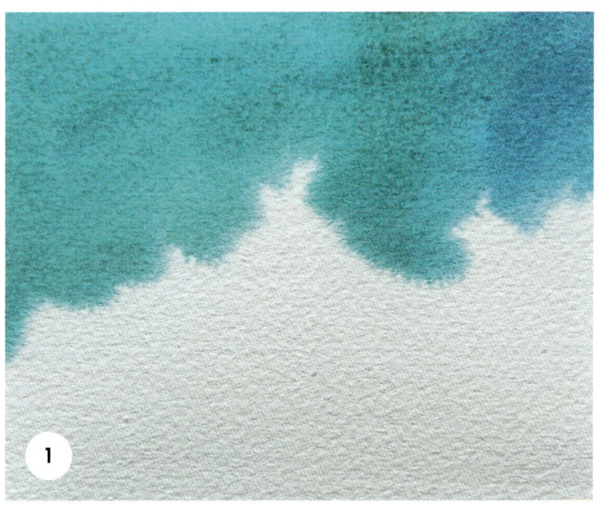

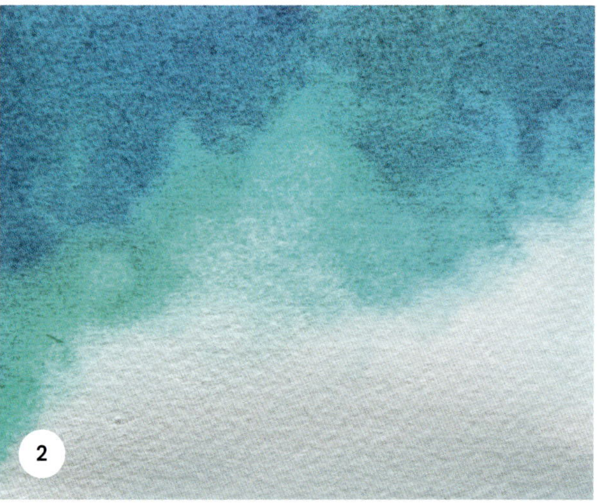

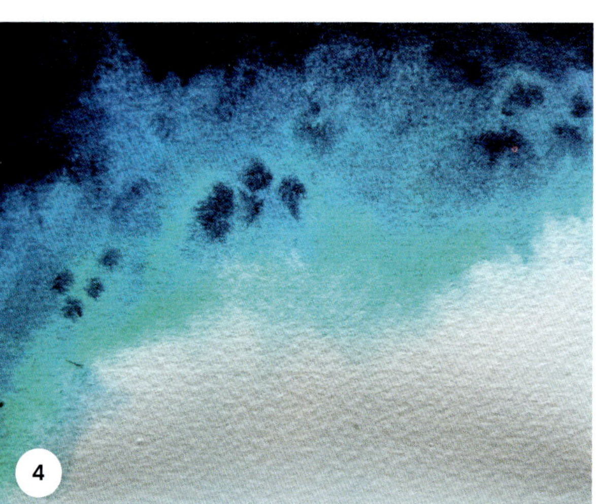

STEP 5: Add in yellow ochre mixed with a tint of lavender to depict the sand areas on the beach. Decrease the color toward the water area; it is all right if some bleeding occurs to create green areas.

STEP 6: Add in some foliage at the bottom by using sap green or olive green for the highlights and dark green and indigo for the shadows. Drop in some random dark-brown strokes to create the effect of rocks on the sand. You can also use a very light tone of brown on some areas of the sand to create a slight discoloration at random places.

STEP 7: Use white gouache or opaque white paint to add in waves at different levels on the water region using the wet-on-dry method. Then, use the drybrush technique to create foam near those areas.

STEP 8: Finish off with more foamy regions and some shadows near the waves. These shadows can be added by using a medium tone of brown and applying it wet-on-dry onto that area, then immediately softening the edge of it with water. Observe how the color of the sand area changed after the paper has dried out. Watercolors always dry out lighter in color than when it was wet.

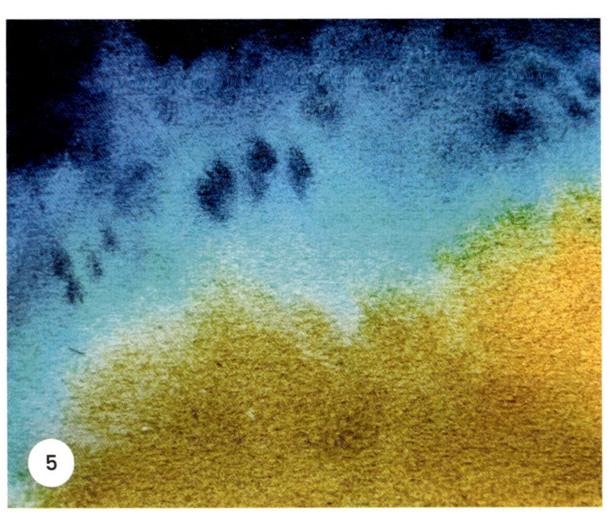

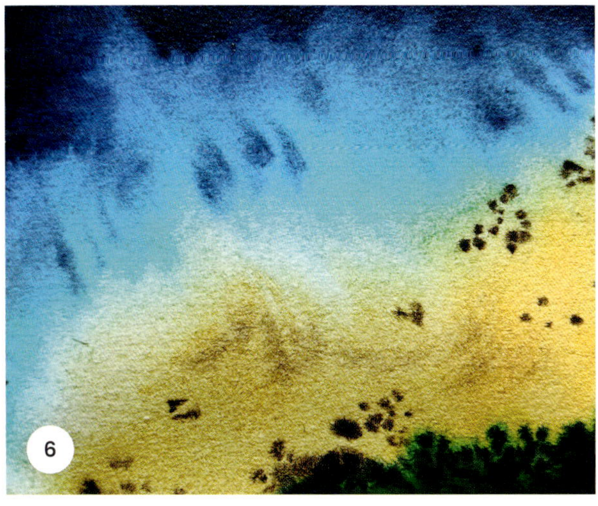

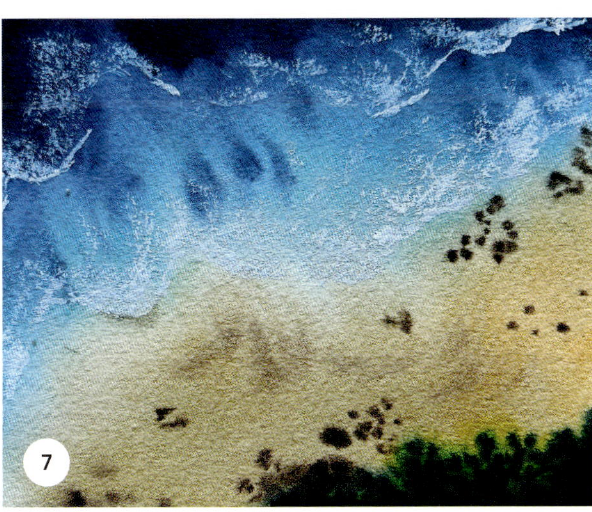

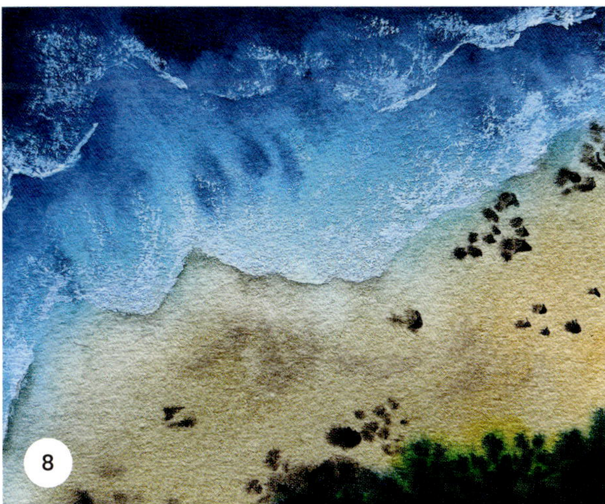

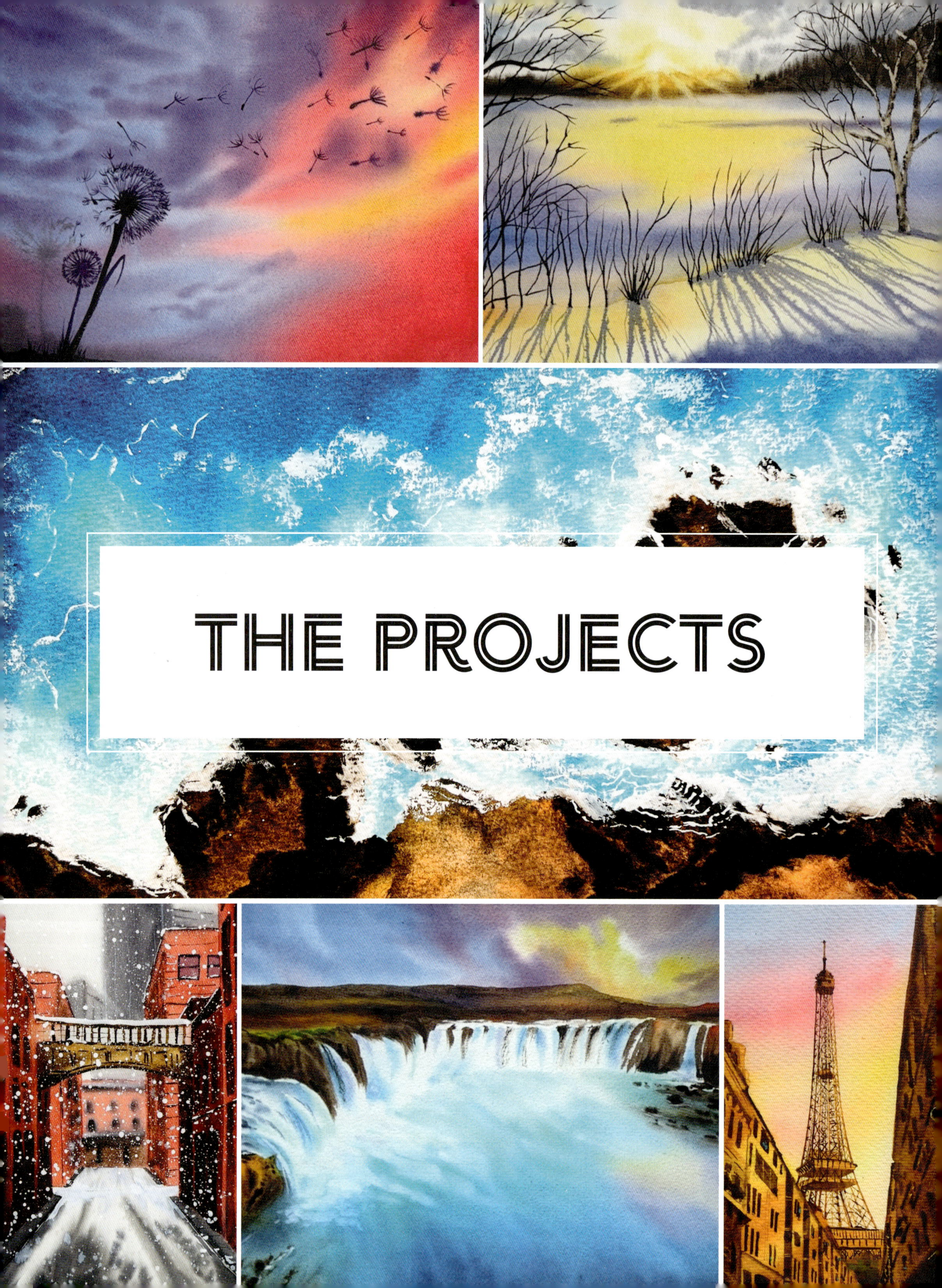

THE PROJECTS

MOUNTAIN RANGE AT SUNSET

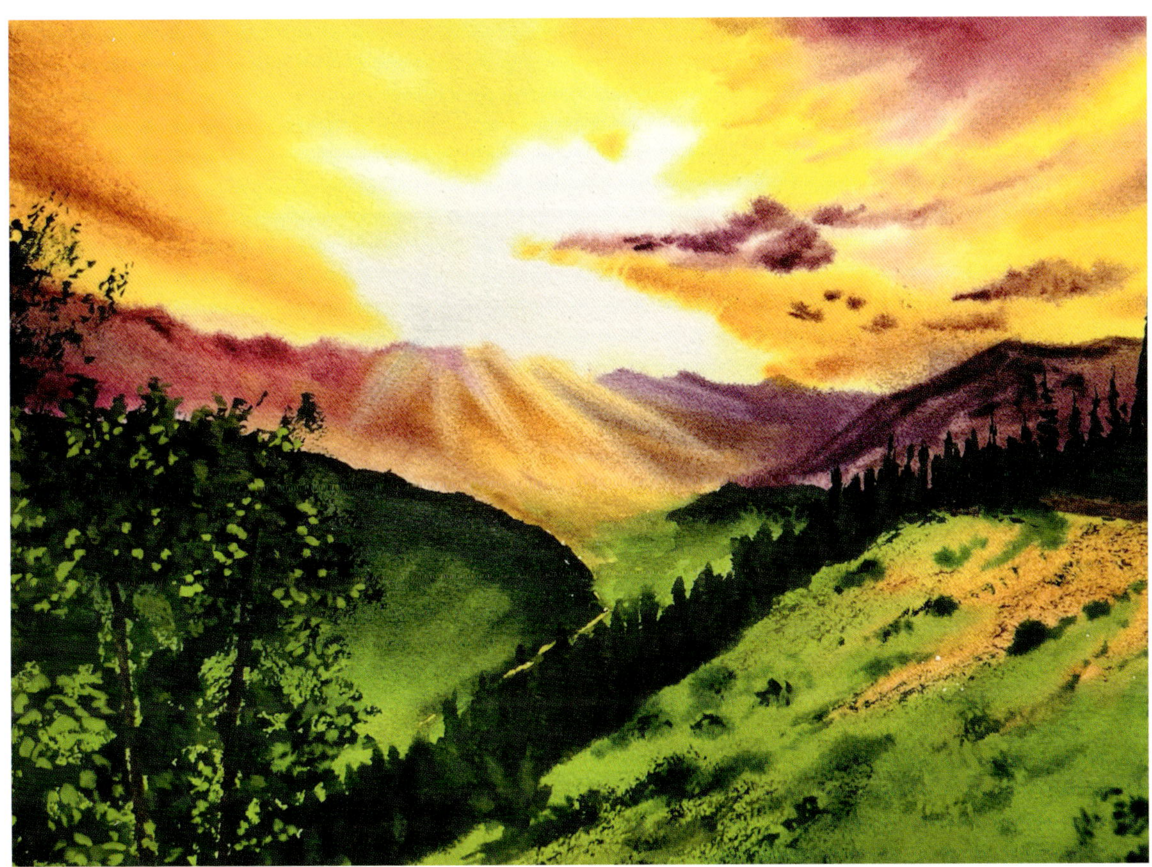

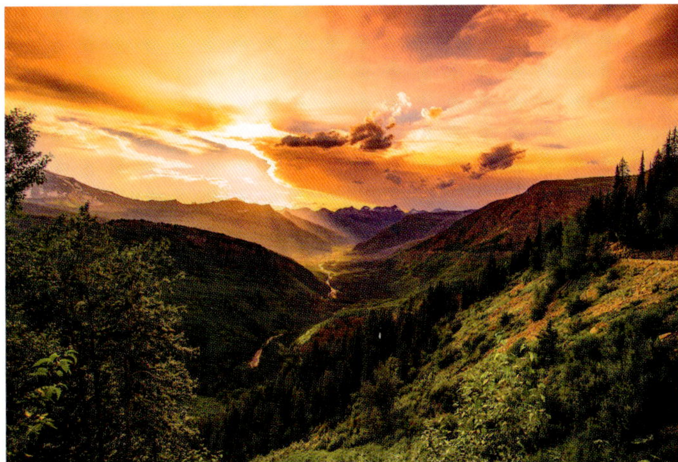

WATER TECHNIQUE: **Taped edges**

PAPER SIZE: **A4**

COLORS: **Transparent yellow, burnt sienna, alizarin crimson, violet, transparent brown, dark green, olive green, Payne's gray, cadmium yellow**

(continued)

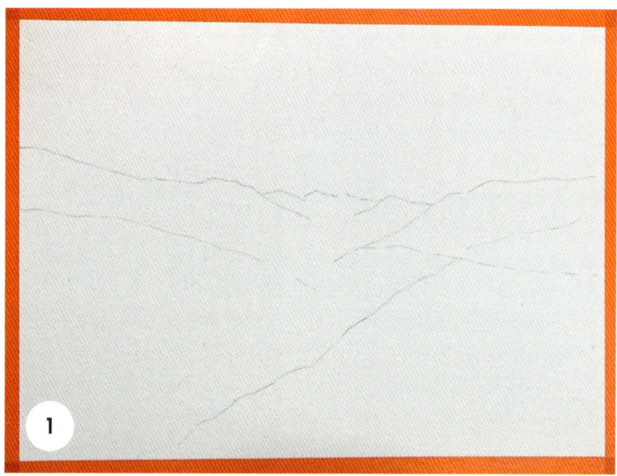

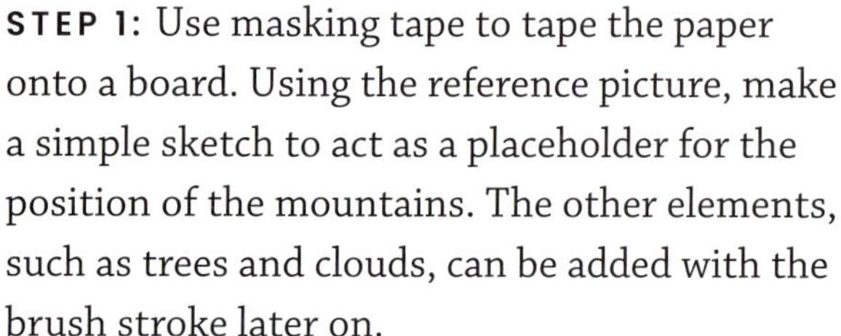

STEP 1: Use masking tape to tape the paper onto a board. Using the reference picture, make a simple sketch to act as a placeholder for the position of the mountains. The other elements, such as trees and clouds, can be added with the brush stroke later on.

STEP 2: Apply water to the whole of the paper and start with painting the sky. Make sure that you take time to apply the water to the whole of the paper and ensure that there are no water blobs on the paper. Using transparent yellow, start making the base cloud layer. Anything with the darker shades of yellow can be added on the top.

STEP 3: Using a mix of burnt sienna and transparent yellow, add the darker clouds on the top. Use the reference picture only as guidance; feel free to change the positions of the clouds. Mix alizarin with violet to create the violet cloudy areas and add a tint of brown to the mixture to make it darker. You can vary the same mixture to add the background mountains in different shades. Remember to keep the area of the sunlight nice and warm using yellow shades.

QUICK TIP

Apply the water evenly, using a large flat wash brush and wait for around 2–3 minutes for the water to sink into the paper. Then, reapply the water. Doing this procedure multiple times will ensure that your paper stays wet much longer; the water gets enough time to sink into the fibers of the paper, and the layers you add on are enhancing its wetness. Always make sure not to create pools of water on the paper.

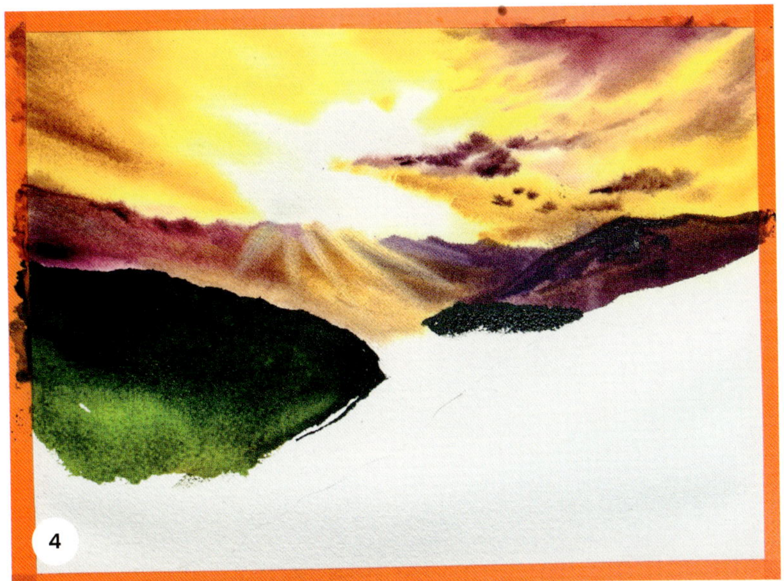

STEP 4: Using the lifting method, lift of some colors from the sunlit area and create streaks of sunlight. Start adding the foreground greenery using dark green. Start mixing yellow into the green to create lighter sap-green shades in the foreground areas.

STEP 5: Use different mixtures of yellow and green to create the foreground and add burnt sienna to some areas to create a muddy effect. Painting the foreground greenery will most probably be wet-on-dry strokes, as the water you applied might have dried. Ensure that you use a good watery mixture with a lot of paint so that you keep these areas wet after you have painted it.

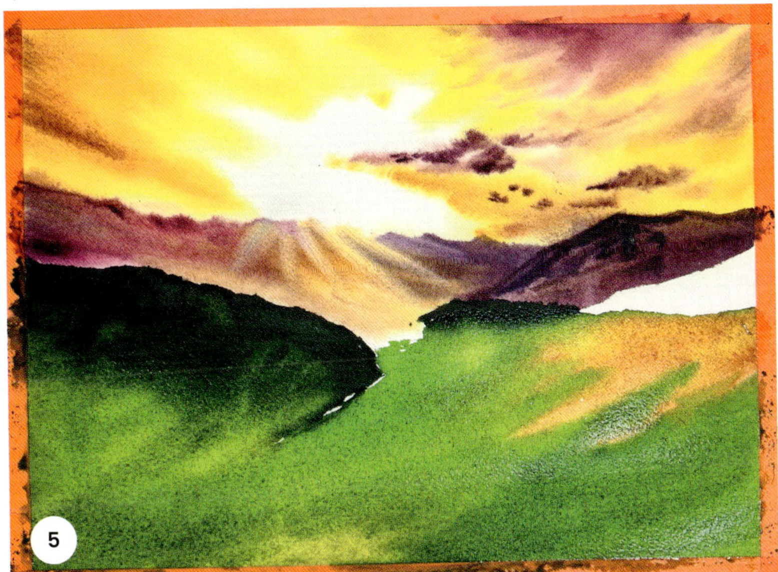

STEP 6: Now add a lot of green details (wet-on-wet) on to the foreground that you just added and add in the pine trees. Remember to vary the heights of the pine trees to get a realistic look.

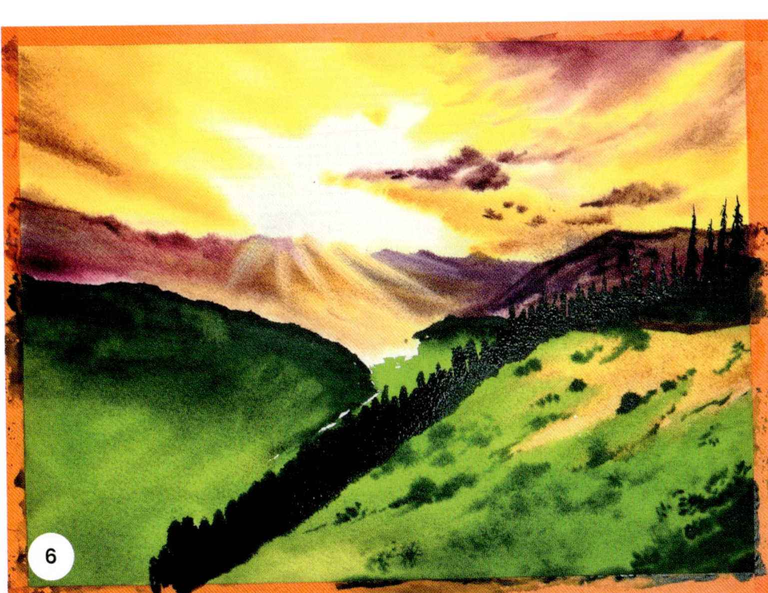

(continued)

STEP 7: Add in random tree-shaped strokes with olive green on top of the dark-green pine trees to create some color change effects on them. Mix dark green with Payne's gray to get a further dark green and use it to add the foreground trees and details. To paint the areas of the foliage toward the sky, use more Payne's gray in the mixture.

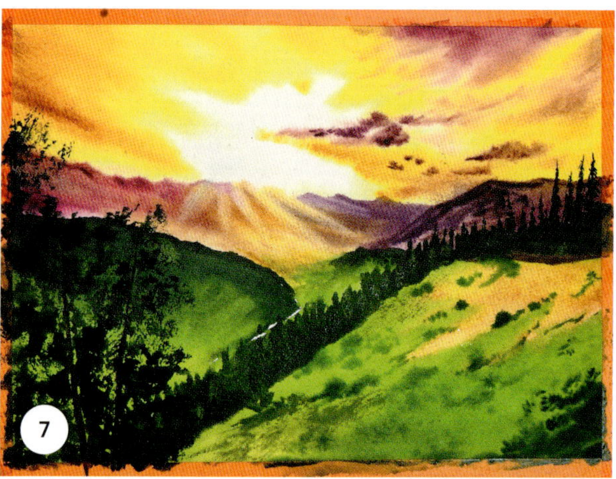

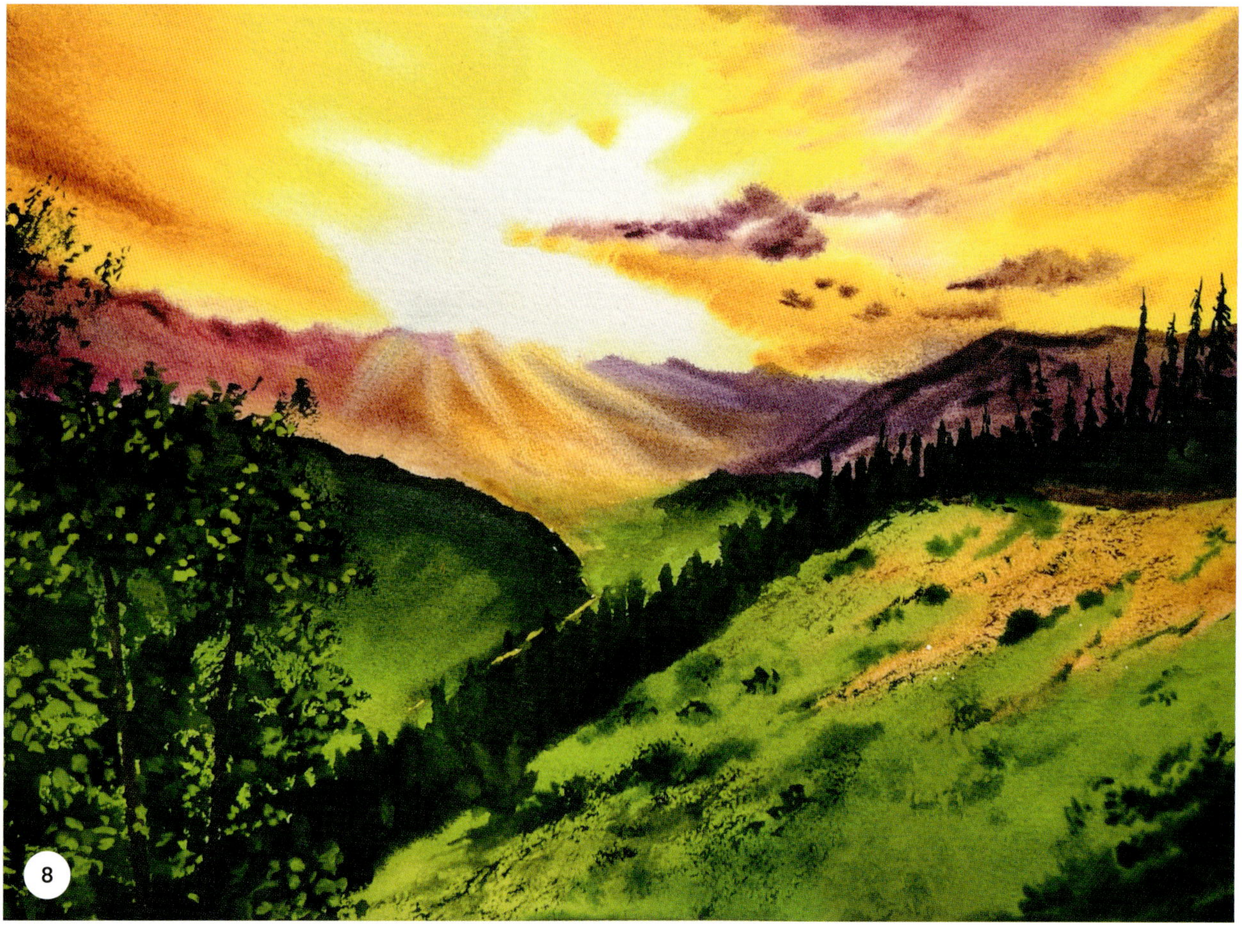

STEP 8: Use olive green and a mixture of cadmium yellow (opaque color) and green to add some highlights to the tree foliage; create varying shades on them. Refine the painting according to your satisfaction and add as many small details as you would like. Toward the bottom, you can add more wet-on-dry details.

MOUNTAIN SHADOW

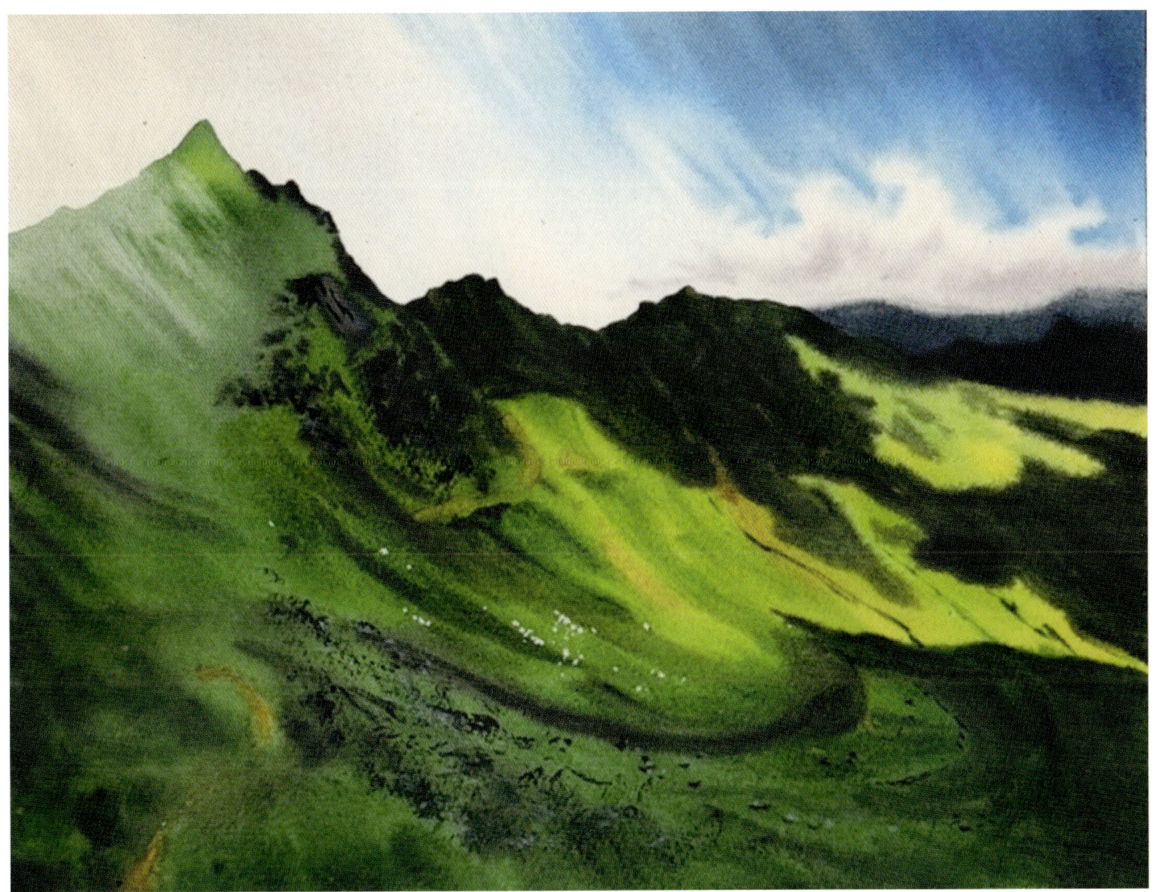

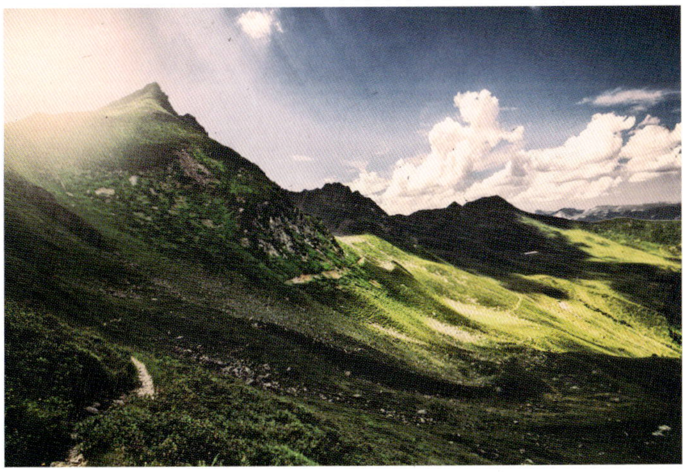

WATER TECHNIQUE: **Applying water to both sides of the paper**

PAPER SIZE: **A4**

COLORS: **Phthalo blue, cobalt blue, transparent yellow, alizarin crimson, ultramarine blue, indigo, green, Payne's gray, sap green, dark green, yellow ochre, lavender, white**

(continued)

STEP 1: Start with a simple sketch of the outline of the main mountains and any important features that you would like to capture. I prefer to do most of my smaller details with brush, hence do not add an extensive pencil sketch when painting landscapes. Apply water on both sides of the paper and fix it firmly on the board. I am using the two-side application method without tape and sticking to a nonabsorbent acrylic board.

STEP 2: Start painting the sky and the clouds using the wet-on-wet method. Since the paper has been wet on both sides, you can start painting with a creamy consistency of paint to get the desired shape for the clouds in the sky. Here, I have used phthalo blue for the blue part of the sky and a mix of cobalt blue, transparent yellow, and alizarin crimson to create a desired gray for the clouds. Enhance the top of the blue sky with a bit of indigo to bring in aerial perspective and depth to the sky.

STEP 3: Paint the background mountain in wet-on-wet using a cool mixture of green, ultramarine blue, and Payne's gray. Make sure to use a thick paint (dry-on-wet technique); otherwise it can spread all around. Additionally, you may use a completely dry brush to remove the hair formed on your background mountain by swiftly running this brush along the edge and absorbing the moisture from that area. Now, let your paper dry on the top surface. You can achieve this by using a hair dryer or heat gun over the top surface or waiting around for a few minutes and coming back to the painting (before the bottom side is dry too!).

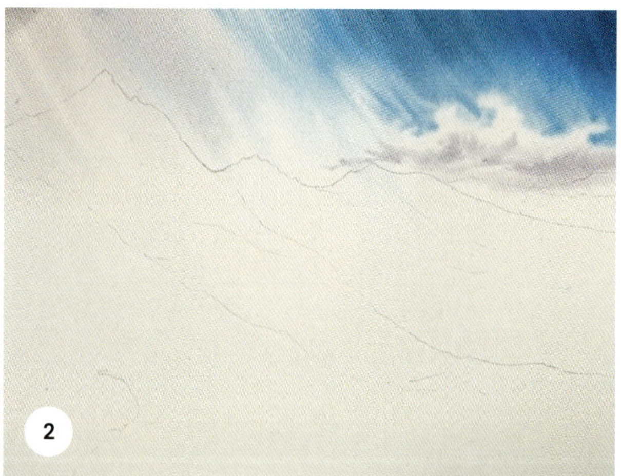

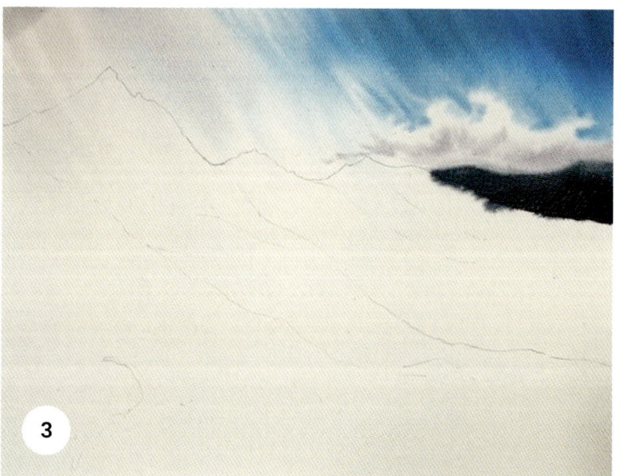

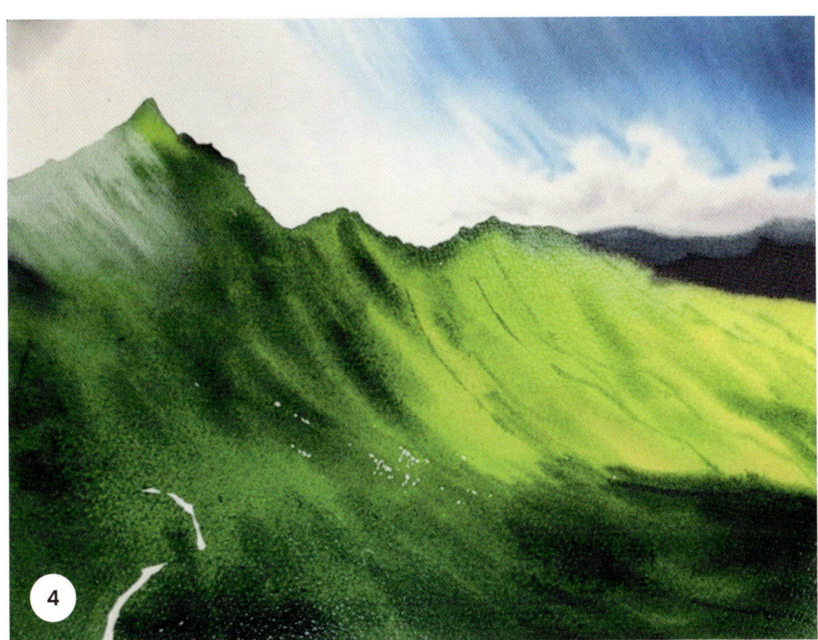

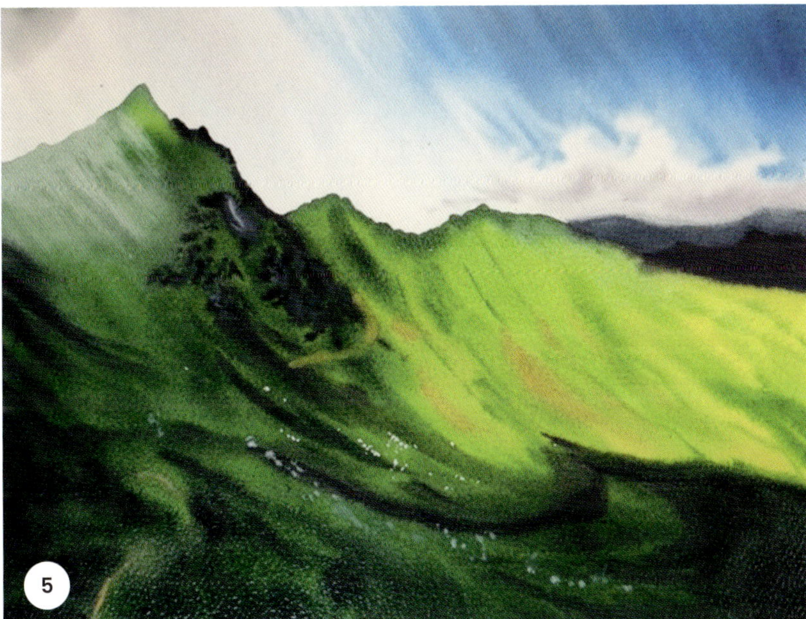

STEP 4: Next use green, sap green, and transparent yellow on the paper directly on the mountain in different areas and blend together to capture the lightest and darkest areas. Try to keep the lightest strokes toward the right side, as we have to capture the shadow there. Remember to leave the areas of the pathway white so that we can add that later on. Toward the left side of the mountain, to create the light streaks, use a paper towel and rub across in the direction of sunlight to remove paint. You will see how that area appears lighter where you lift off using the paper towel.

STEP 5: Using a dark green and indigo mixture, or dark green and Payne's gray mixture, add in the darkest spots on the mountain. Add them in wet-on-wet. Your paper should retain the wetness again if your paper had moisture on the back side after step 3. Use yellow ochre with a tint of lavender for the pathways and a mixture of lavender and white for the highlights on the rocky areas of the mountain. Add in shapes on the mountain for dirt tracks and tiny details with dry-on-wet technique.

(continued)

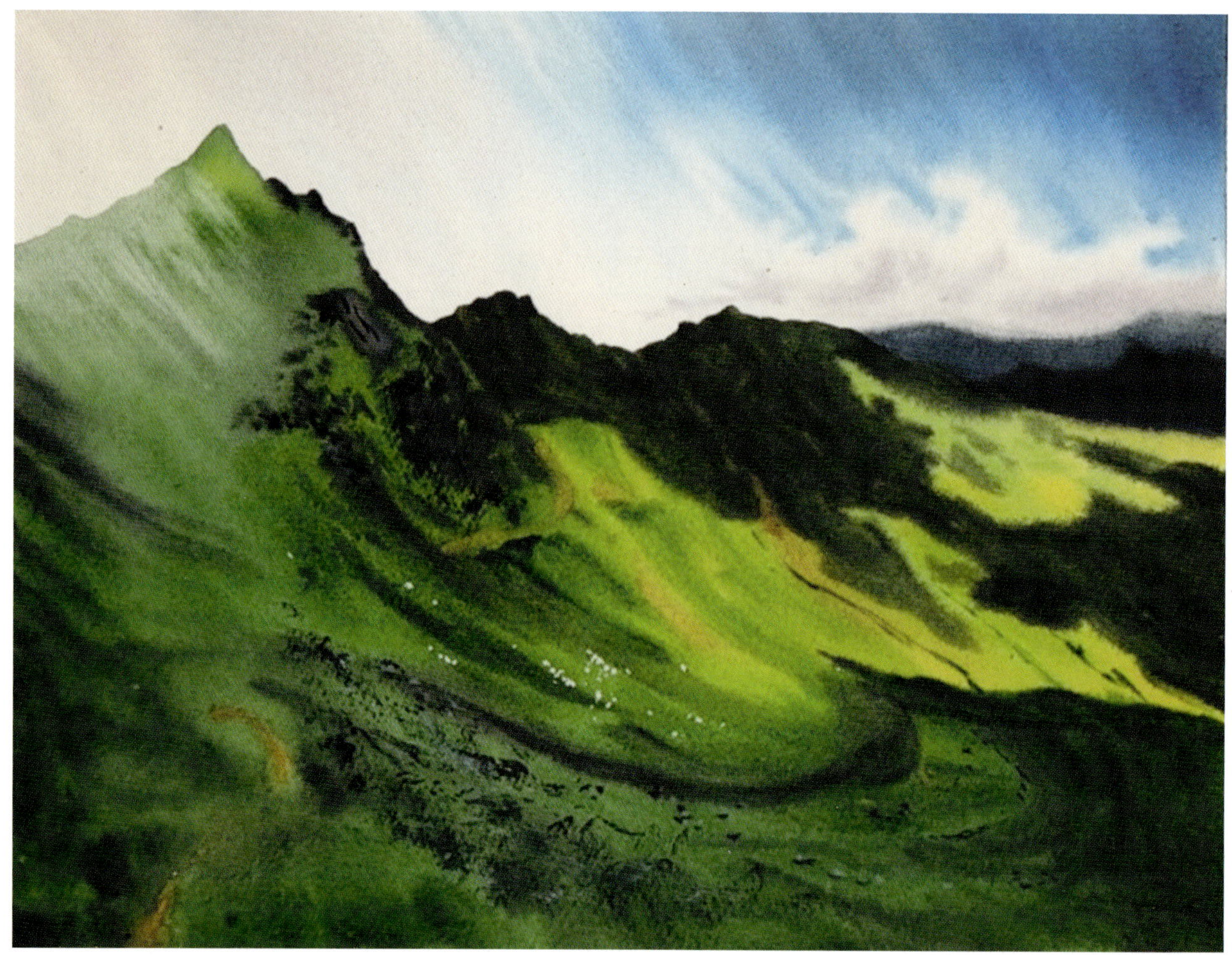

STEP 6: Mix in the darker shadow color with dark green and Payne's gray and add it to the mountain using the dry-on-wet method. Create different shapes, as seen in the reference, for the shadow areas. Soften any edges that are harsh using a second brush. Once the mountain has completely dried, you can finish it off with some dry brush strokes with dark green or Payne's gray on random areas.

FLYING DANDELIONS

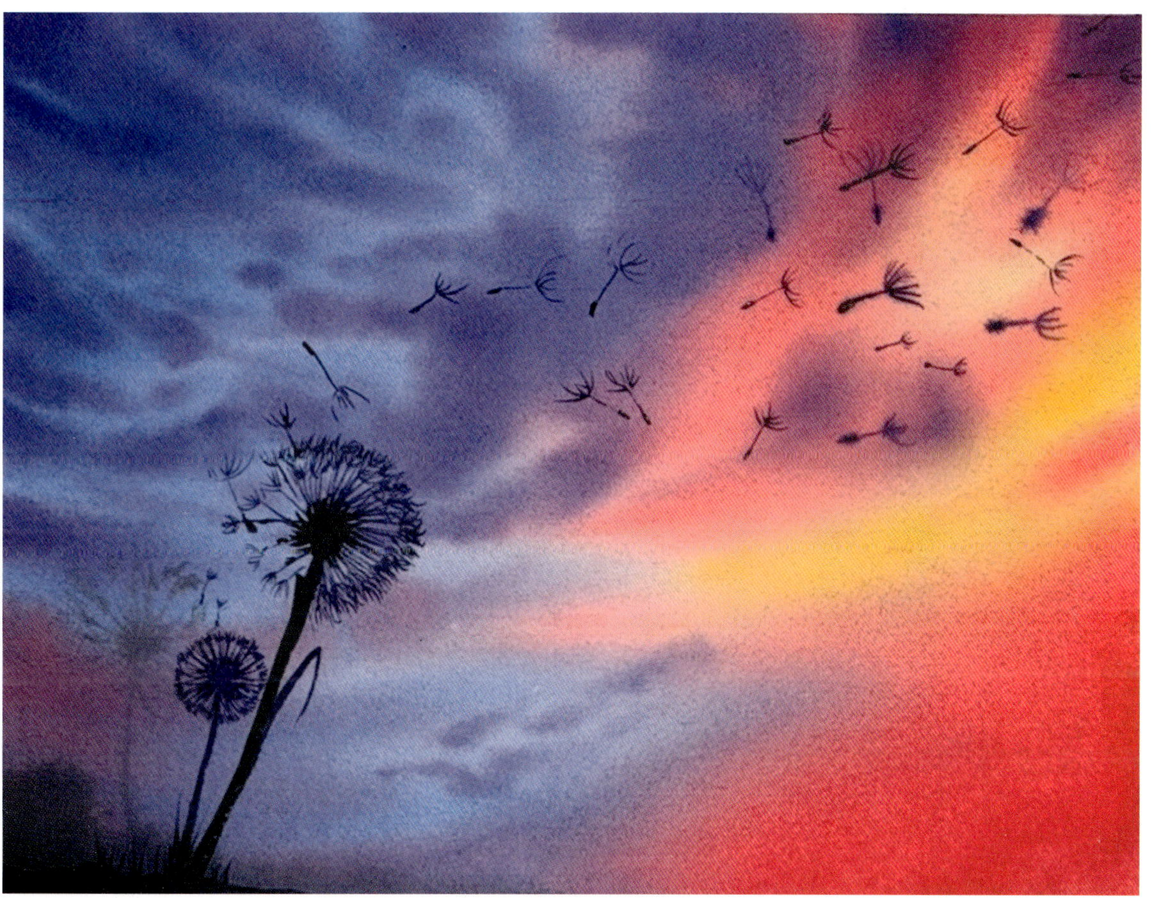

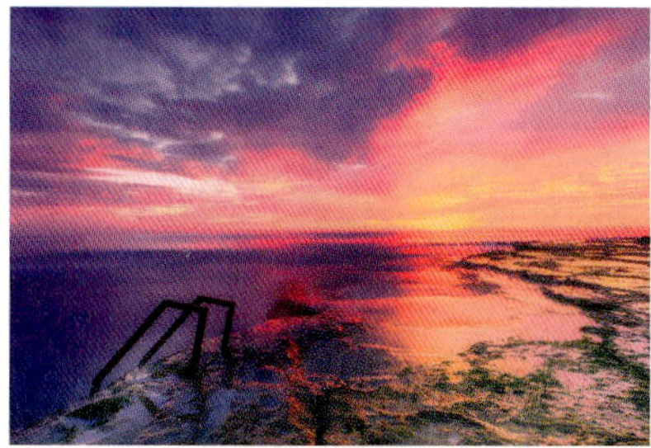

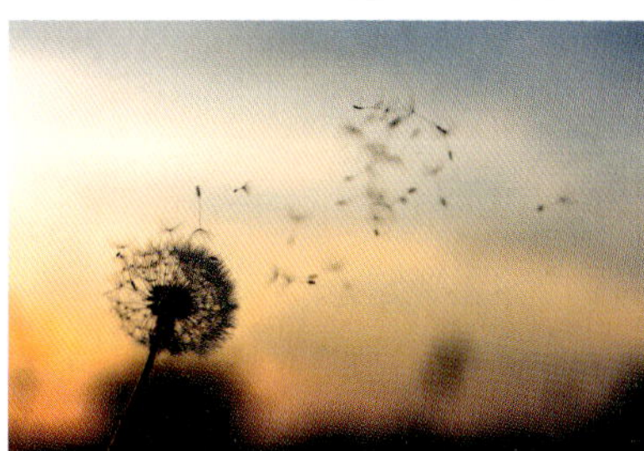

WATER TECHNIQUE: **Applying water to both sides of the paper**

PAPER SIZE: **A4**

COLORS: **Transparent yellow, quinacridone violet rose, cobalt blue or ultramarine blue, violet, Payne's gray**

(continued)

This project has been painted by combining two reference pictures. You can always add other elements of interest to your composition to enhance the painting for the viewer's eyes.

STEP 1: Start by applying water onto both sides of the paper. Once the paper has been fixed on the board you are using, start with a transparent yellow to depict the lightest glowing areas in the sky.

STEP 2: Blend quinacridone violet rose (PV19) into the sky areas. Do not cross over too much into the yellow areas, as we do not want it to turn red at this point.

STEP 3: Fill the rest of the sky with cobalt blue or ultramarine blue such that the areas adjoining the pink turn into a bright purple hue. Be very careful that the blue and yellows do not mix together.

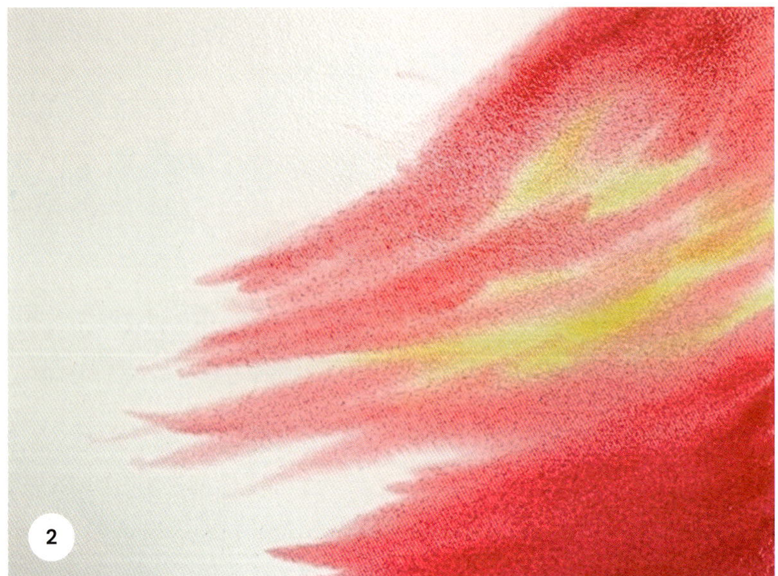

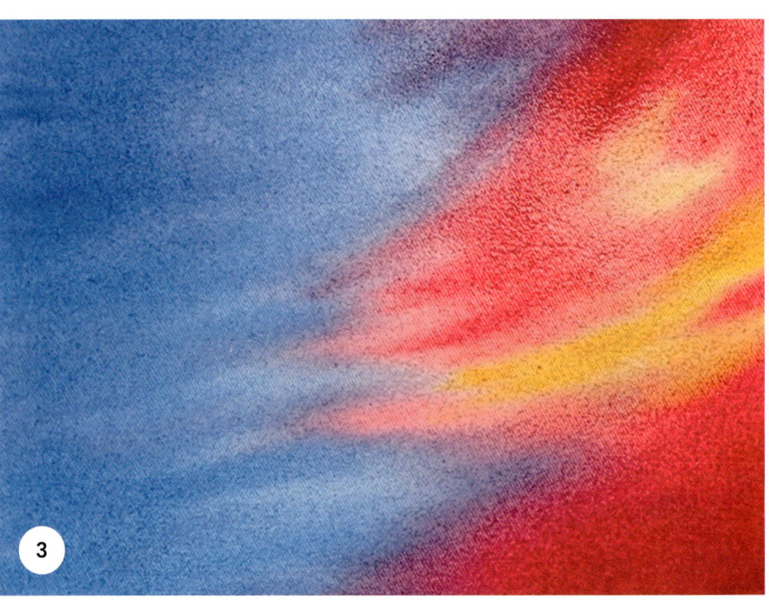

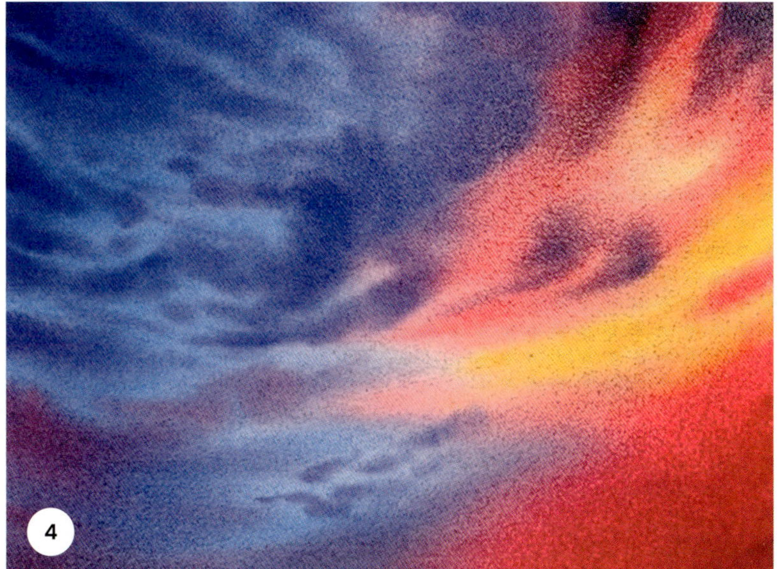

STEP 4: Add in violet clouds on the top in various directions. Use the entire bristles of a pointed round brush; change the angle of the strokes to get the clouds turned and twisted in different directions. You can also add more clouds to the areas adjoining the blue and rose so that the transition looks smooth.

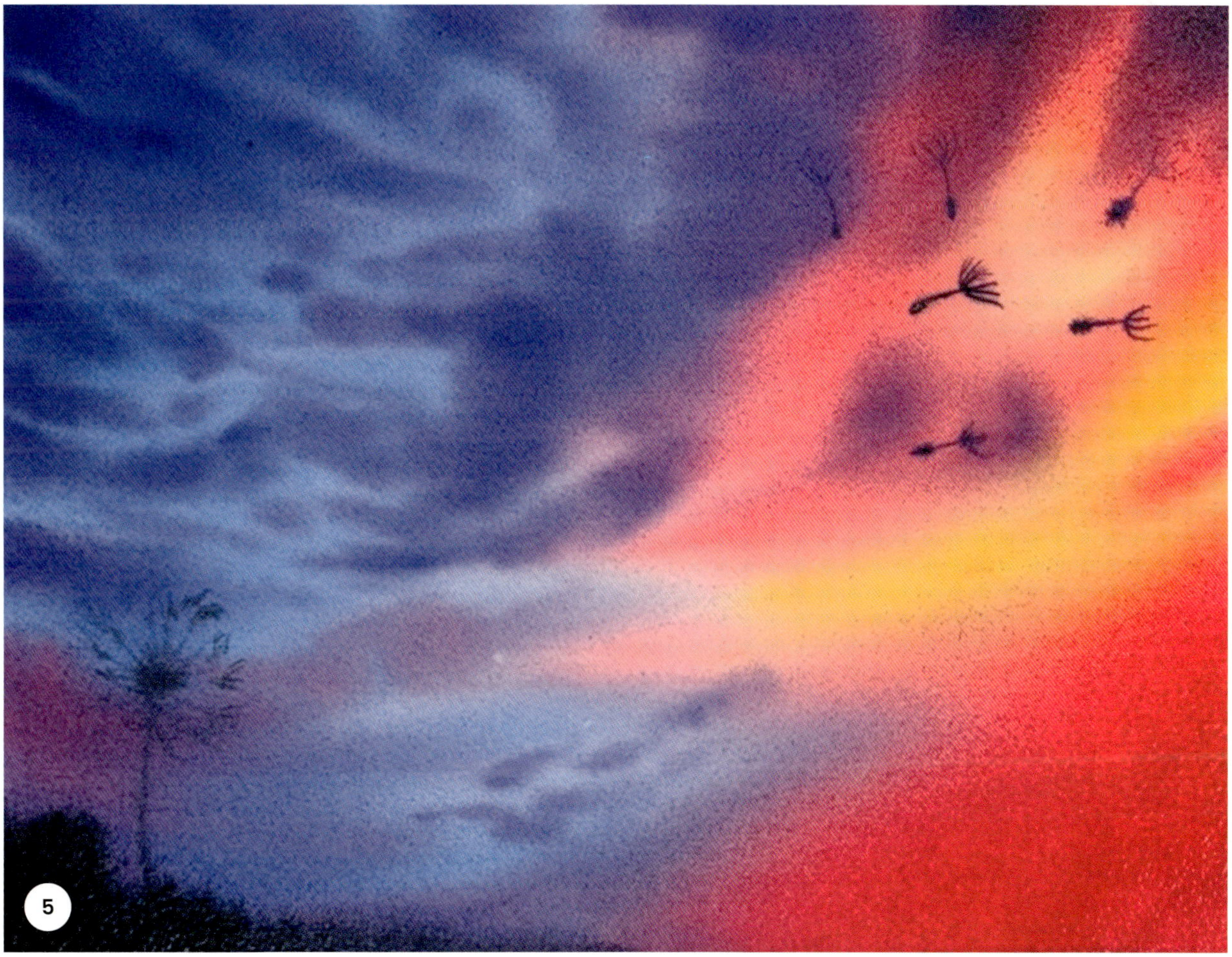

STEP 5: While the paper is still wet, add in some dry-on-wet background details—some floating dandelion seeds and some soft dandelions at the bottom areas—with a mixture of violet and Payne's gray. You can add more details to your liking at this point. Then wait for the entire paper to completely dry.

(continued)

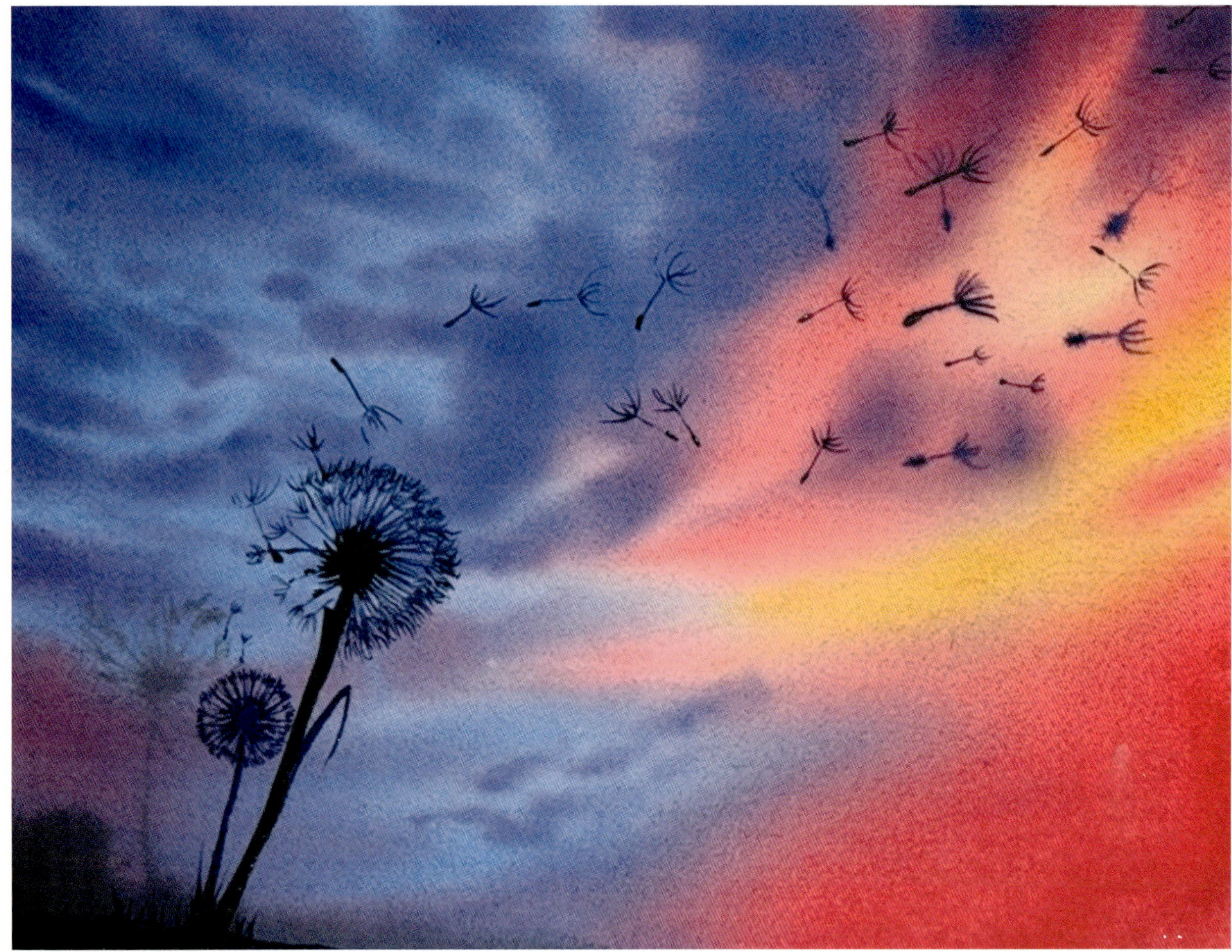

STEP 6: Once the paper has dried, add in detailed foreground dandelions with the wet-on-dry method using the same violet and Payne's gray mixture. Add more floating seeds as well so that the wet-on-dry strokes appear clearer than the background strokes.

THE WINTER SUN

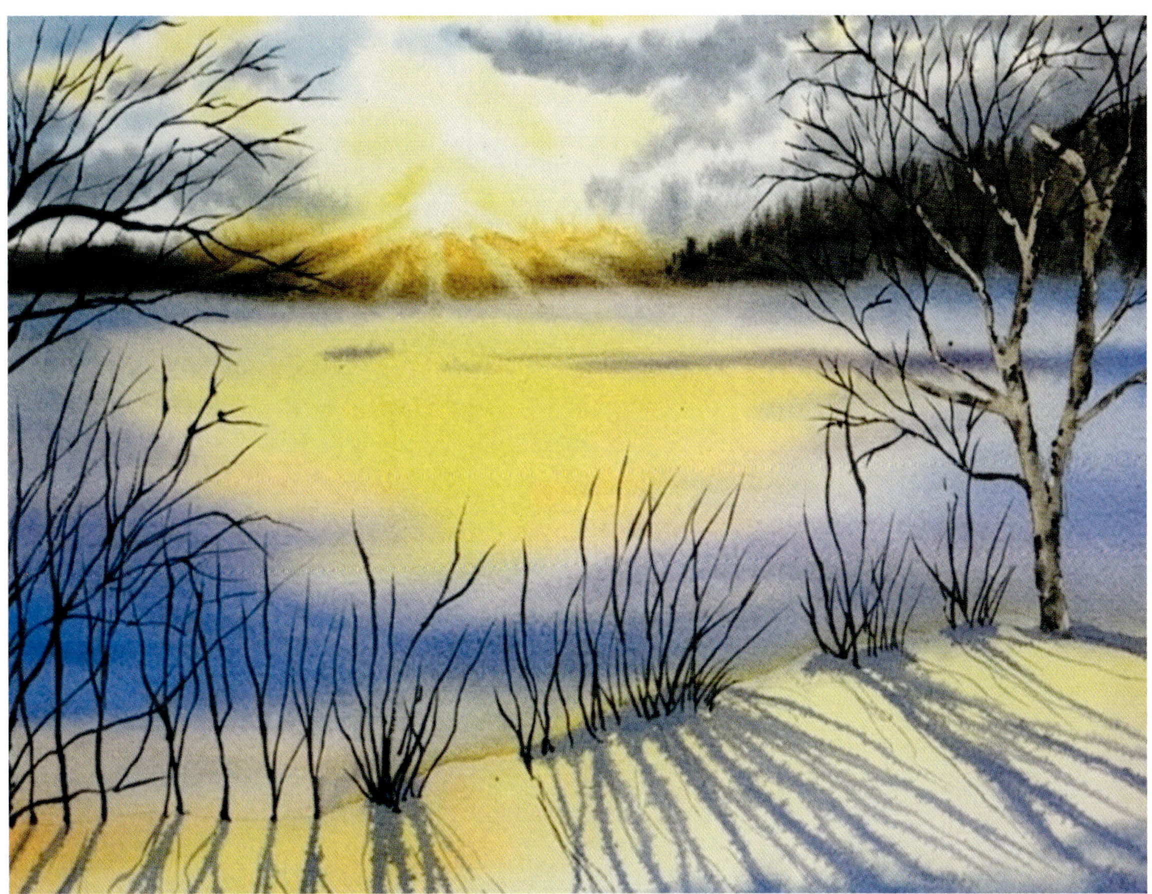

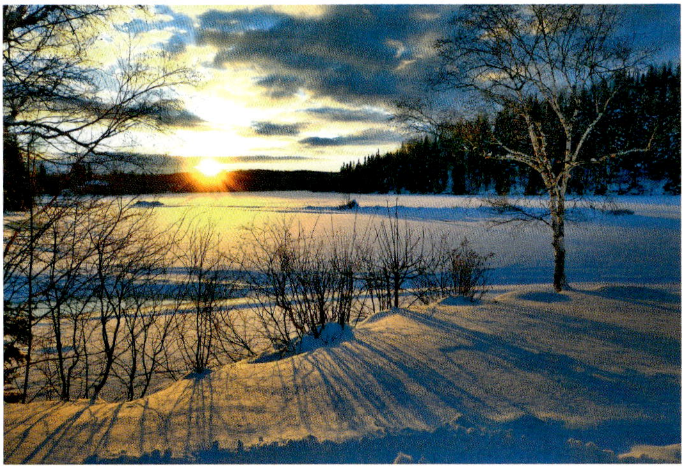

WATER TECHNIQUE: Applying water to both sides of the paper

PAPER SIZE: A4

COLORS: Transparent yellow, phthalo blue, Payne's gray, transparent brown, quinacridone gold or burnt sienna and yellow, sepia or brown and Payne's gray, cobalt blue, violet, orange, lavender, yellow ochre

(continued)

STEP 1: Start with a simple sketch to depict the most important elements from the reference. Anything that can be added with the brush can be skipped. Apply a thin layer of masking fluid to the tree on the right side so that it remains white while we paint the rest of the painting.

STEP 2: Apply water to both sides of the painting and then add in the clouds using a transparent yellow, phthalo blue, and a gray mixed from the primaries. Be careful not to let the blue and the yellow touch each other on the paper.

STEP 3: Add in the furthest bushes using a Payne's gray and brown mixture toward the left side, moving to brown, and finally a quinacridone gold shade (or a mixture of burnt sienna and yellow) toward the sun. Add the pine trees on the right side with wet-on-wet using sepia (or brown and Payne's gray mixture). Add in some cobalt blue to depict the snow underneath the pine trees. Use the lifting method with a small pointed round brush to lift off the sun's rays in different directions.

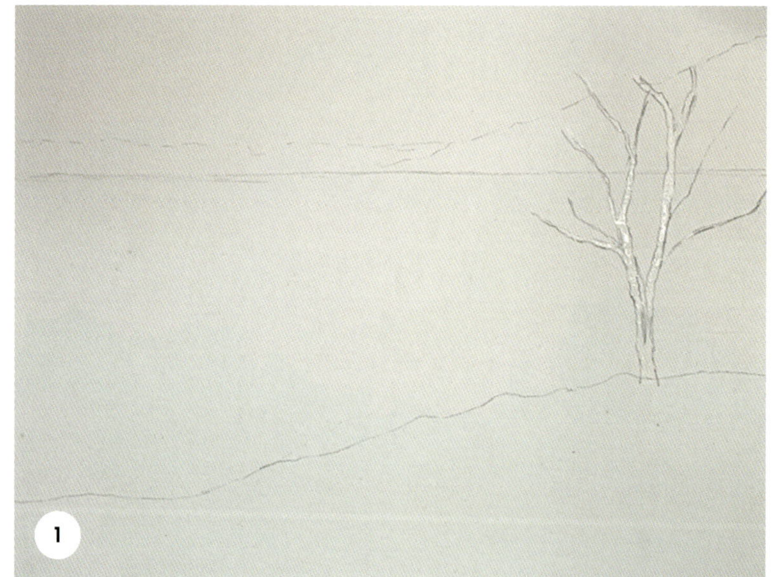

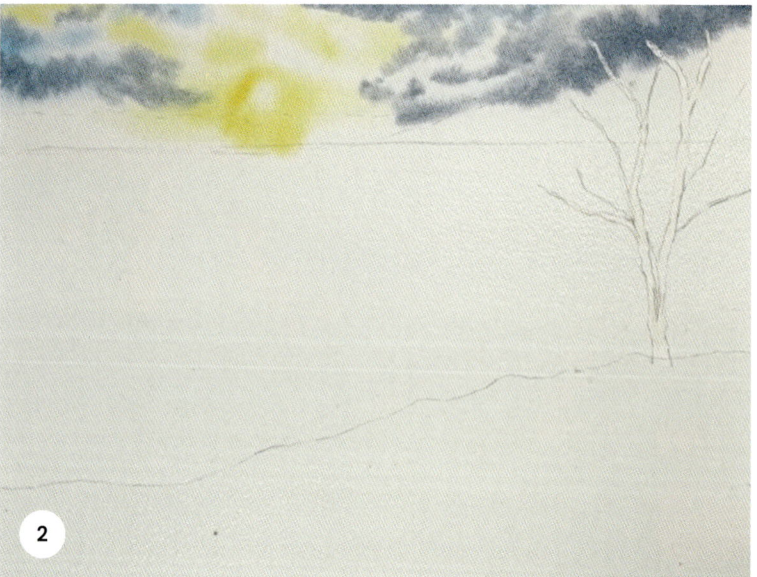

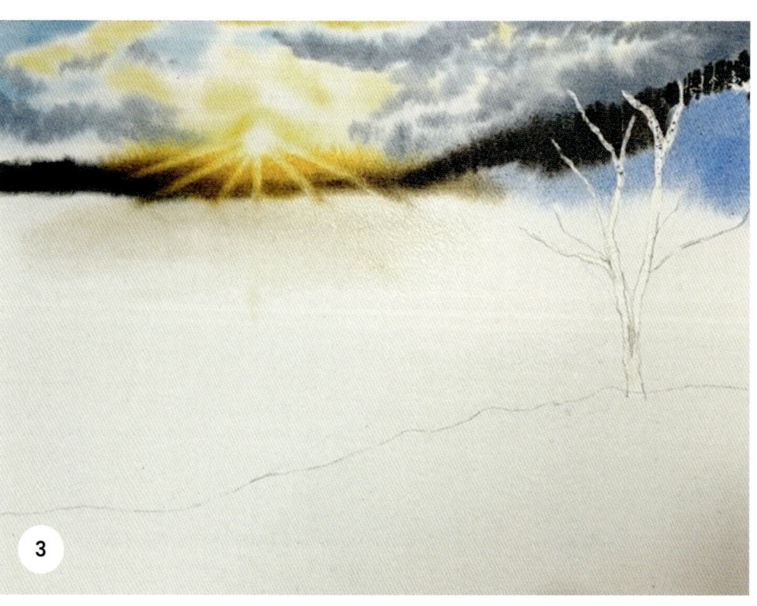

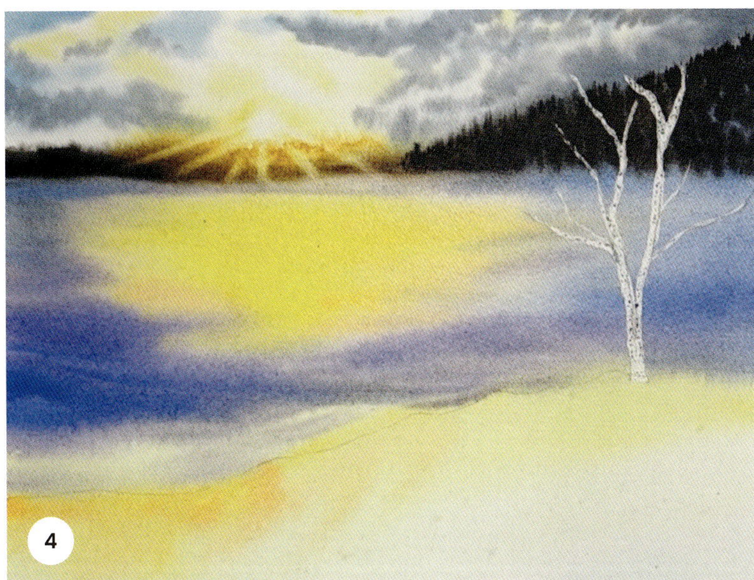

STEP 4: On to the snow regions: add in transparent yellow toward the areas right in front of the sun and the foreground. All the areas closer to the yellow can be painted in violet (complementary color of yellow) to depict the shadows on the snow. The areas furthest away from the sun can be painted with cobalt blue. Mix in some orange in random areas of the foreground to get some glowing areas there. Fill in the background pine trees with Payne's gray, but remember to leave some gaps here and there so that the blue can be reflected through.

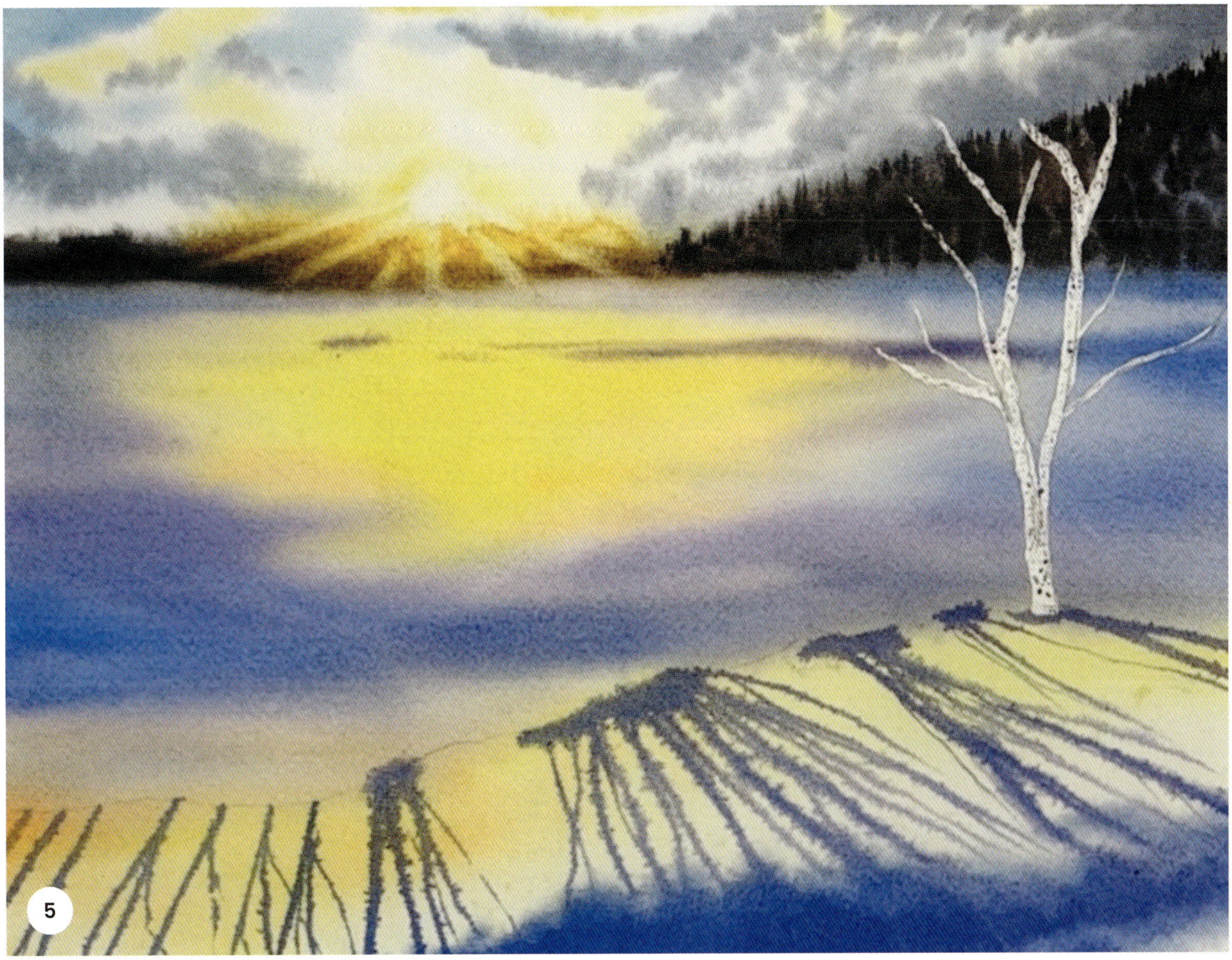

STEP 5: Add in violet shadow marks of various twigs and branches on the foreground areas. Note that you need to capture the direction of the shadows correctly.

(continued)

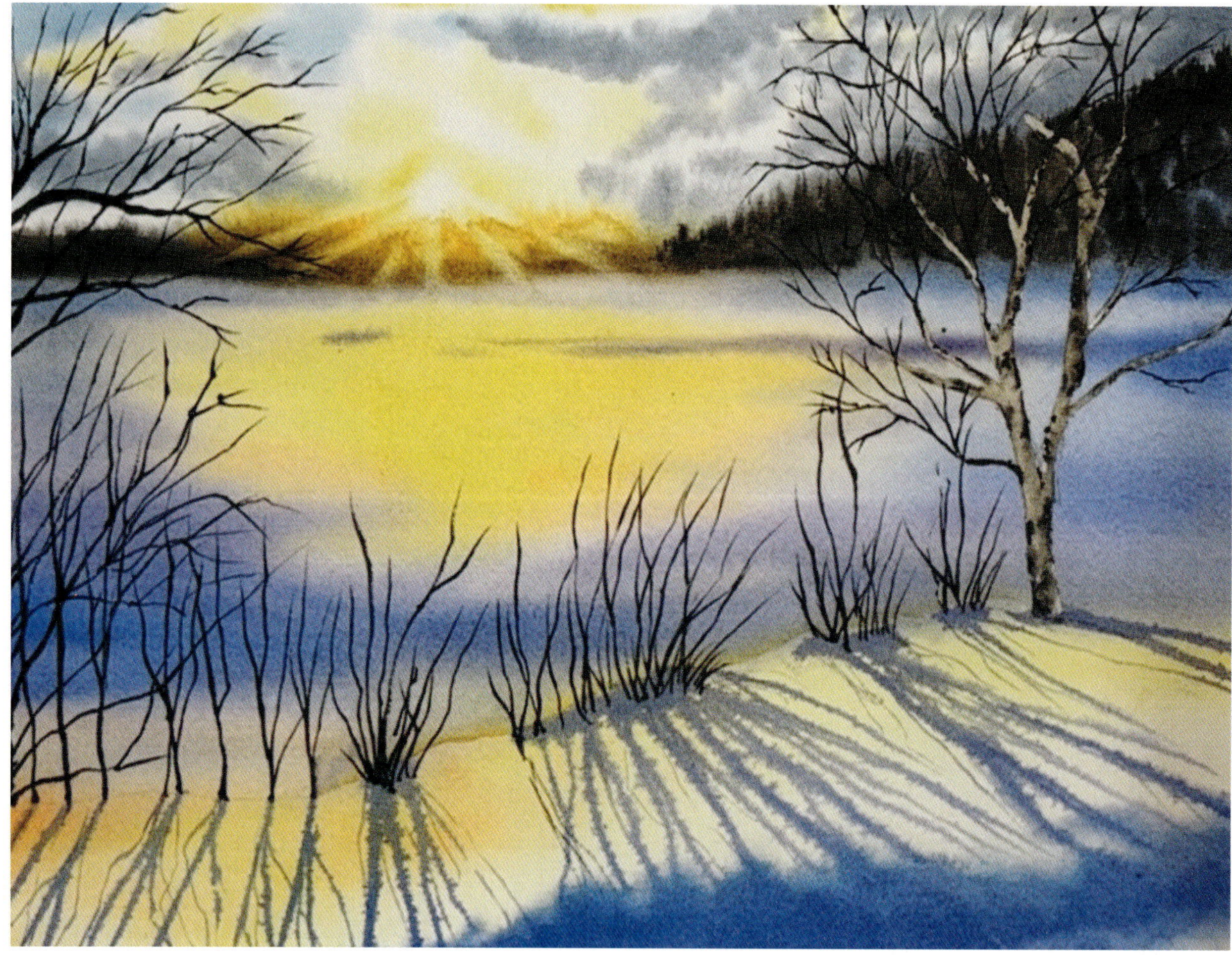

STEP 6: Remove the masking fluid from the tree and paint it using a mixture of lavender, yellow ochre, and brown with some random black spots in between using Payne's gray. Using a thin liner brush and Payne's gray, finish off the tree branches, other branches, and twigs on the snow areas that complement the shadows.

DRAMATIC SKY IN SUMMER

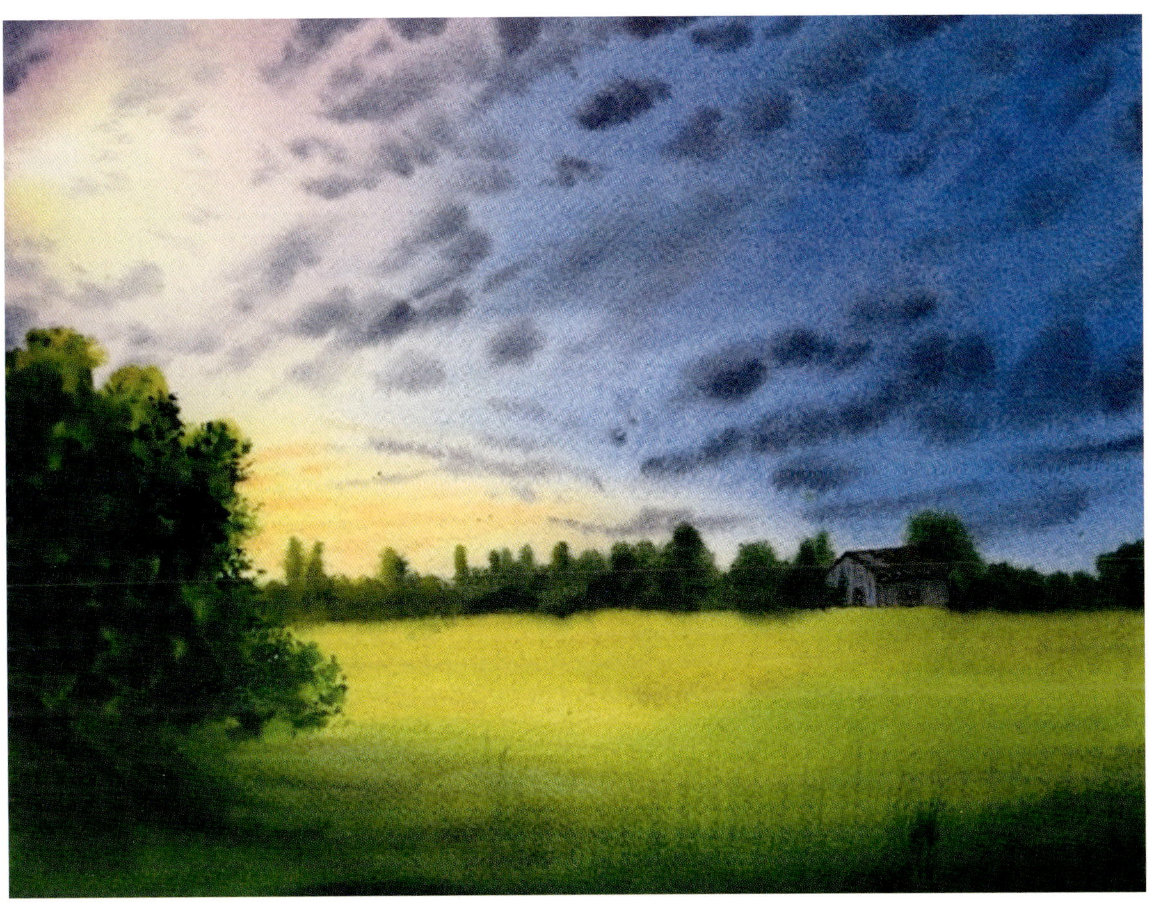

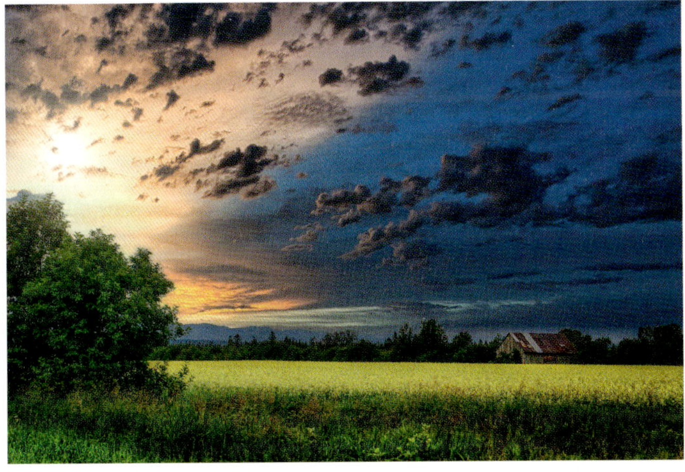

WATER TECHNIQUE: Applying water to both sides of the paper

PAPER SIZE: A4

COLORS: Transparent yellow, violet, alizarin crimson, cobalt blue, indigo, transparent orange, dark green, olive green, Payne's gray, sap green, lavender, transparent brown, dark brown

(continued)

STEP 1: Make a simple pencil sketch of the reference to capture the tiny house and the horizon line.

STEP 2: Apply water to the painting in whichever way you prefer and start with the sky. I have used the two-side water application method. Using transparent yellow, a mixture of violet and alizarin, cobalt blue, and indigo, paint the background sky by following the reference picture. Use indigo over the cobalt blue to create darker areas in the sky.

STEP 3: Add in darker clouds with the wet-on-wet technique using indigo for the bluish regions, a mix of violet and indigo for the purple areas, and orange for the yellow areas.

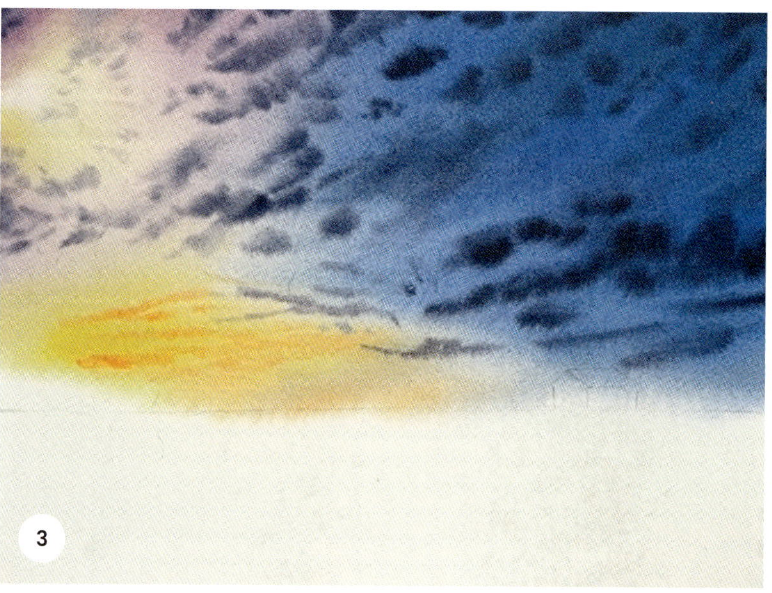

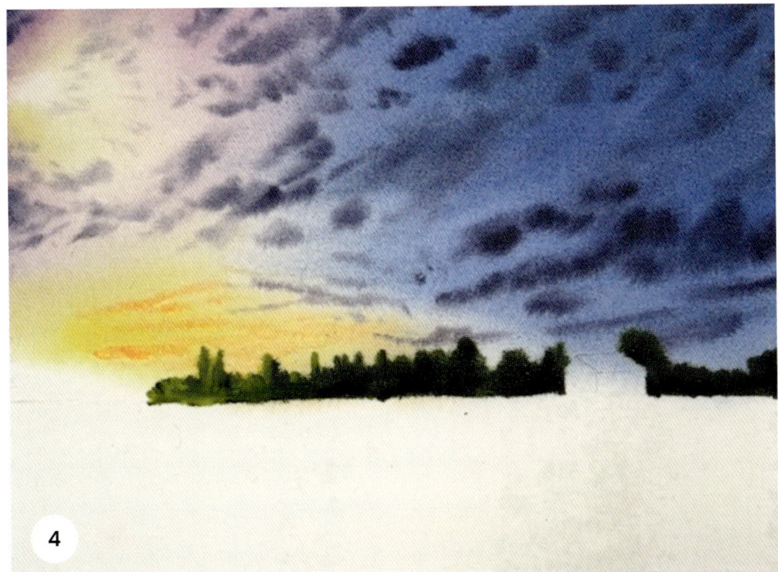

STEP 4: Start the bushy structure at the horizon with a dark green on the right side; remember to capture the lighter areas with olive green as you reach toward the sunlit areas on the left side. At the same time, add in darker shadows to some areas of the bush with indigo or Payne's gray.

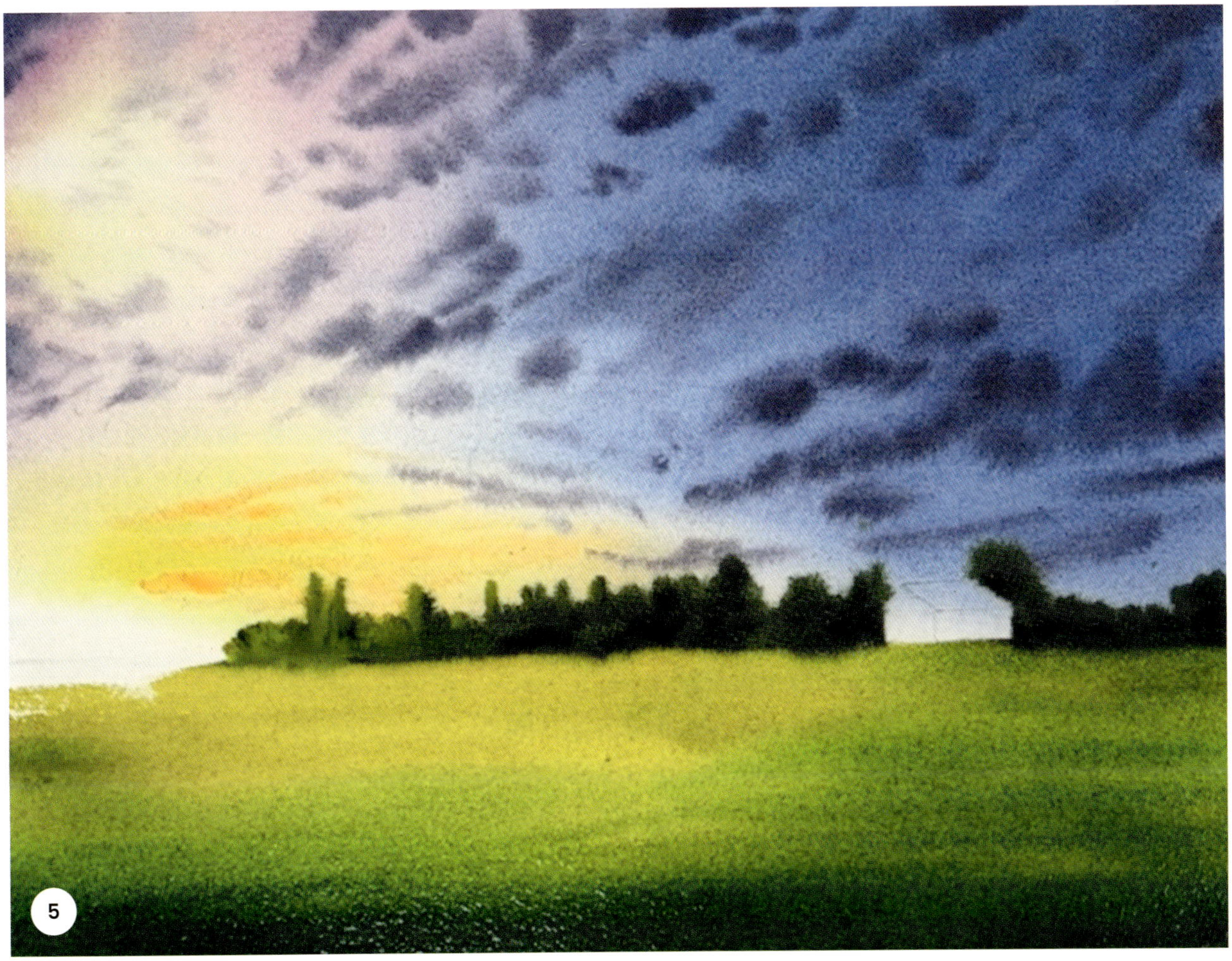

STEP 5: Paint the foreground grass with a mix of yellow, sap green, olive green, and darker green. Capture lighter areas toward the left where the sun is and darker areas toward the bottom and right side.

(continued)

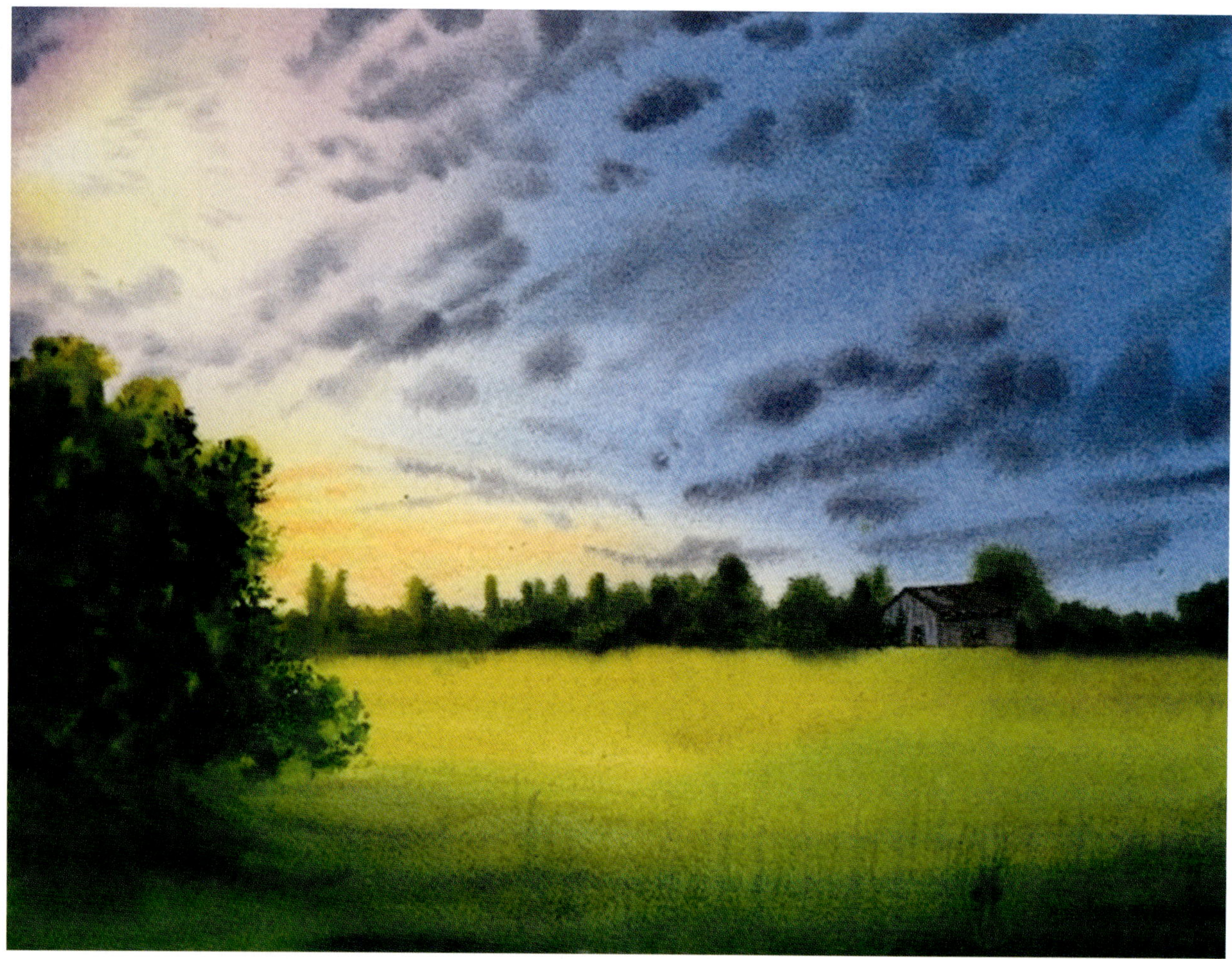

STEP 6: Add in the large bush in the foreground with a mix of greens. Start with olive green at the top to depict the highlight and use sap green to paint the midtones. Add the dark details with dark green and further darkest details with indigo. Blend the bottom of the bush into the foreground grass toward the right side to depict the shadow of the bushy region. Paint the house with a lavender and brown mixture and its roof, doors, and windows with dark brown. Finish off with a liner brush, adding vertically upward strokes on the foreground grass region.

UNDERWATER BUBBLES

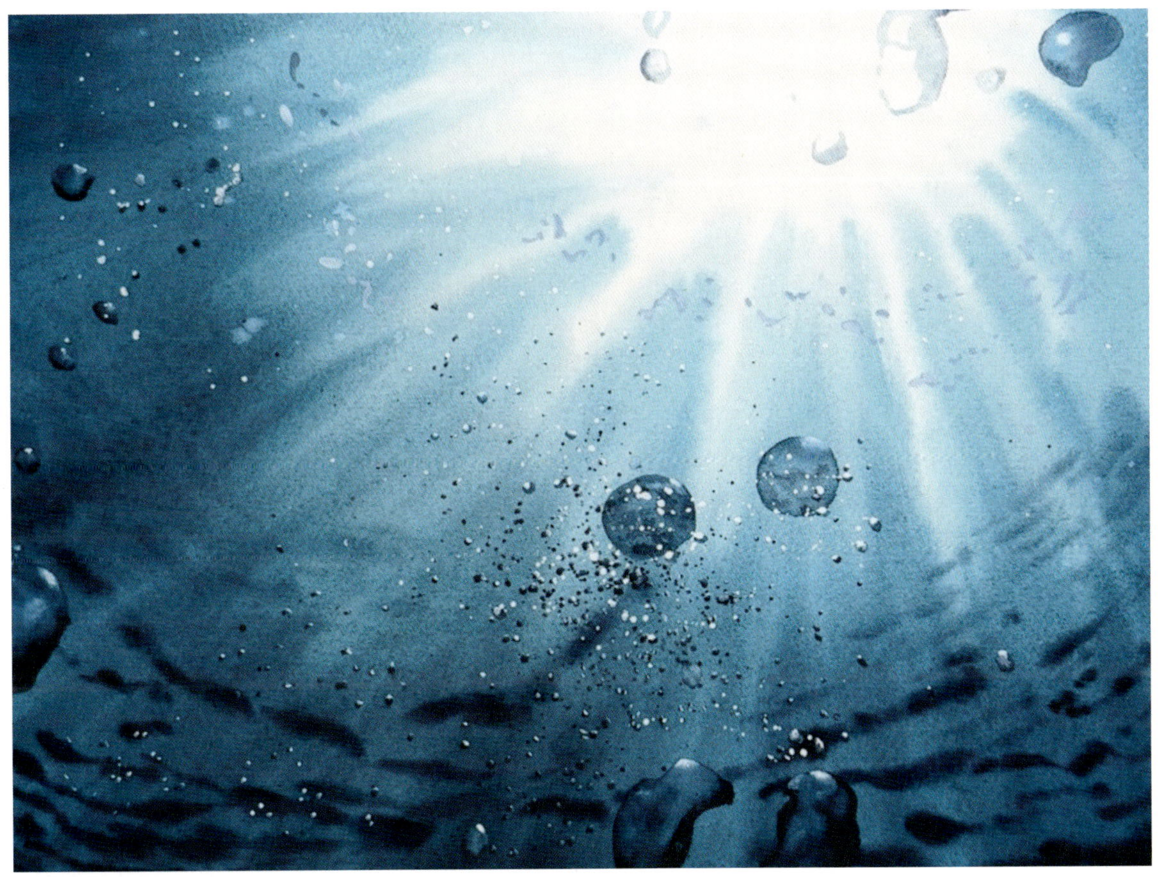

WATER TECHNIQUE: **Taped edges**

PAPER SIZE: **A4**

COLORS: **Turquoise green, indigo, white gouache, lavender**

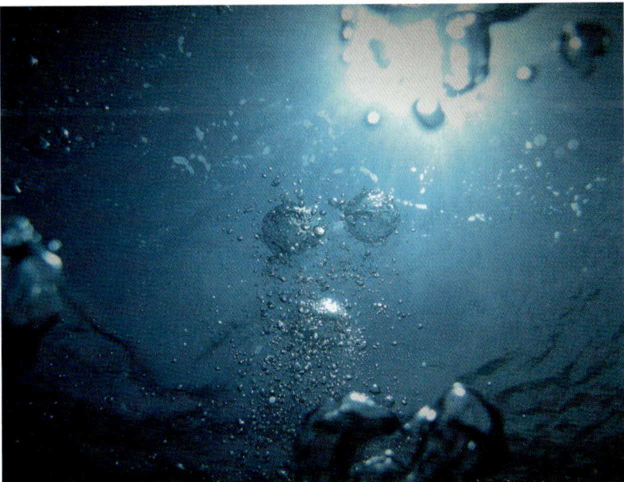

(continued)

STEP 1: Using a bright turquoise green color (I used aqua green from Winsor & Newton), make a nice, blended movement of the water such that all your strokes are toward or away from the light. Make sure to keep the light area as clean as possible. Capture depth by having the darker tones toward the outside and the lighter tones toward the light source.

STEP 2: Using a mixture of indigo with the turquoise green, add in some wet-on-wet random underwater wave strokes following a semicircular curve. This depicts the wave movement following the light source. Add in white splatters toward the top while the paper is still wet.

STEP 3: Once the first layer is completely dry, start adding bubbles onto the paper at random. To add larger bubbles, start with indigo toward the bottom edge, then use turquoise green to fill up the shape of the bubble. The indigo then becomes the shadow edge. Add in a tiny drop of white paint to make the highlight inside the bubble that is the reflection of the light.

STEP 4: Add in many more bubbles of different sizes. To add in tiny bubbles, add in a lot of splatters with white paint. Once they have dried, add a touch of indigo right next to each of the splattered white drops. This marks both the highlights and the shadow on the bubble, giving the neutral effect and effectively giving more depth to the painting. Finish off with some random strokes toward the top with a mixture of white and little lavender (2 parts white and 1 part lavender).

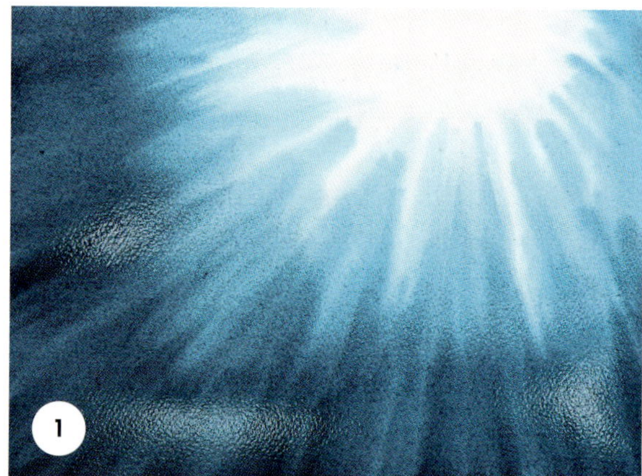

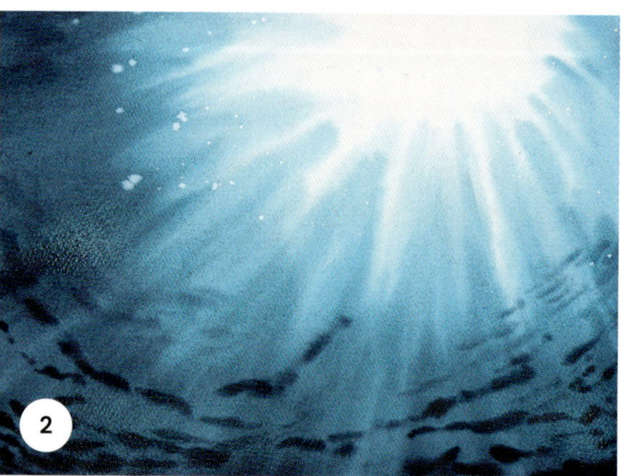

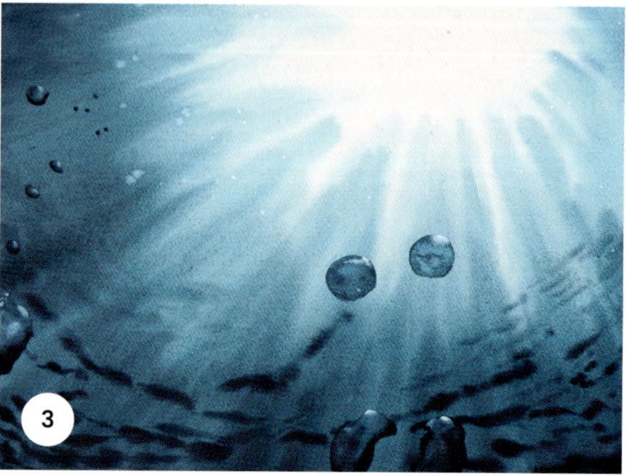

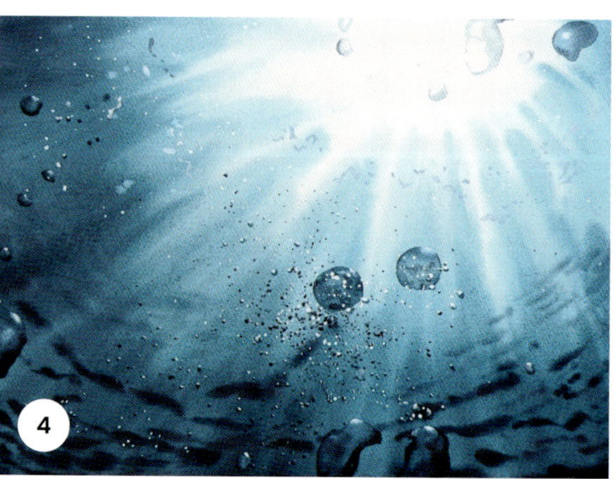

OCEAN AERIAL DRONE SHOT

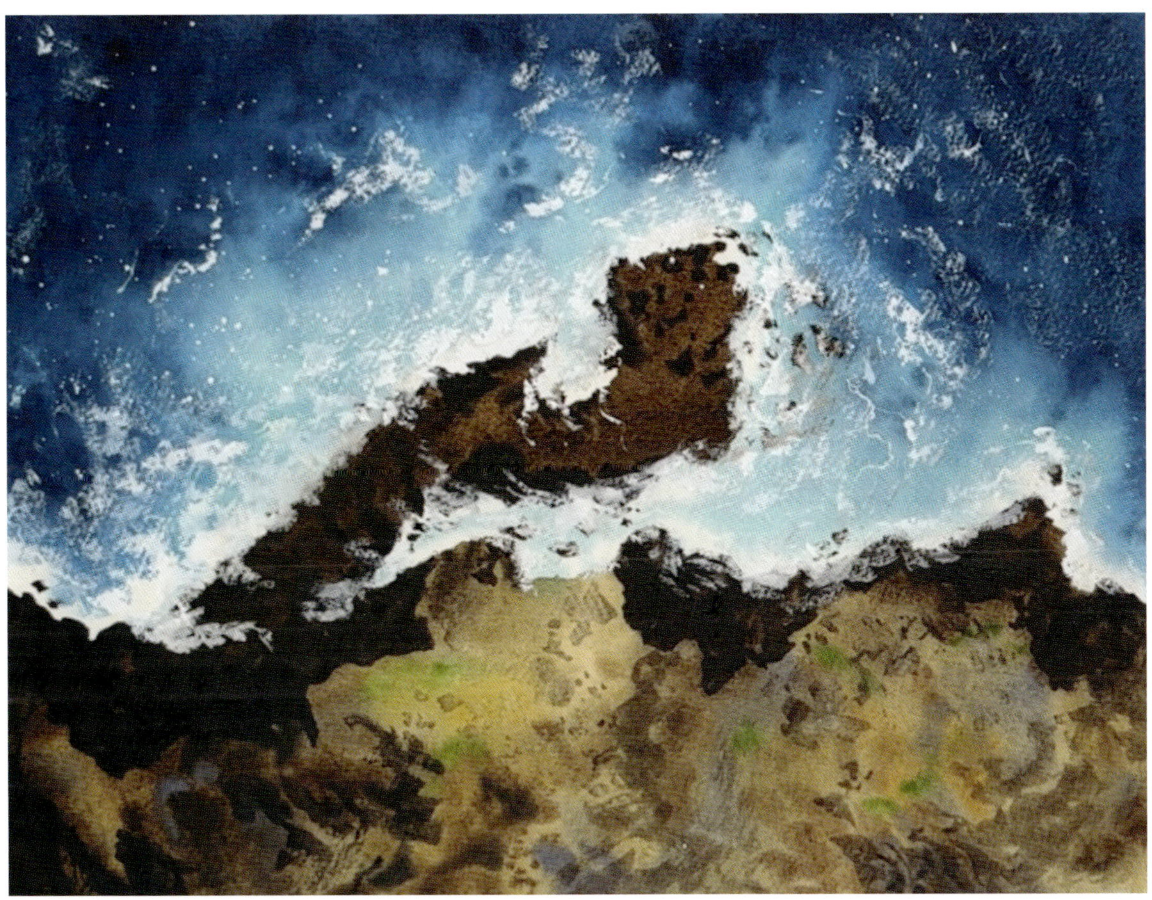

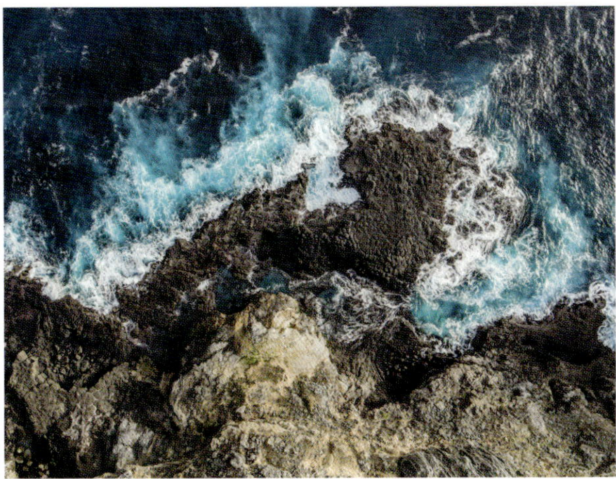

WATER TECHNIQUE: **Applying water to both sides of the paper**

PAPER SIZE: **A4**

COLORS: **Phthalo blue, phthalo green, indigo, dark brown, yellow ochre, lavender, transparent brown, olive green, Payne's gray, white gouache**

(continued)

STEP 1: Sketch out the important lines and curves from the reference. There is no need to add the tiny stones in the ocean or every single detail on the rocks. Just the outline of the shape will do. Optional: Apply masking fluid to some areas with a thin liner brush in random shapes.

STEP 2: After applying water to both sides of the paper and fixing your sheet on the board that you are using, add the first layer of the ocean water area in phthalo blue.

STEP 3: Blend in phthalo green along the areas toward the rocks. Add in darker layer of indigo on the top of the phthalo blue, especially toward the top of the paper and random dots here and there. Leave a lot of white gaps between the rocks and the water region.

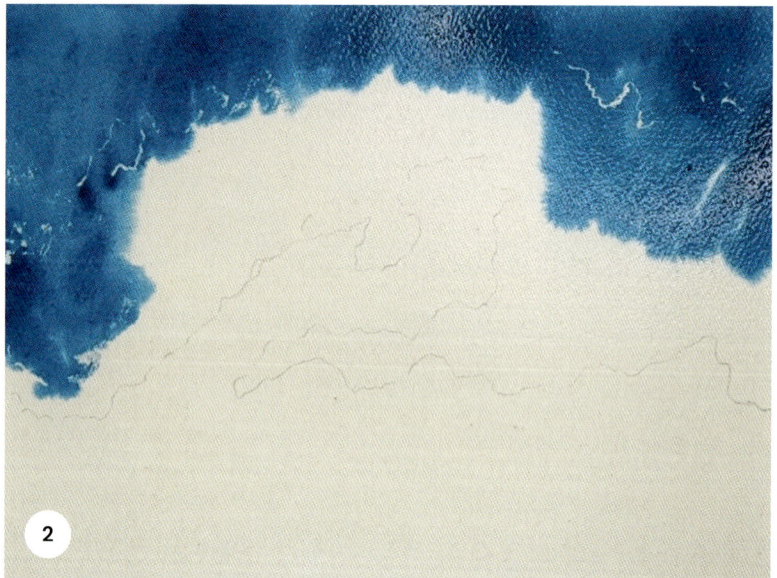

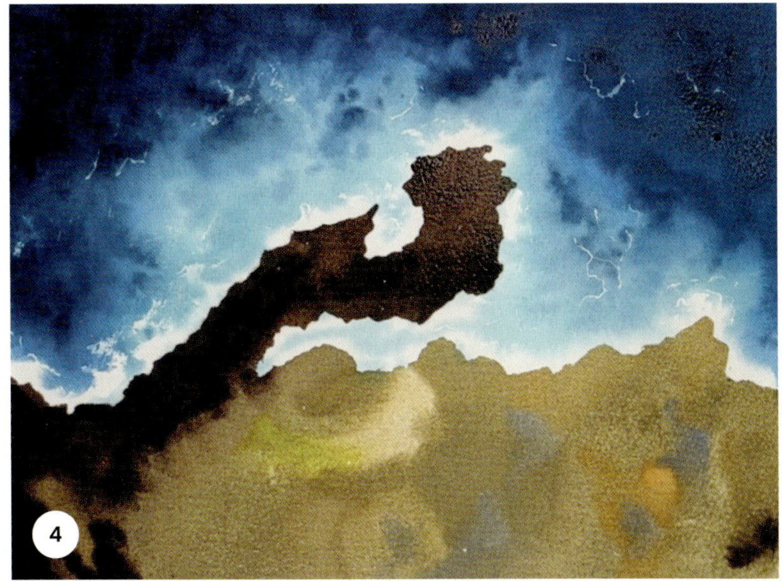

STEP 4: Once the top surface of the paper has dried, paint the rocks using dark brown for the darkest areas and a mix of yellow ochre, lavender, and brown for the lighter areas. You can capture highlights using a lighter tone of this mixture and add in slight color variations using lavender, olive green, and brown.

STEP 5: Add in more structure and shape to the rocks using the same set of colors in a darker shade. Keep the reference picture close to you so you can check where to add these details and in which shapes.

STEP 6: Use darker brown to add separations of the rocks and other small details. The shadows in these areas can be created using a mix of Payne's gray and brown (or sepia).

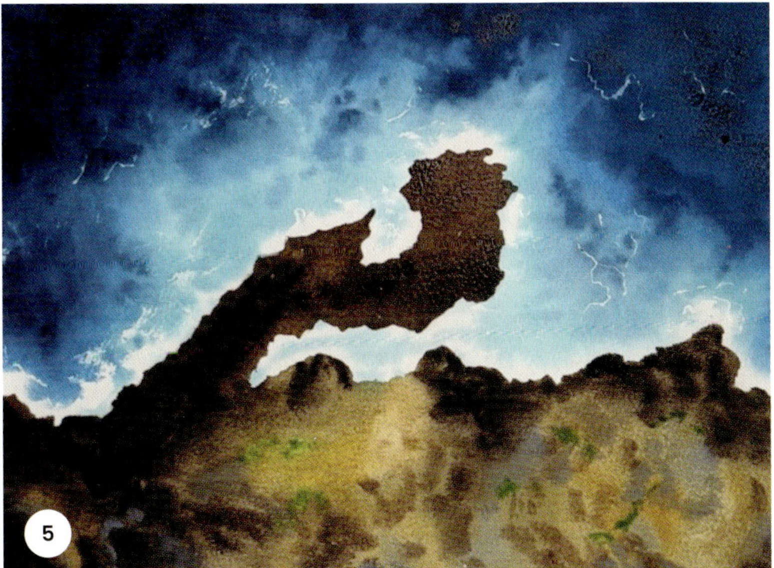

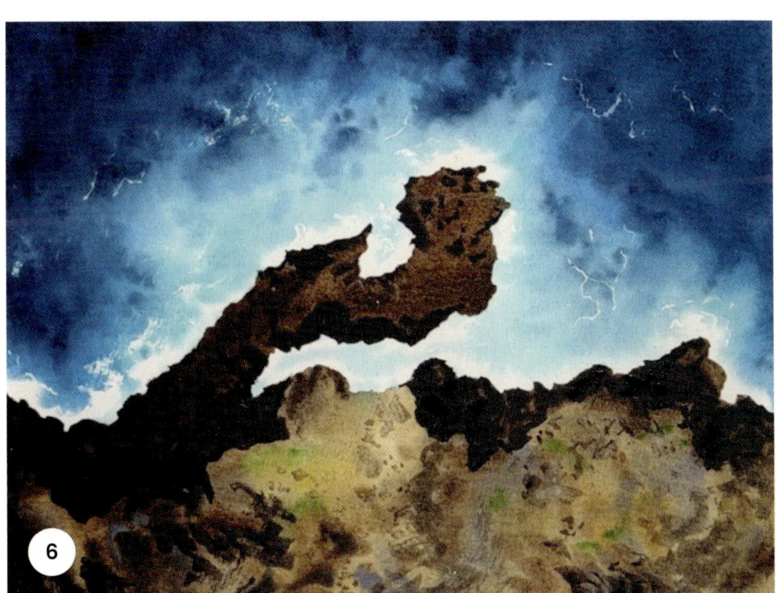

(continued)

STEP 7: Add in random rocks on the water region using dark brown. Add in shadows with an even darker mixture.

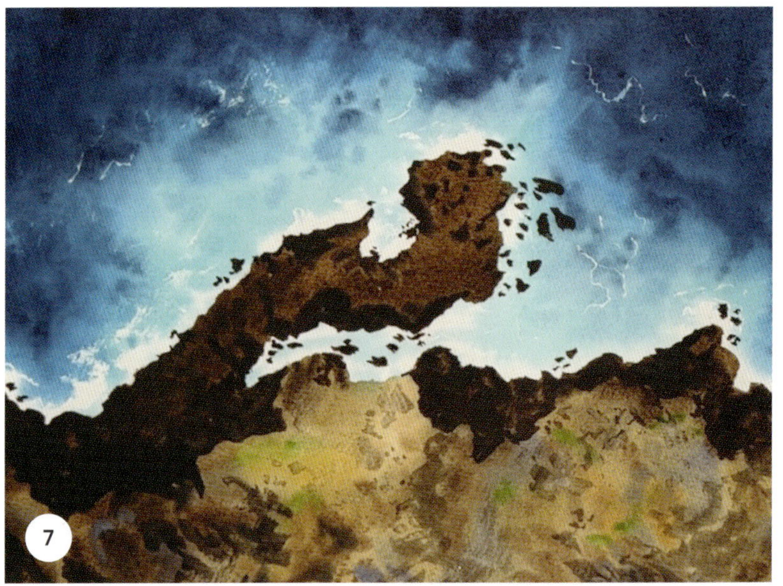

STEP 8: Finish the painting with a lot of foamy areas near the rocks; place some in the water region and some toward the masking fluid areas, if you applied any (remember to peel off the masking fluid). Use the drybrush technique with an opaque white paint. You can add some additional dry areas on some crevices between the rocks to depict the foamy water splashing there and flowing in between the rocks. Add some splatters in the water region to enhance the painting further.

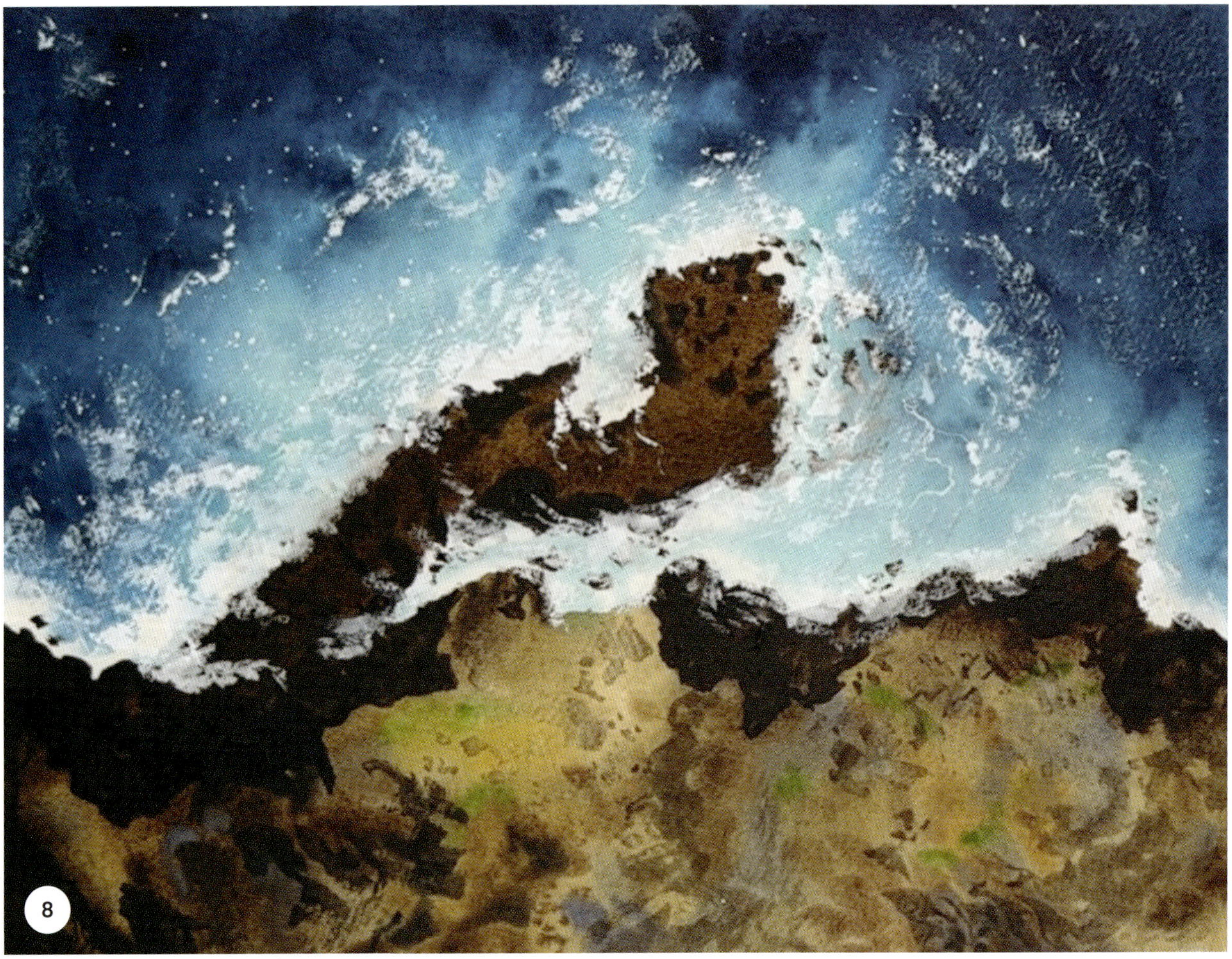

A DOLPHIN UNDERWATER

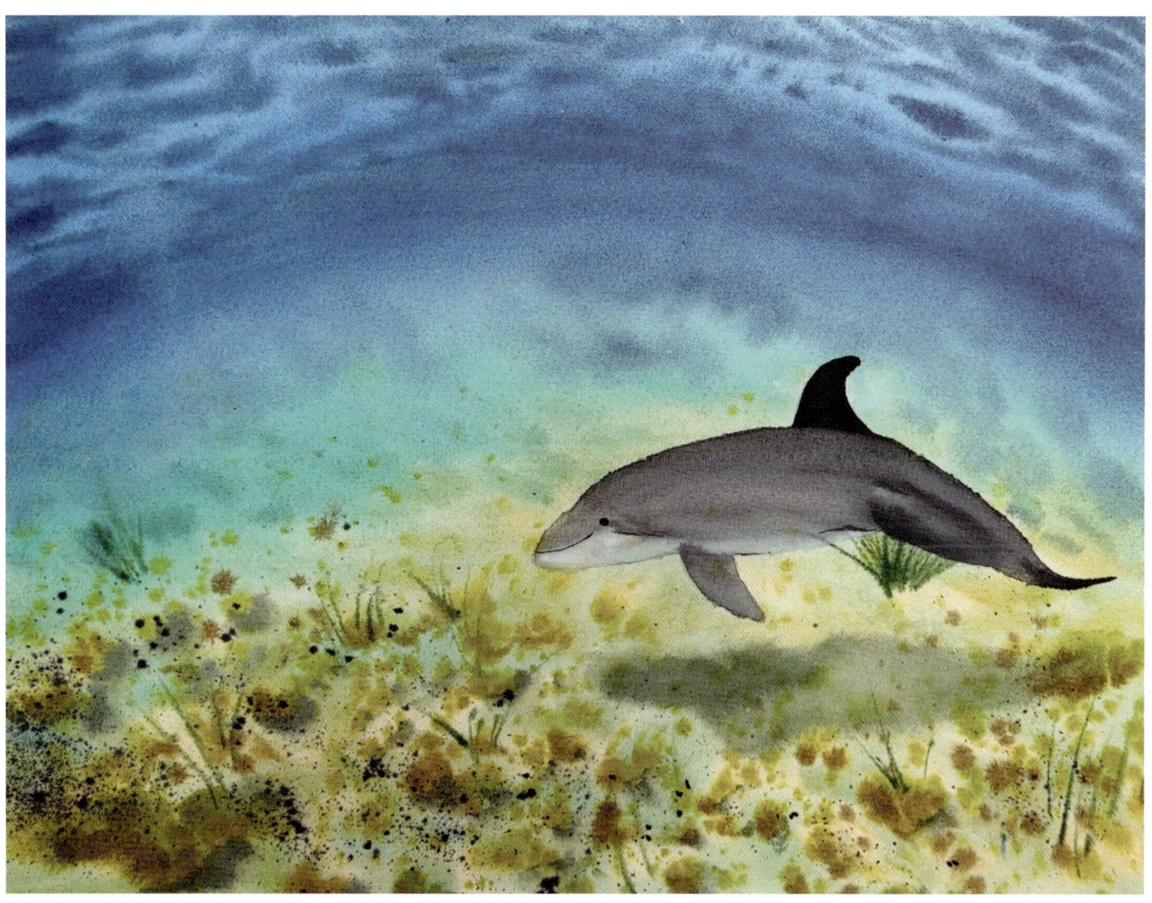

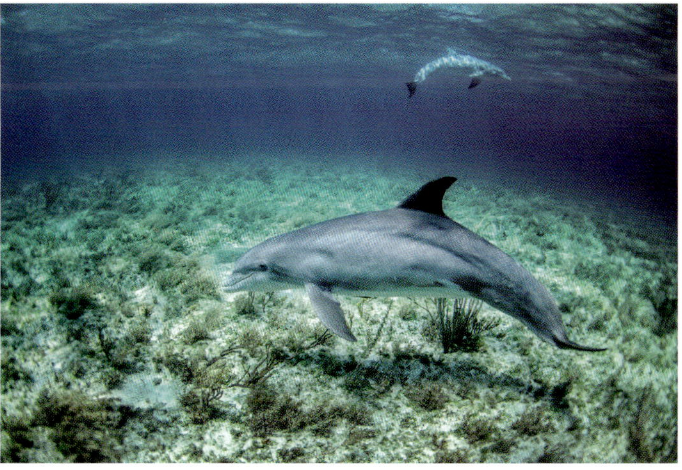

WATER TECHNIQUE: **Applying water to both sides of the paper**

PAPER SIZE: **A4**

COLORS: **Phthalo blue, phthalo green, raw sienna, indigo, transparent brown, olive green, dark green, Payne's gray, white gouache**

(continued)

STEP 1: Sketch out the dolphin. There are two ways to approach this painting: masking the dolphin with masking fluid or not. I am going to paint without the masking fluid. Apply water onto both sides of the paper and fix it to the board.

STEP 2: Start with phthalo blue and paint in the water. The brush strokes should depict the movement of the water; I have started with a curvy flow.

STEP 3: Mix in phthalo green with the phthalo blue and complete the water area. Toward the bottom, add in raw sienna. Ensure that the dolphin is in the raw sienna region and not in the blue-green water area.

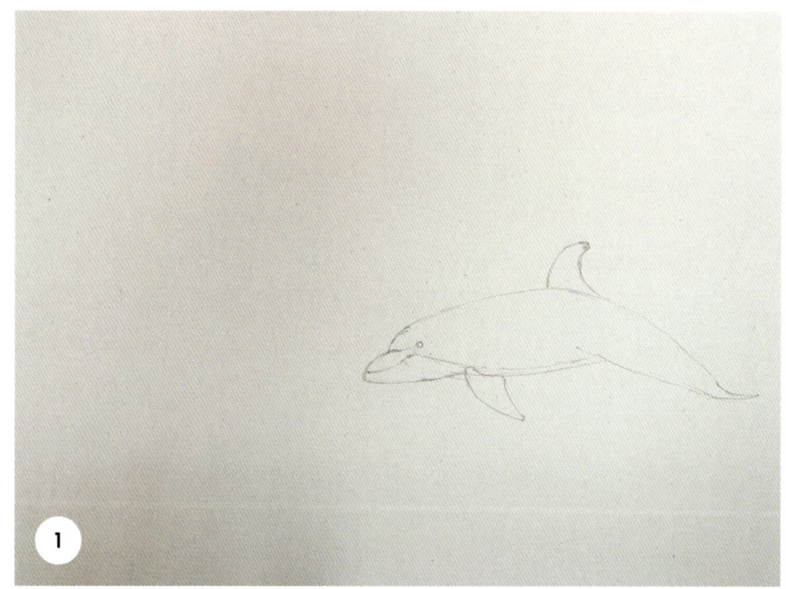

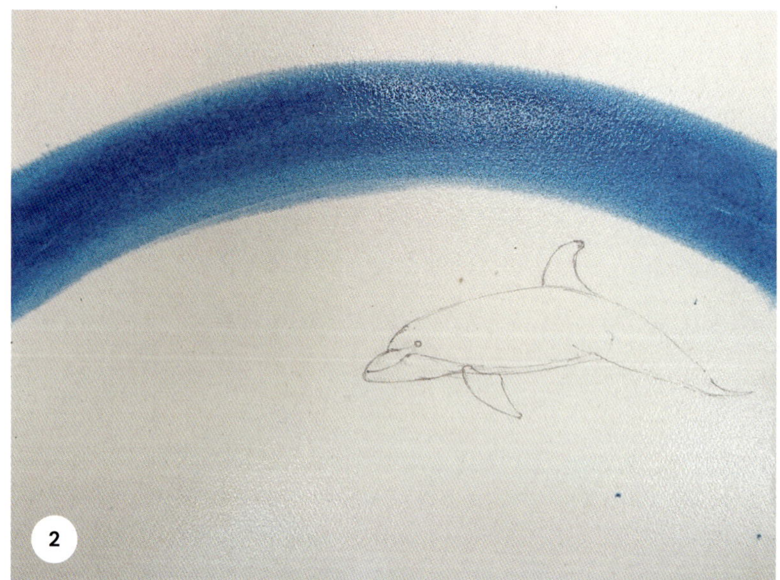

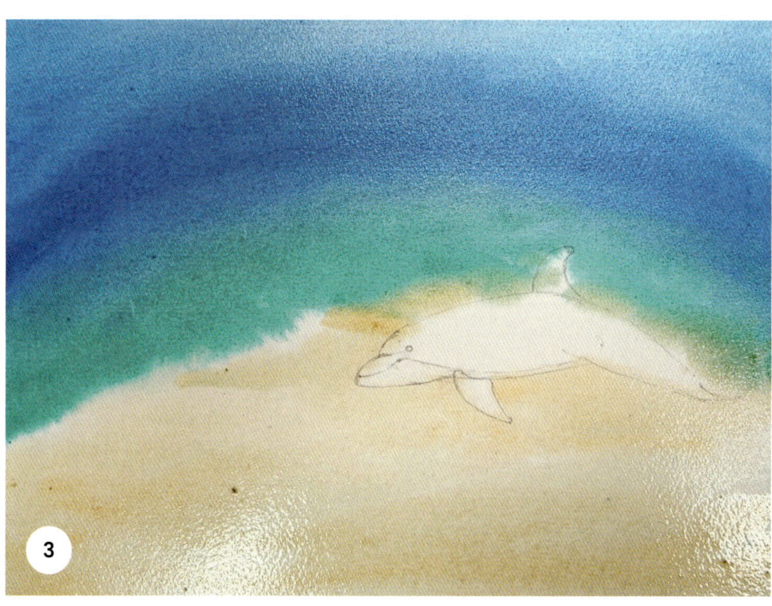

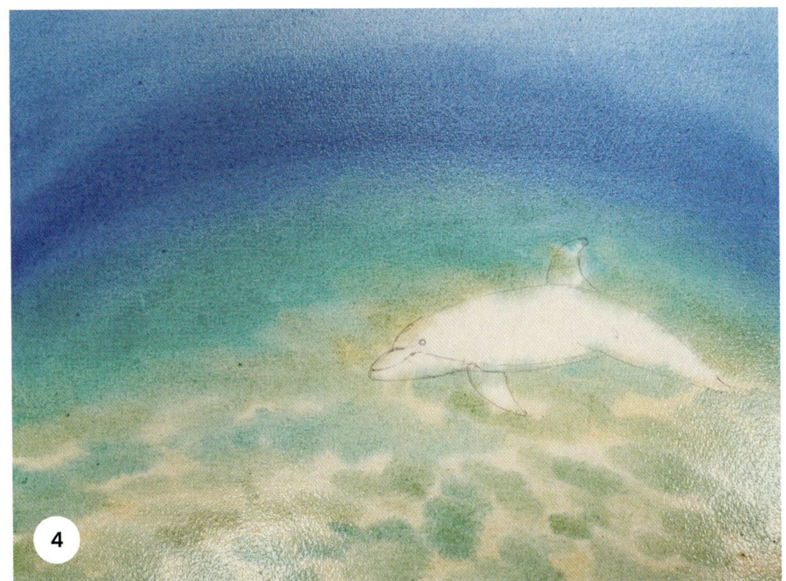

STEP 4: Add in phthalo green in random strokes on top of the raw sienna to depict the irregular ocean floor.

STEP 5: Add the waves in the water using a mixture of indigo and phthalo blue. Remember to capture the movement of the water with your strokes.

STEP 6: Add in a lot of splatters to the bottom ocean floor region with a mixture of transparent brown, olive green, and dark green. Add in random grass to depict the underwater flora as well.

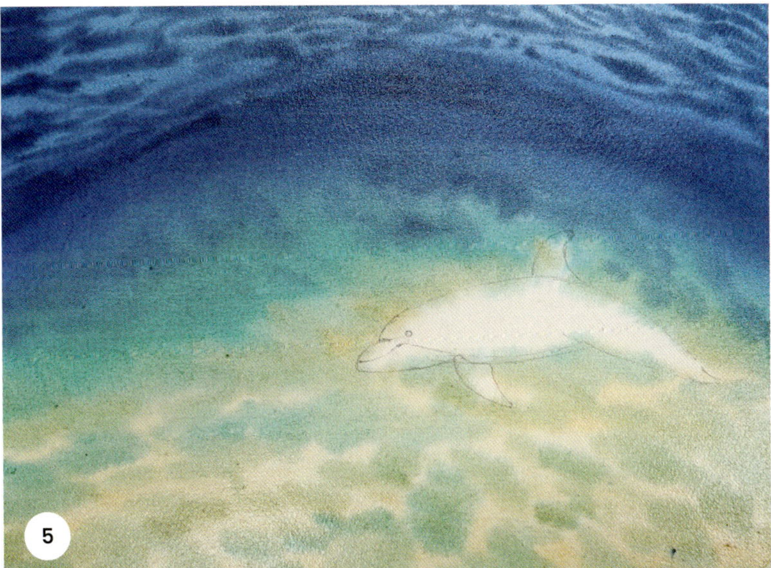

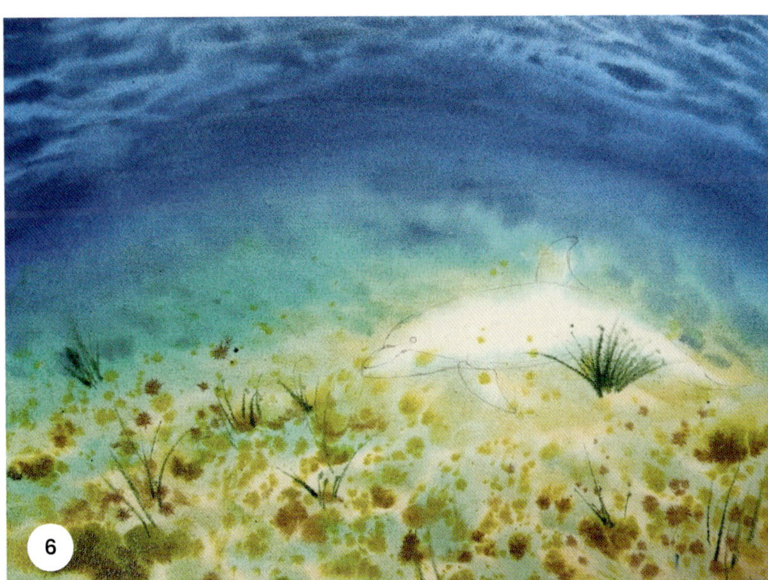

(continued)

STEP 7: Using a very subtle gray mixture (Payne's gray and dark green mixed together), add in the shadow of the dolphin on the ocean floor. It doesn't have to be a perfect shape.

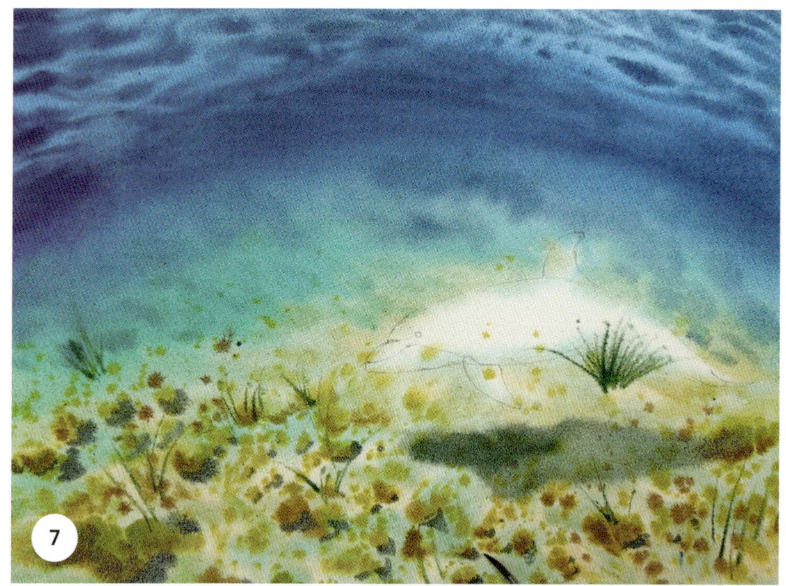

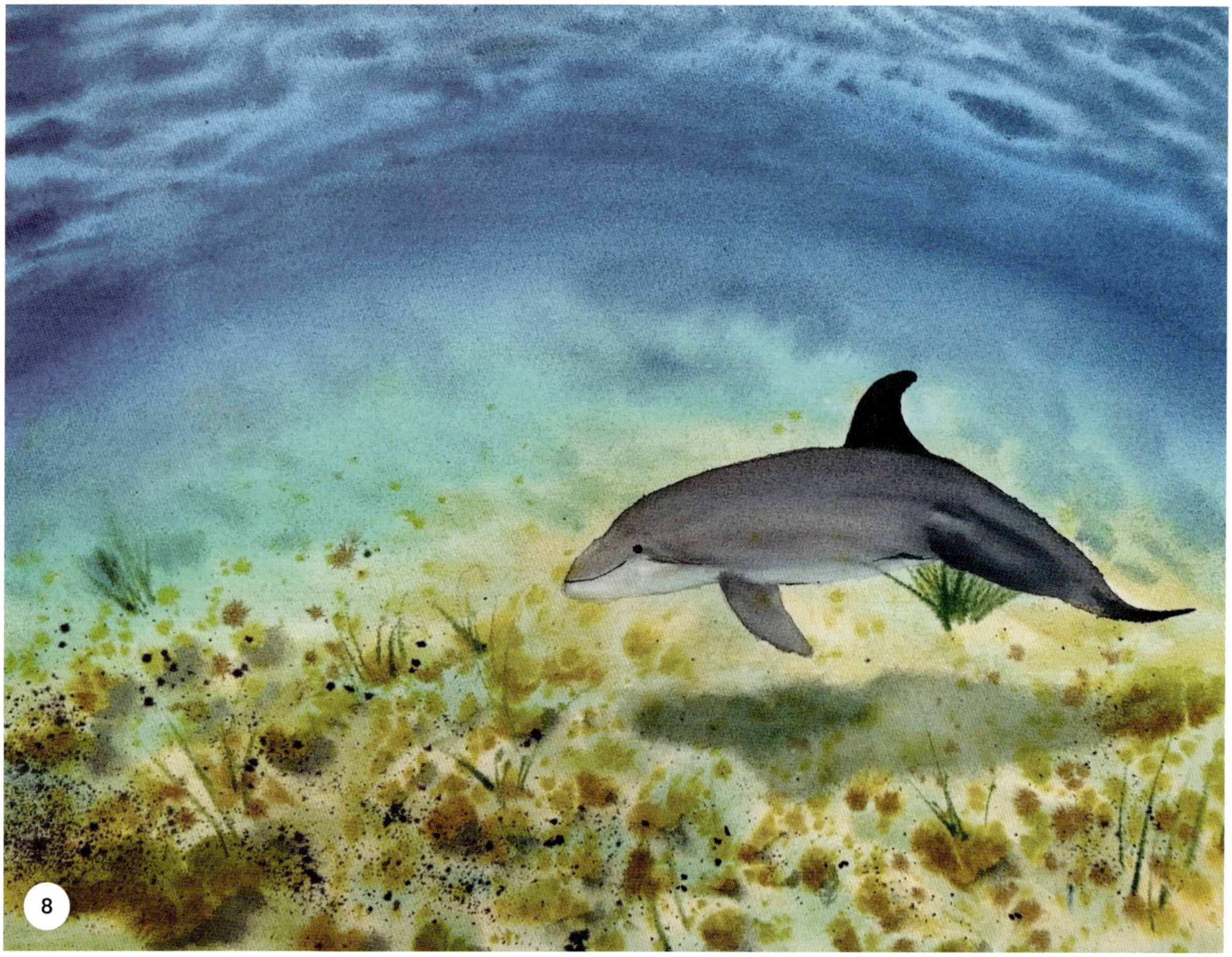

STEP 8: Paint in the dolphin using Payne's gray. Use various color tones of the gray to clearly mark the curves of the dolphin's body and give a rounded shape. Use white paint if necessary to add in highlights. Finish with toothbrush splatters of dark green and brown on the ocean floor area.

THE WATERFALL

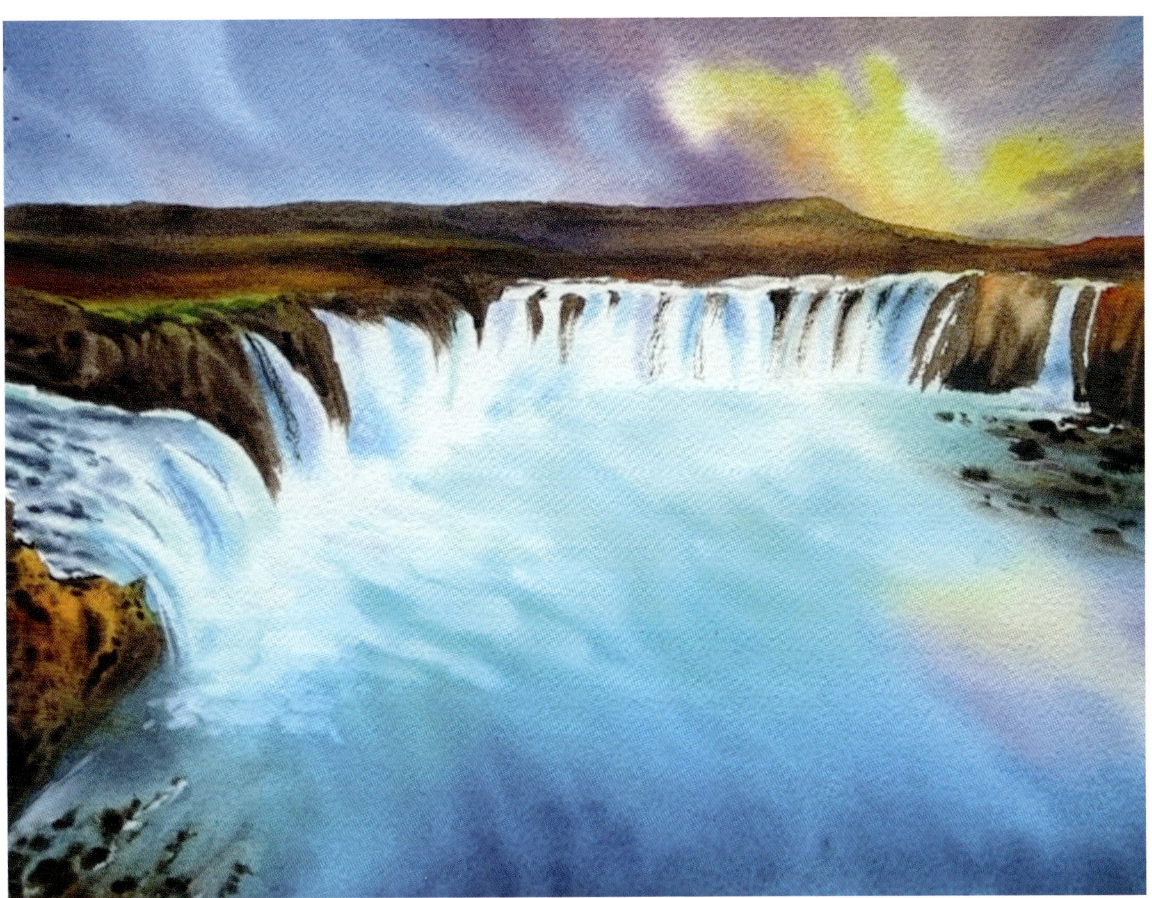

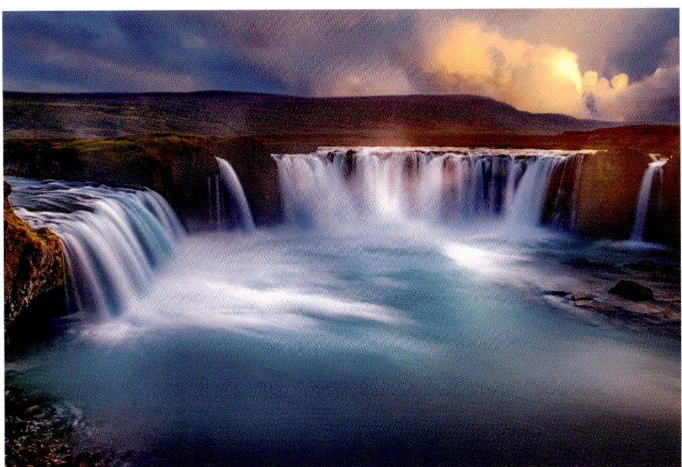

WATER TECHNIQUE: Applying water to both sides of the paper

PAPER SIZE: A4

COLORS: Transparent yellow, quinacridone rose, cobalt blue, phthalo blue, violet, phthalo green, indigo, burnt sienna, transparent brown, yellow ochre, olive green, orange, Indian gold, dark brown, white gouache

(continued)

STEP 1: Mark out the important lines from the reference for the mountains and the cliffs. Do not sketch the waterfall lines; we need them to be white in the end. Apply water to both sides of the paper.

STEP 2: Paint the sky using the techniques learned previously. Use transparent yellow, quinacridone rose, cobalt blue, phthalo blue, and violet. Remember, you don't have to paint the sky exactly as in the reference. You are free to change any aspect of it.

STEP 3: Start painting the water area with phthalo blue and add in the reflection of the dramatic sky in the water area on the right side. Note here that you have to invert your strokes in the sky, as this is the reflection.

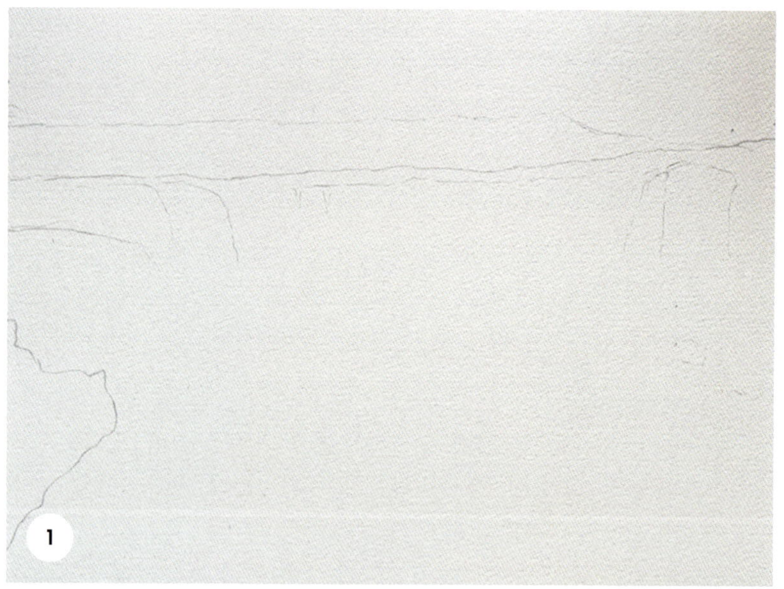

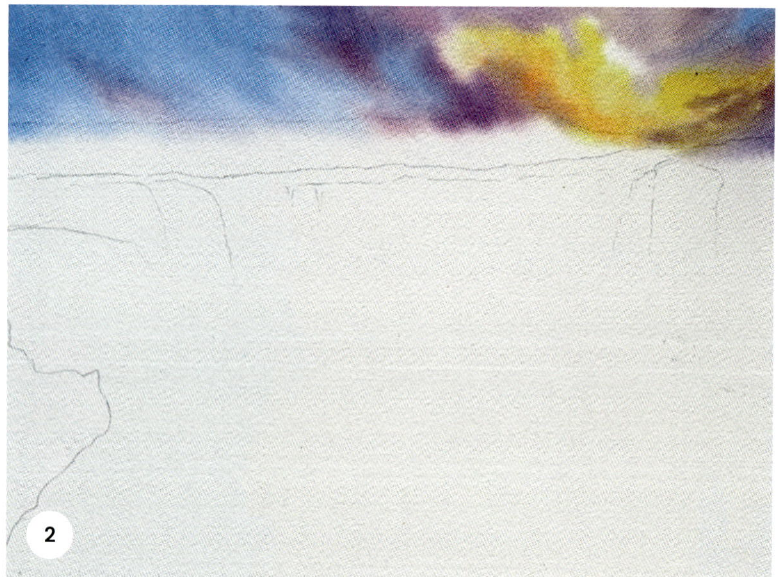

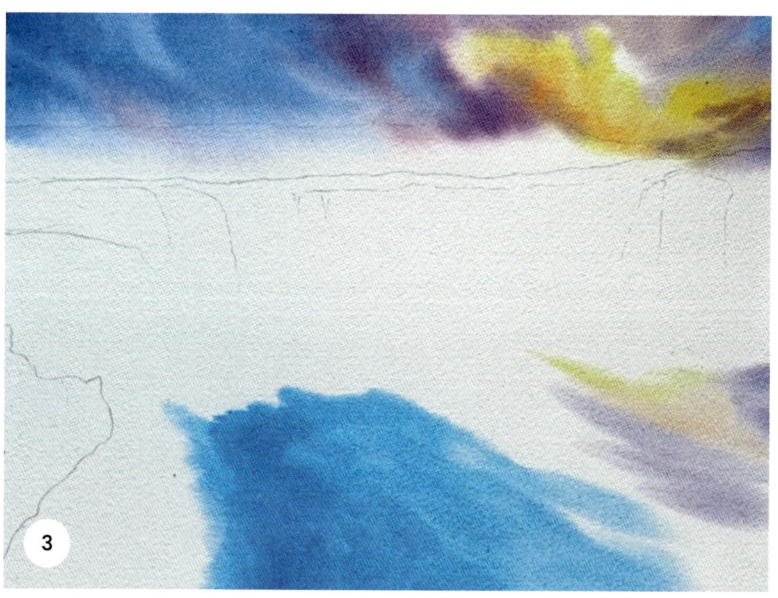

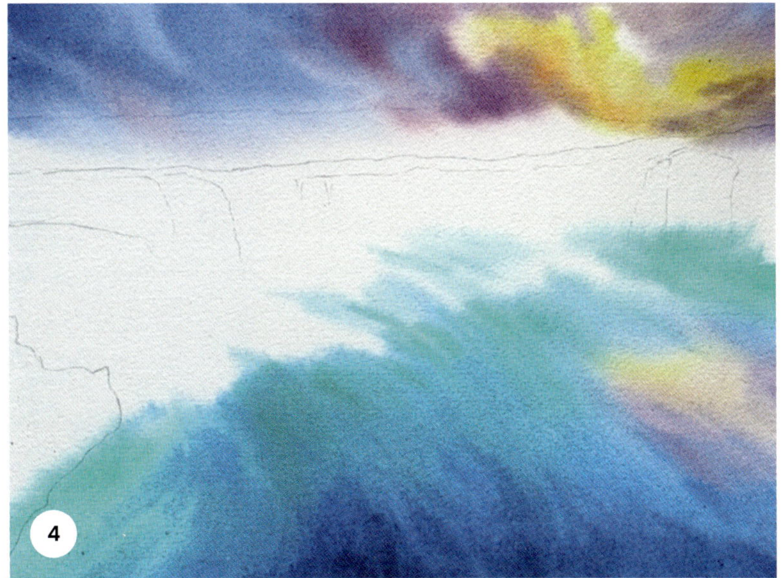

STEP 4: Using phthalo green, blend into the blue to create the water area. You can add darker strokes with a mix of indigo and phthalo blue as well. Leave white areas in the region closer to the waterfalls.

STEP 5: Add in the waterfall strokes with a mix of phthalo blue, phthalo green, and indigo at random places. Leave as much white area in the waterfall region to create the highlights. Also, make sure that your waterfall strokes are vertical to depict the movement of the water.

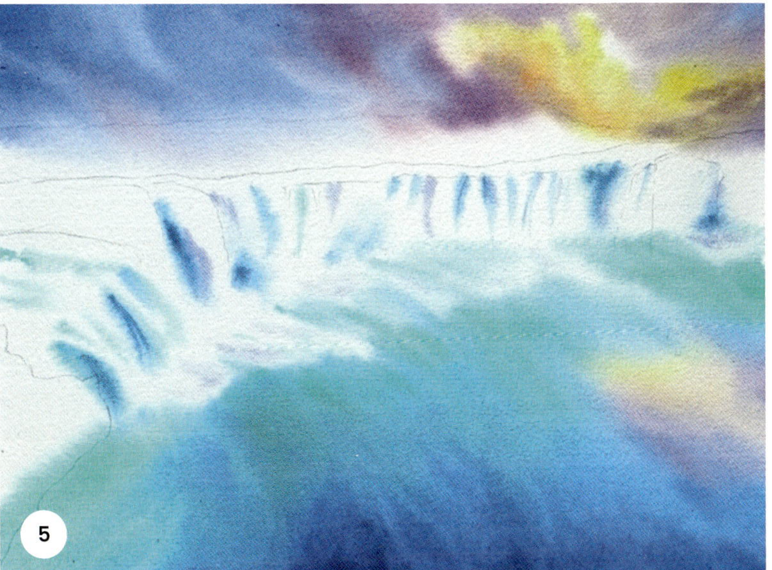

STEP 6: Add in the background mountains using a very creamy mixture. Painting the mountains last with an almost dry creamy mixture will ensure that your strokes don't flow much into the sky. Use a mix of burnt sienna, transparent brown in the darker regions, yellow ochre in the lighter region, and olive green for the vegetation.

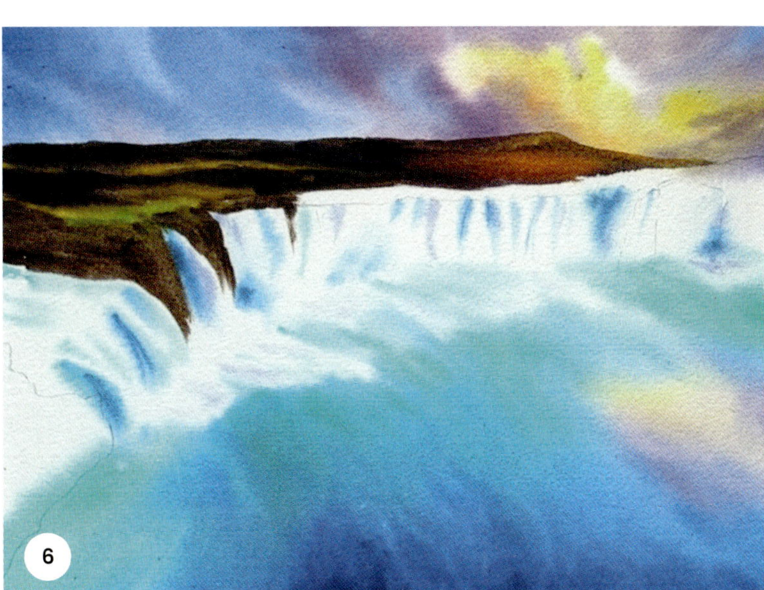

(continued)

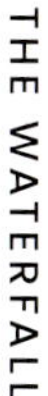

STEP 7: Paint the foreground cliff with a mixture of orange, Indian gold, and transparent brown, along with some dotted spots of dark brown. Using the drybrush technique, add in vertically downward strokes for the areas in between the falls to show the part of the rocky cliff seen through the water.

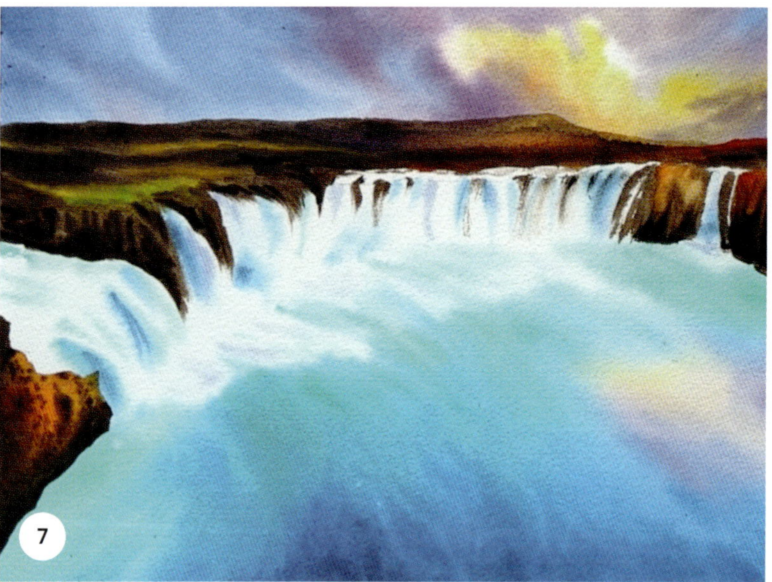

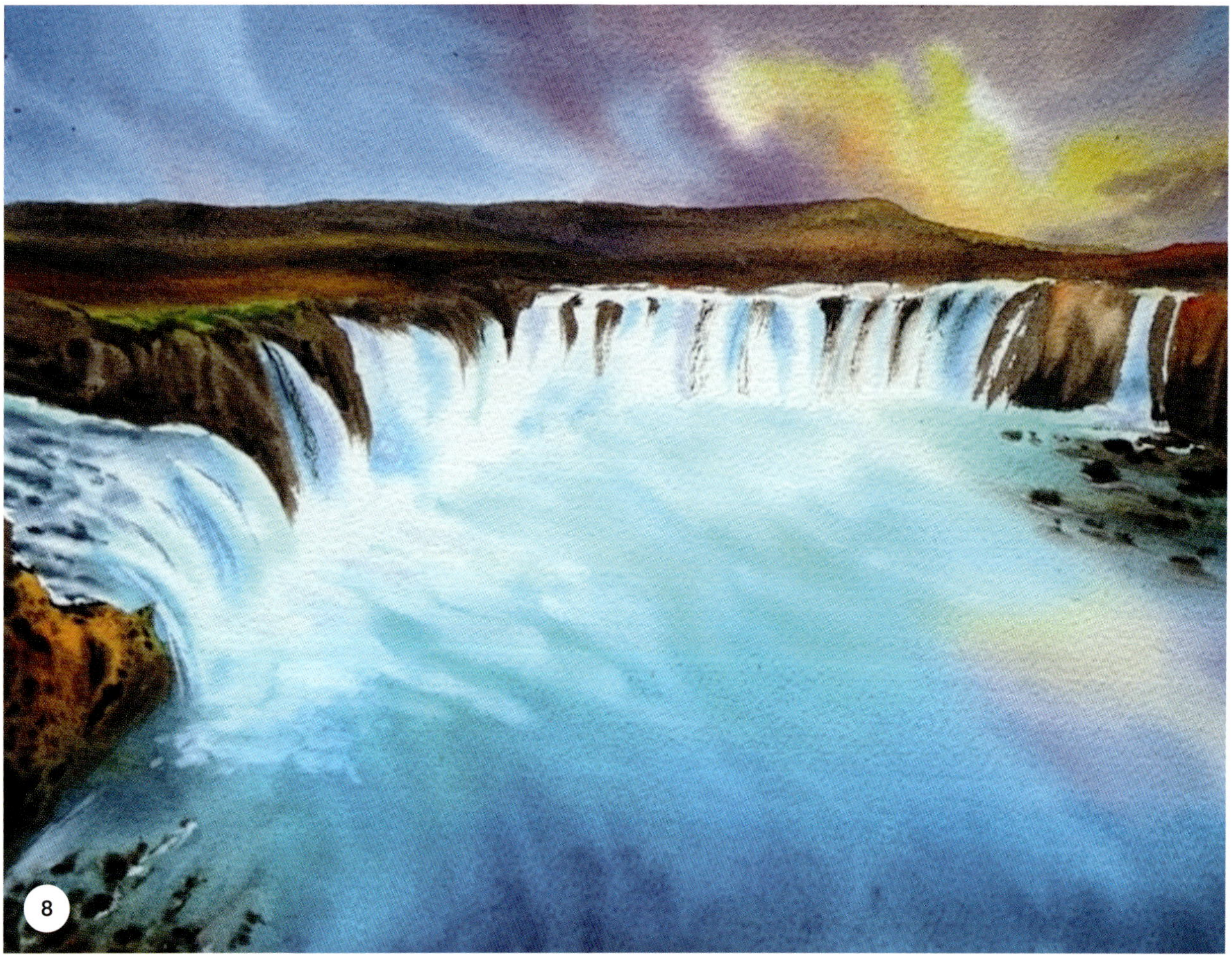

STEP 8: Paint the underside of the foreground cliff with indigo to ensure that you capture the shadow areas there. Add in smaller rocks in the water with dark brown and a little indigo to depict darker accents in the water. Finish with additional white strokes wherever necessary.

SPLASH ON THE ROCK

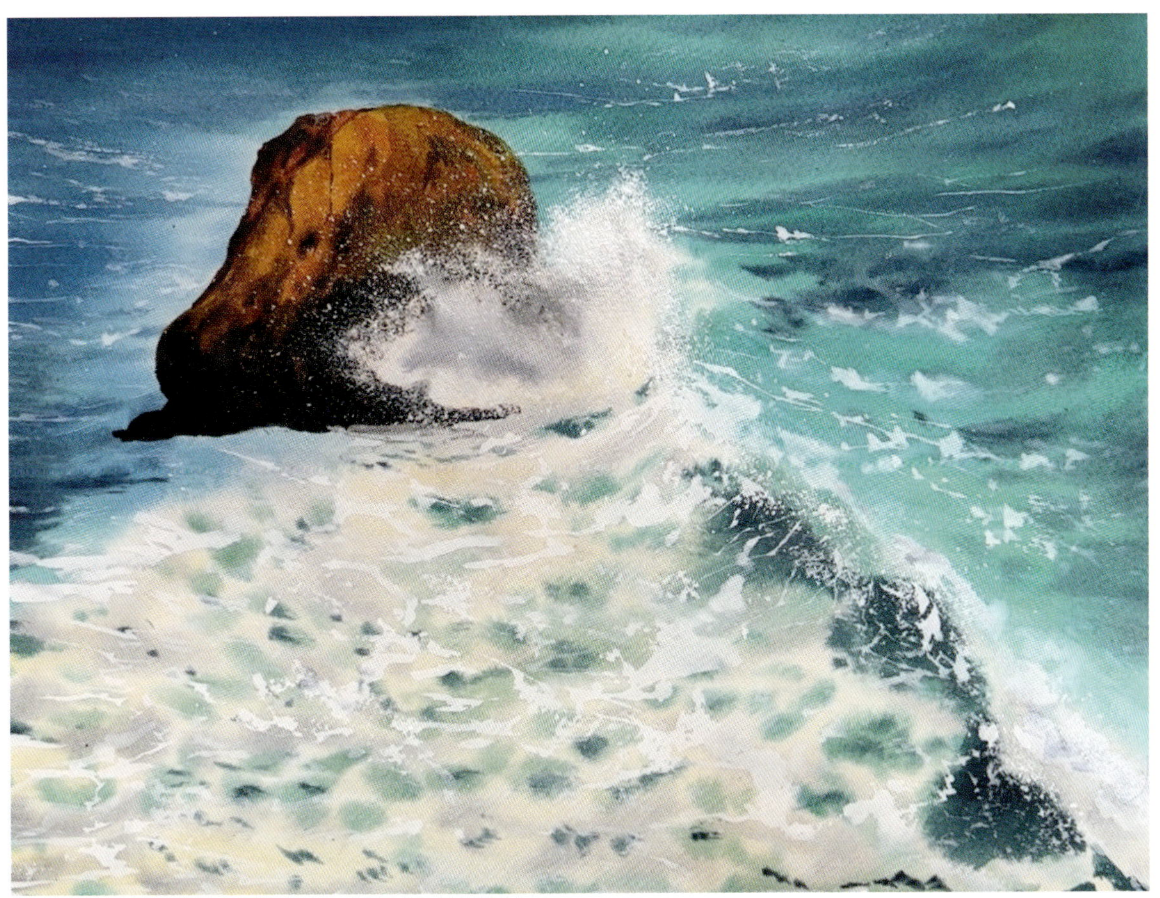

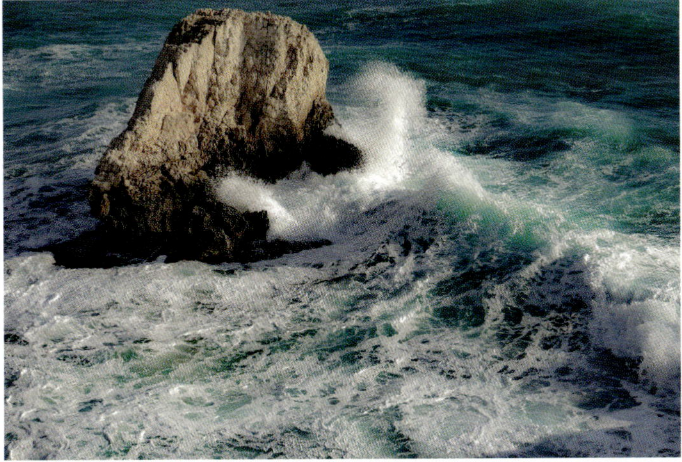

WATER TECHNIQUE: Applying water to both sides of the paper

PAPER SIZE: A4

COLORS: Phthalo blue, phthalo green, raw sienna, Payne's gray, lavender, turquoise green, yellow ochre, burnt sienna, transparent brown, olive green, white gouache

(continued)

STEP 1: Sketch the shape of the large rock in water. Observe how the rock has been placed in the ideal composition position (the reference actually helps!). Apply water to both sides of the paper.

STEP 2: Paint in the horizontal strokes of the water with phthalo blue and phthalo green. Blend them nicely. Be careful near the rock; leave a lot of white space where the splash is going to be.

STEP 3: To paint the foam in the sea, add in some raw sienna strokes at irregular places first. These are the highlights. Adding warm and cool tones together will create a good contrast.

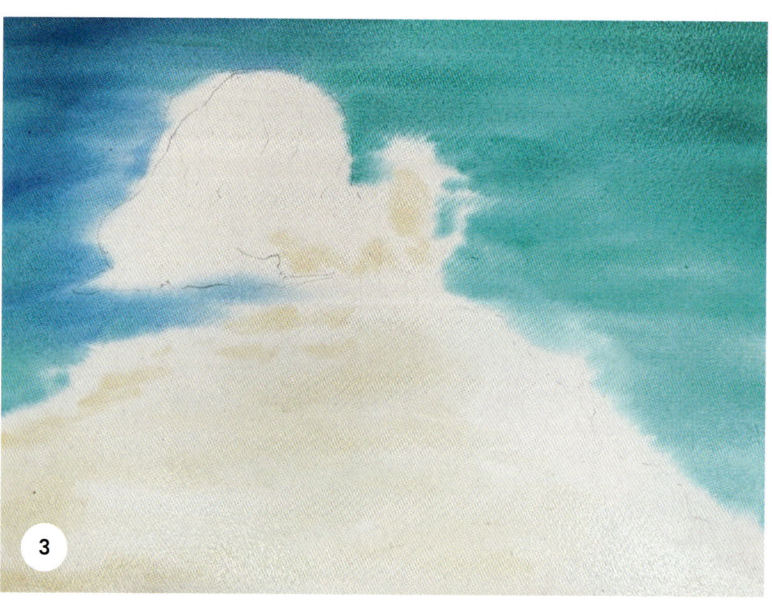

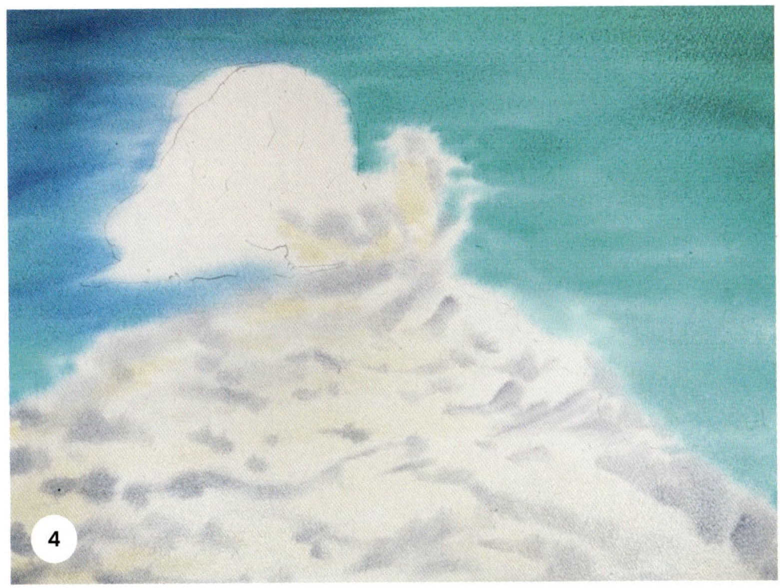

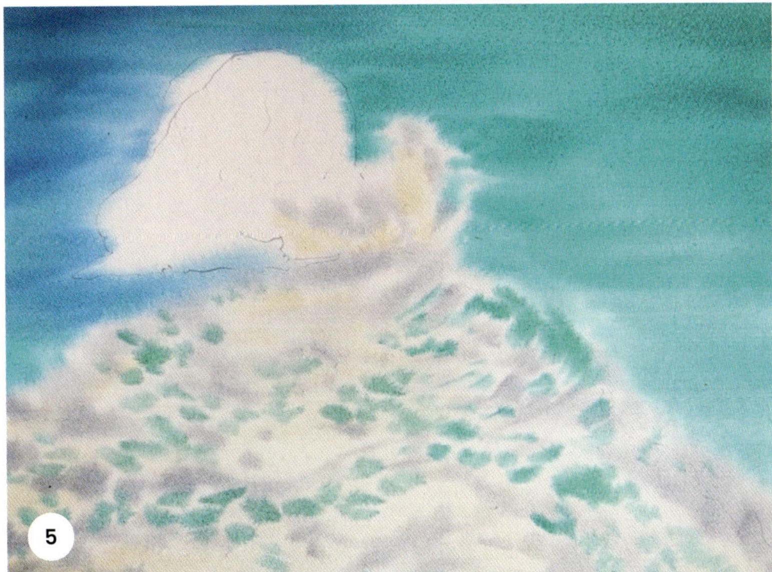

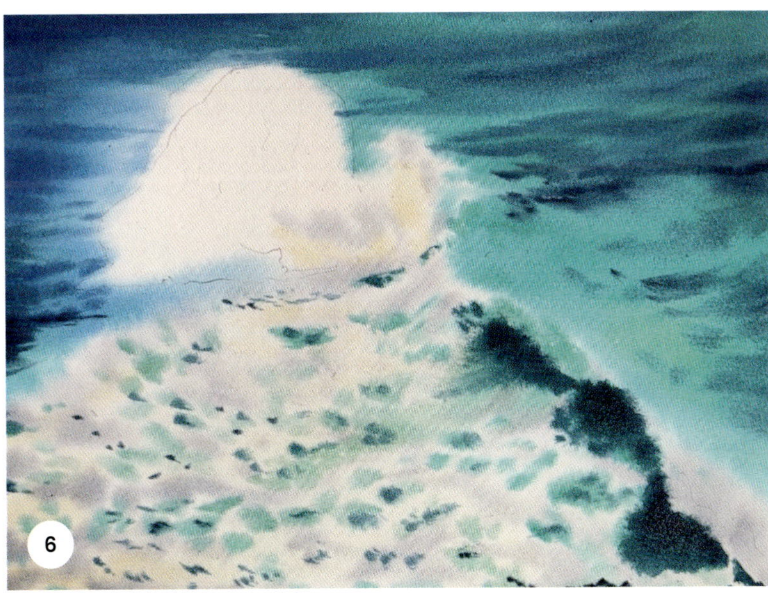

STEP 4: Add in the shadow areas of the foam with Payne's gray. You can mix a little bit of lavender into the mixture to give a slightly different shade at random.

STEP 5: Now add in the water areas in the foam using phthalo green. You can be as irregular as you want and don't have to follow the reference picture exactly.

STEP 6: Add in the darker regions of the wave with a turquoise green shade. Add in some shadows on the foam and the splash of the wave with a mix of lavender and Payne's gray.

(continued)

STEP 7: Paint the rock with a mixture of yellow ochre, burnt sienna, and transparent brown. Add in Payne's gray on the darker areas. You may add some tiny strokes with olive green to depict the moss on the rock.

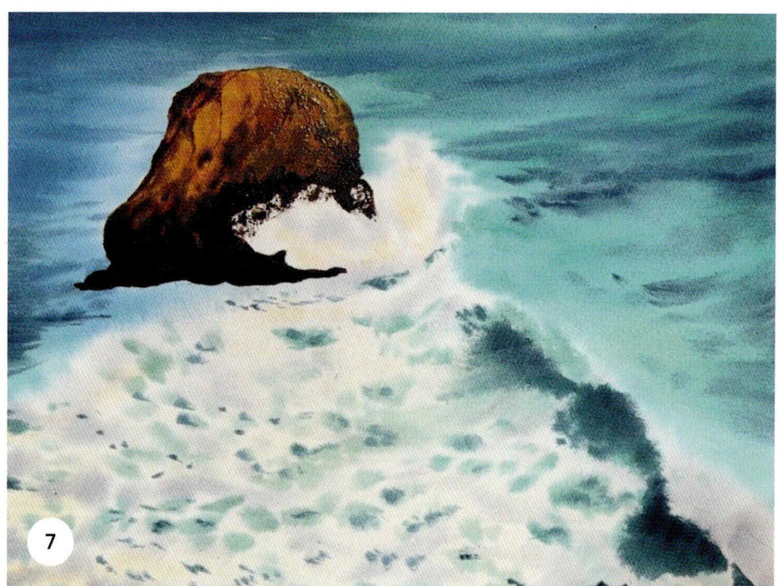

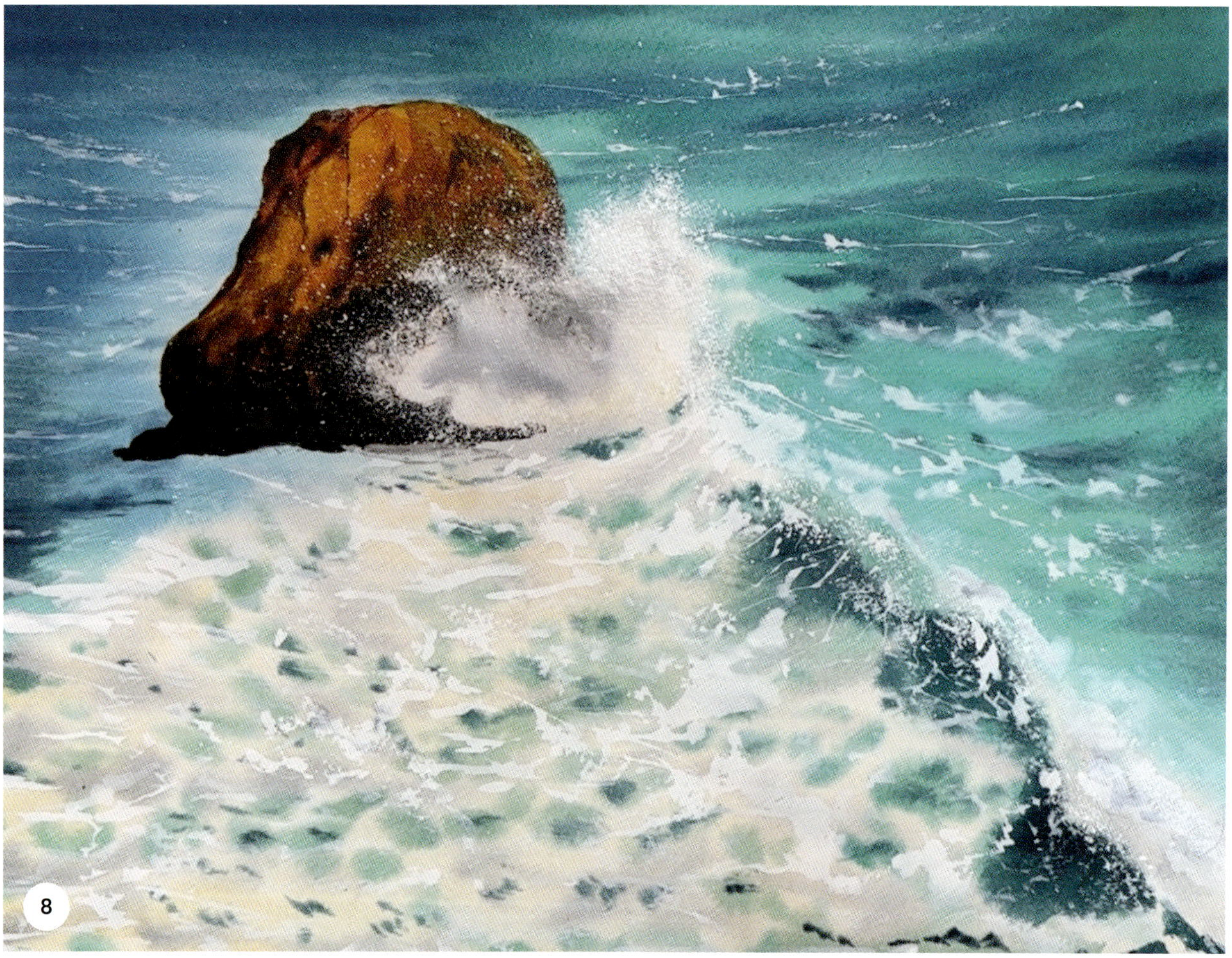

STEP 8: Add in a lot of additional foamy areas with white paint. You can add further white highlights in the large foamy region. Finish the painting with a lot of tiny splatters using the toothbrush splattering method.

PROJECT 11

MISTY PRAGUE

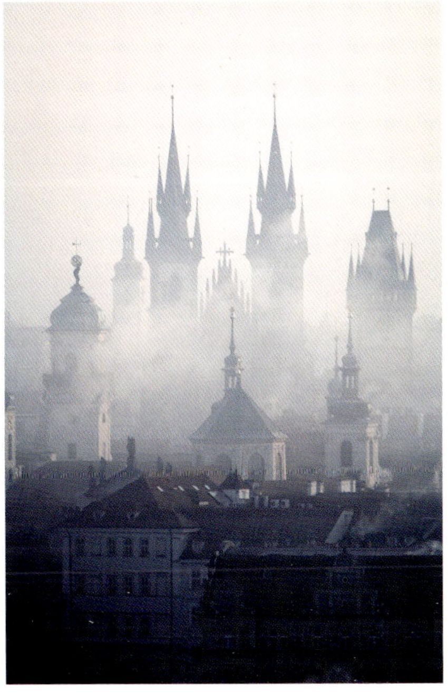

WATER TECHNIQUES: **Taped edges; monochromatic**

PAPER SIZE: 10" × 7" (25.4 × 17.8 cm)

COLOR: **Indigo**

(continued)

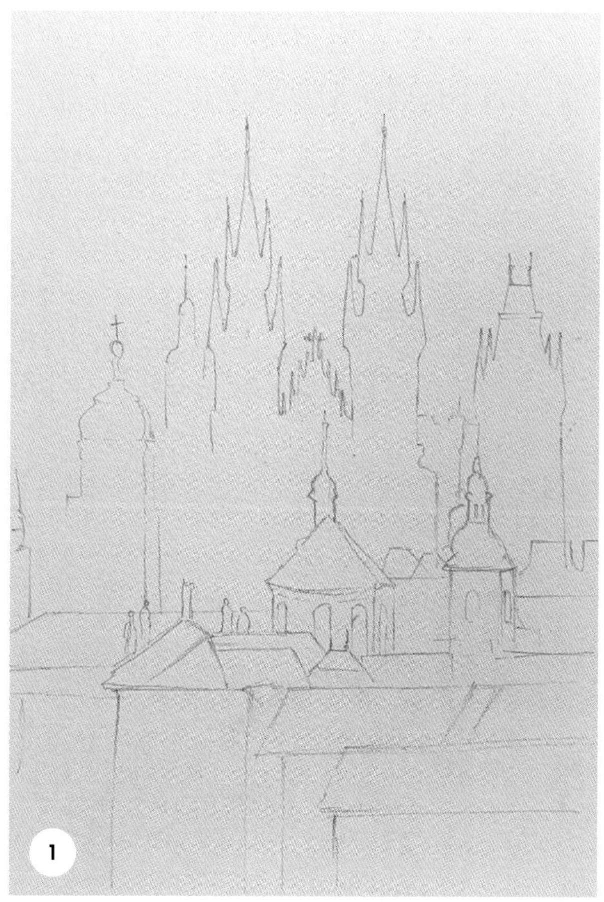

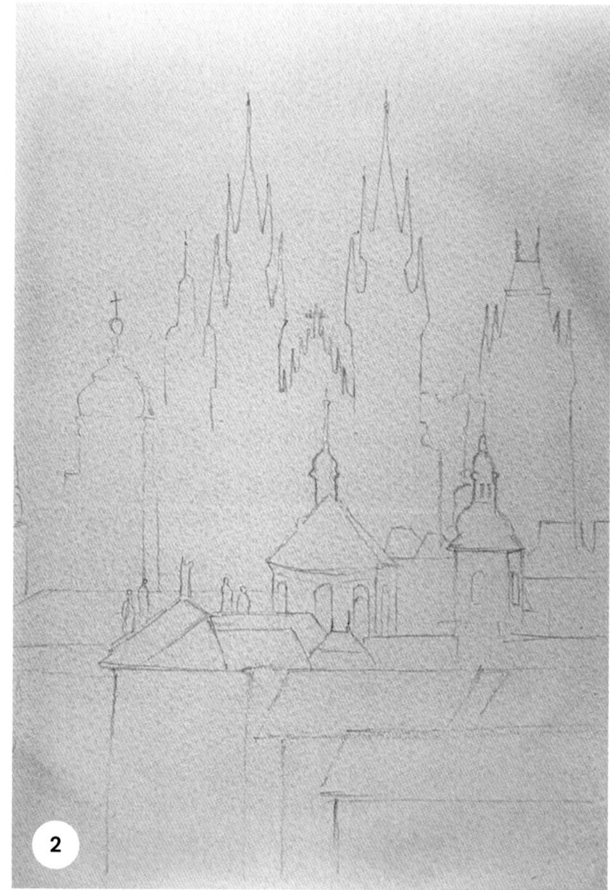

STEP 1: Sketch the outline of the entire city. You can skip any details within the buildings. We will be painting this in multiple layers; it involves a lot of drying out. Feel free to use a heat gun or hair dryer to speed up the drying time.

STEP 2: Apply water to the whole paper and add a very light wash of indigo to the entire painting.

STEP 3: Start with a lighter tone of indigo that is darker than the previous wash and add in the silhouettes of all the buildings in the background. Remember, we will be painting this over and over again, so make sure the mixture you use is very light. Mixing 1 part indigo and 5 parts water (milky consistency) would be ideal here.

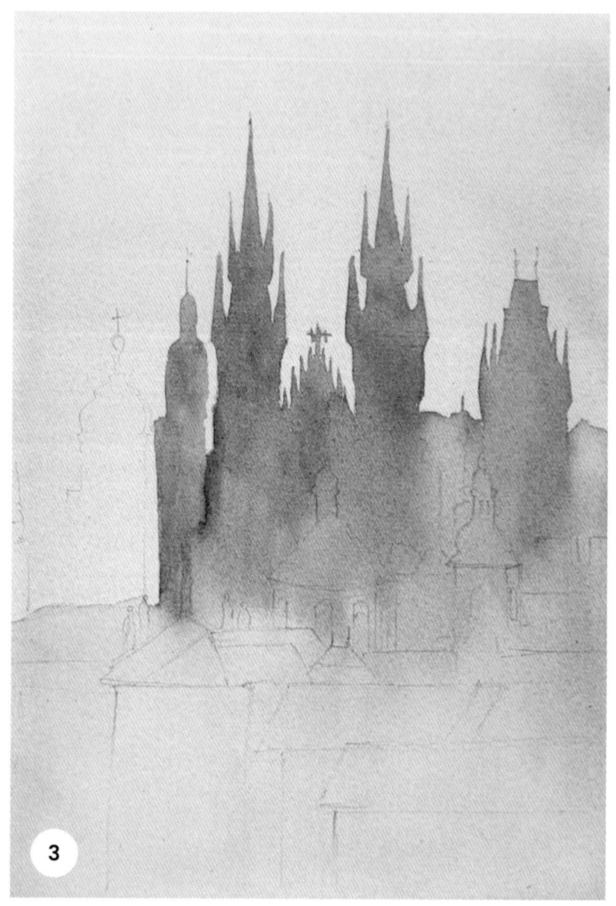

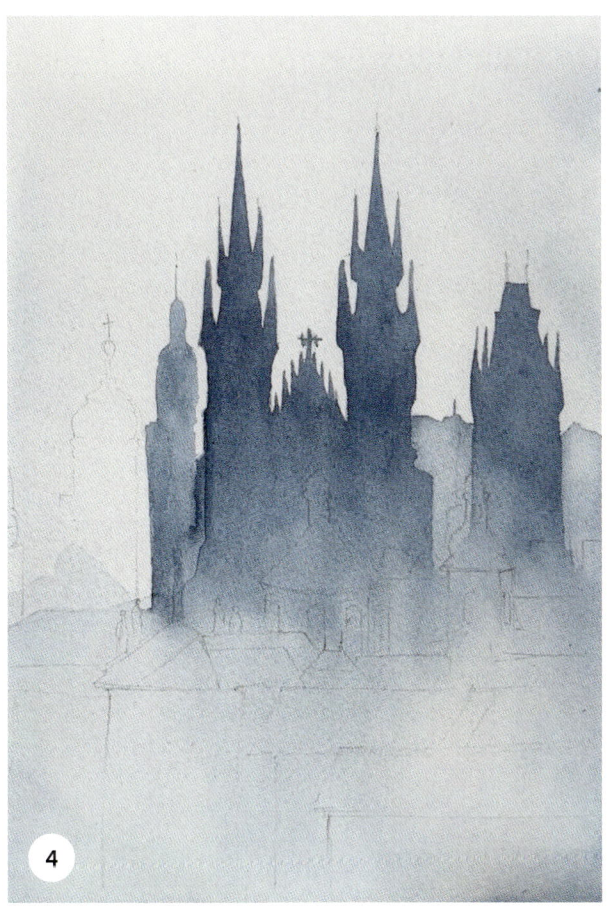

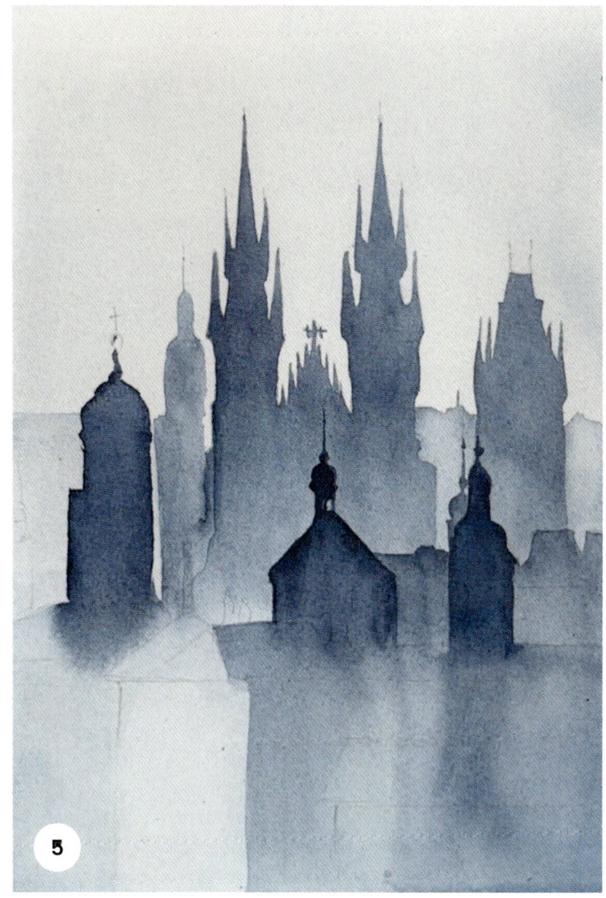

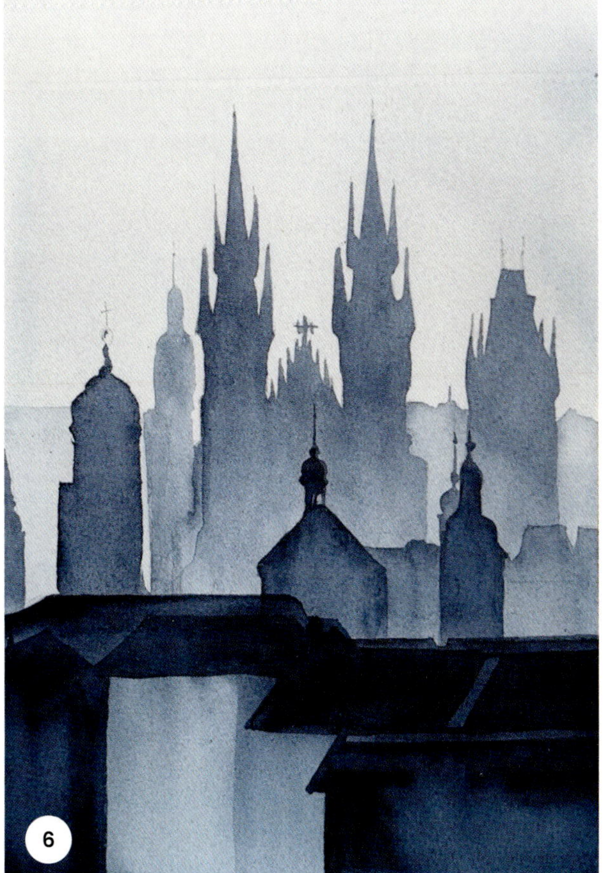

STEP 4: Continuing with the mixture of 1 part indigo and 5 parts water, add in the silhouette of the main buildings once more so that it comes forward from the ones in the background. We had to paint these in the previous step and again in this step because the buildings in step 3 would leave a definite outline that would be harder to erase with the lighter tone that we are using.

STEP 5: Mix 2 parts indigo and 4 parts water for the next silhouettes: the buildings in the middle. Let the color bleed toward the bottom and use water to blend it all the way downward. Do not let any edges form a distinct line.

STEP 6: Using 3 parts indigo and 2 parts water, add in the foreground buildings.

(continued)

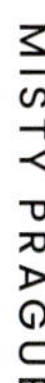

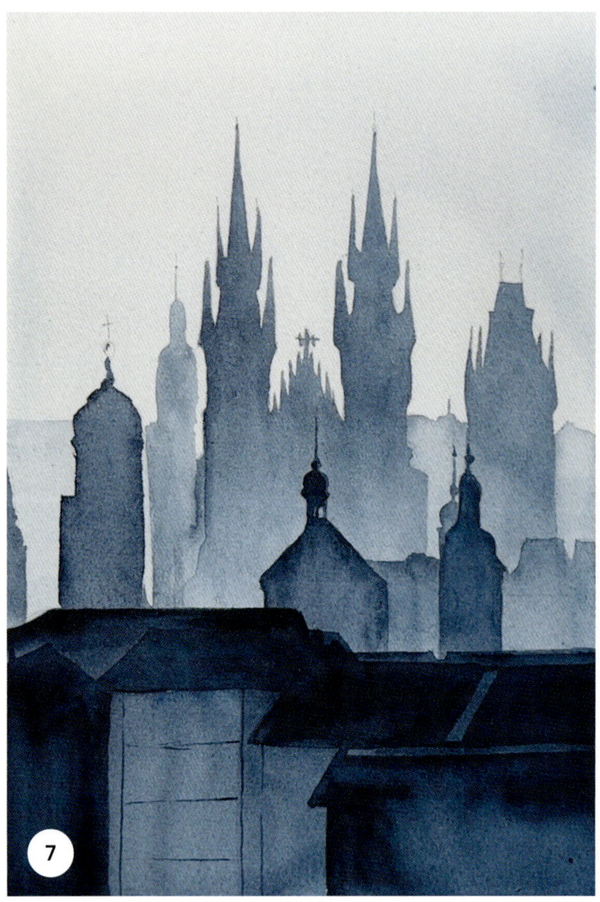

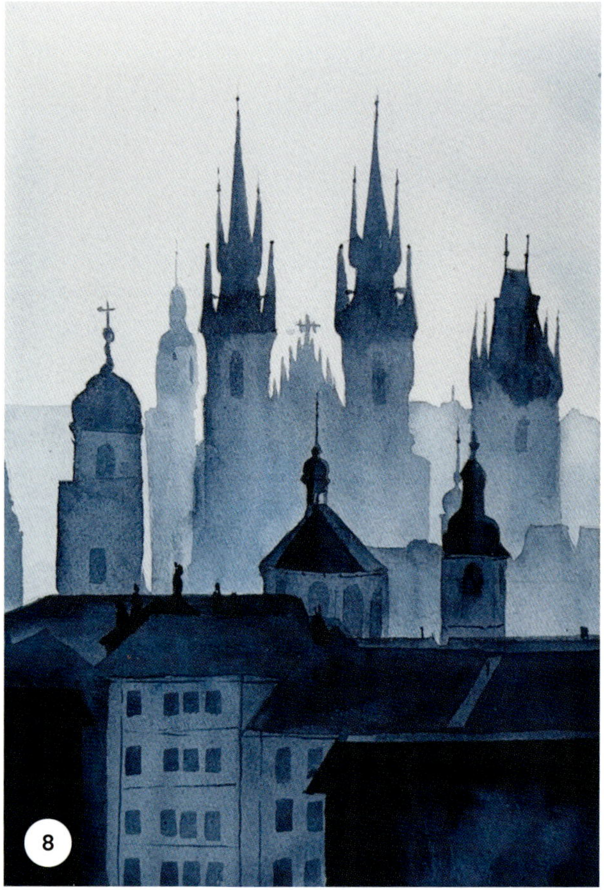

STEP 7: Use the reference picture to adjust the tones wherever necessary and to give varying height and depth to the picture.

STEP 8: Using a creamy mixture of the darkest value, add in the darker shadows and objects (i.e., the statues on the rooftop on the bottom left side). Use a medium tone to add in the roofs of the background buildings to make them stand out. Try to add them without a definite line and in a washed-out manner by using water to soften edges at random. Finish the details, such as poles and windows.

WINTER IN NEW YORK

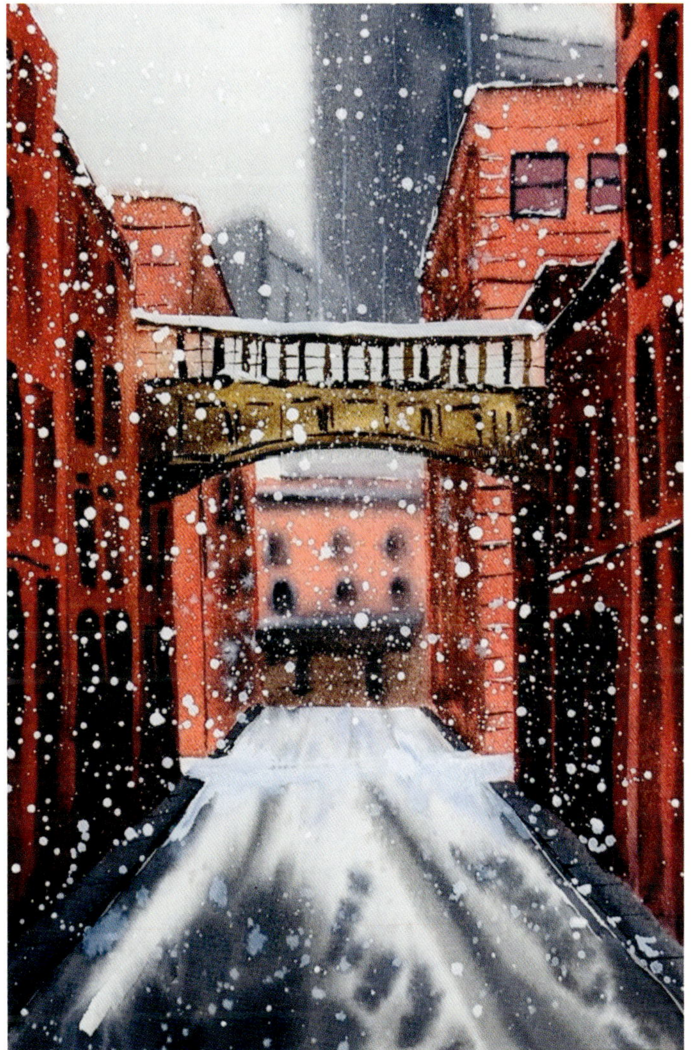

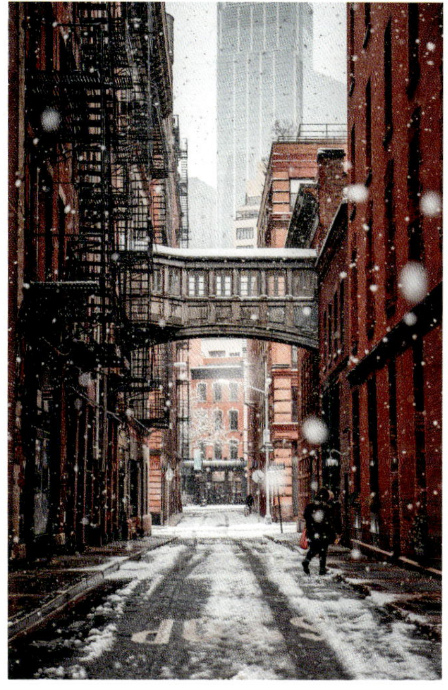

WATER TECHNIQUE: Taped edges

PAPER SIZE: 10" × 7" (25.4 × 17.8 cm)

COLORS: Quinacridone rose, sap green, Payne's gray, lavender, transparent brown, white gouache, alizarin crimson, yellow ochre

(continued)

STEP 1: Sketch the outline of the buildings following the one-point perspective. Here, the vanishing point is right in the middle of the buildings, underneath the bridge (see the dot in the picture). Use the vanishing point to add the lines for each of the buildings on the side.

STEP 2: Apply water to the whole of the paper. Using a creamy mixture of 2 parts quinacridone rose and 1 part sap green, add the buildings on the left and the right with the wet-on-wet method. Using 2 parts Payne's gray and 1 part lavender, add in the background buildings as well before the paper dries up. This is the first layer. Run your brush along the edges of strokes multiple times to prevent the paint from running and creating a lot of hairs. However, we do need some softer edges. Using Payne's gray, add some random strokes to the foreground path. Keep the area toward the background white.

STEP 3: Before the paint from step 2 dries up, add in the windows using transparent brown. Also add some lines to the buildings in the background with white gouache. This needs to be in the wet-on-wet method to capture the depth; the softness in your strokes creates the illusion of these buildings being

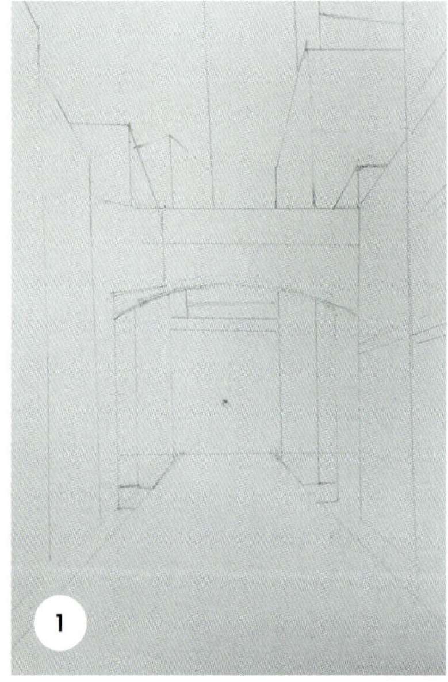

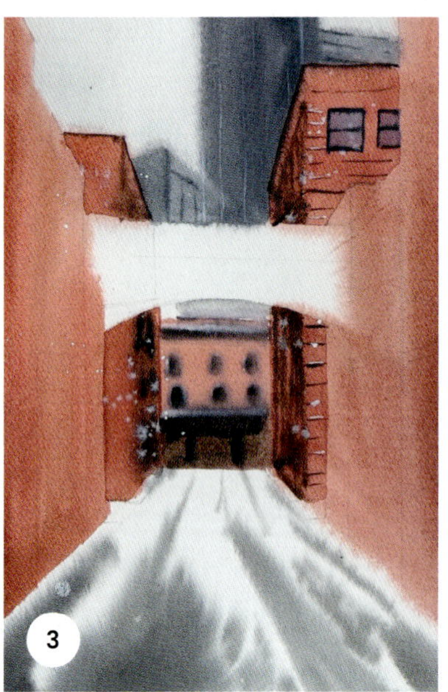

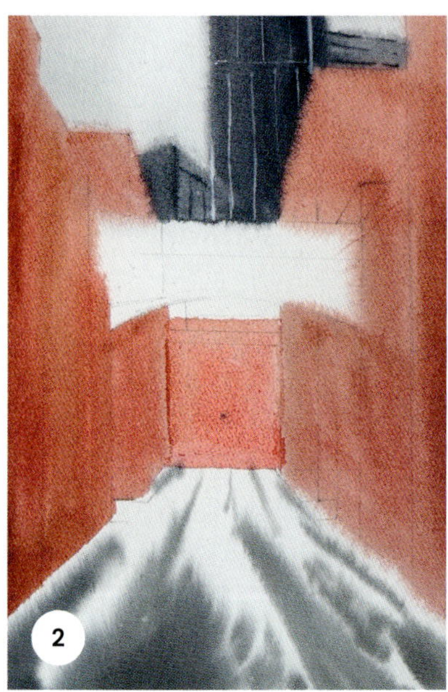

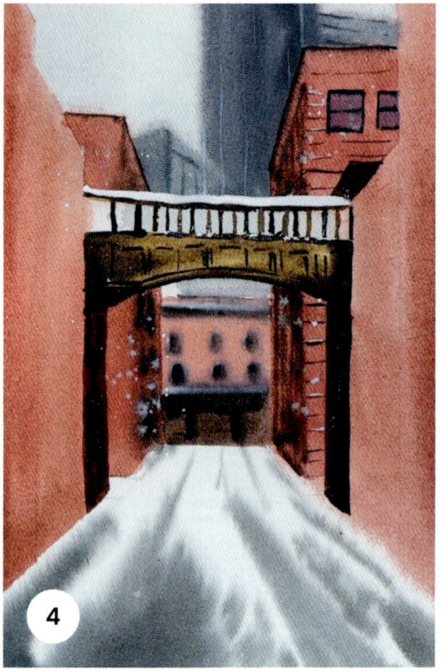

far away. After this, dry this layer and start painting each of the buildings from the back to the front. Use a mixture of 2 parts quinacridone rose and 1 part sap green to paint over the building. The wet-on-dry method will get a definite edge on your buildings. Using transparent brown, add in windows and lines on the wet red shade of the buildings. Optional: Use the wet-on-wet

splatter technique, splatter some white paint onto this wet building. This enhances the depth in your painting when you add snow at the end.

STEP 4: Add in the next building using a mixture of 2 parts alizarin crimson and 1 part transparent brown. Notice that this building is darker and needs a darker tone. Add in the windows using a much darker tone

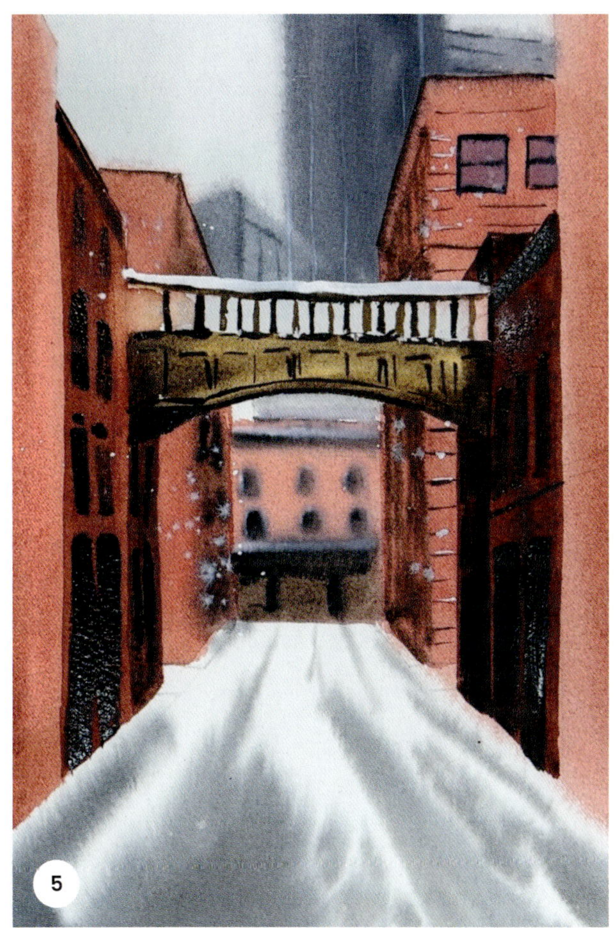

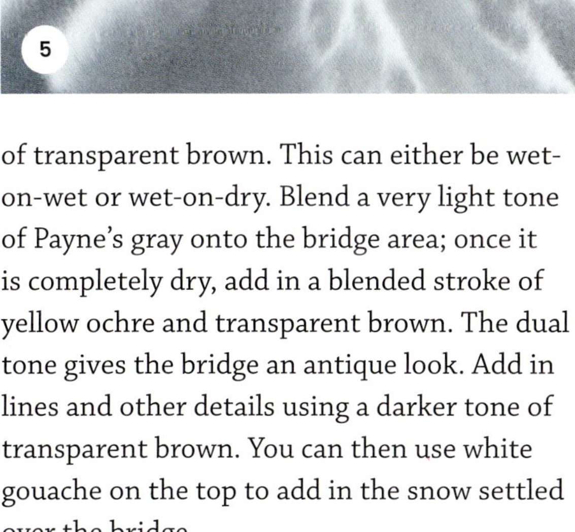

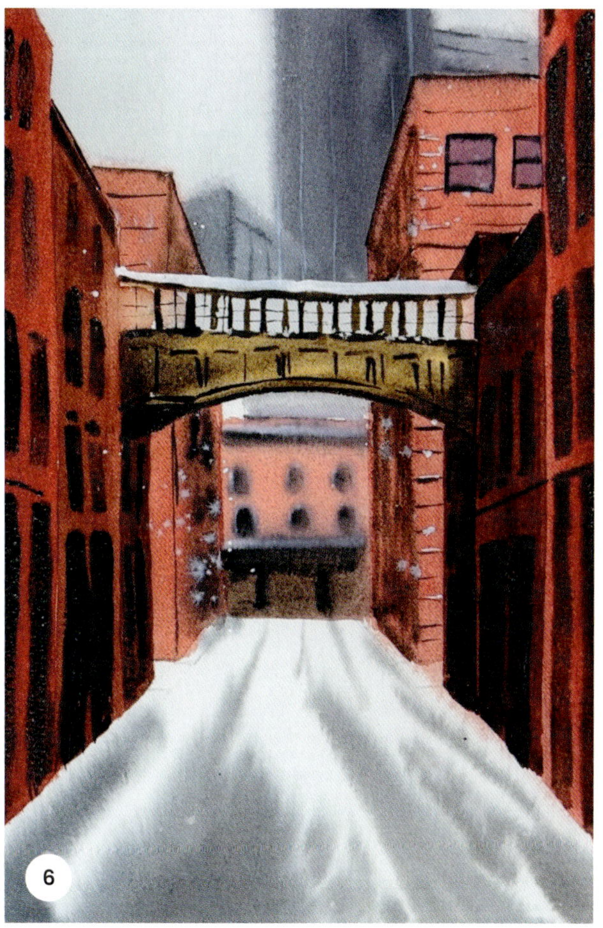

of transparent brown. This can either be wet-on-wet or wet-on-dry. Blend a very light tone of Payne's gray onto the bridge area; once it is completely dry, add in a blended stroke of yellow ochre and transparent brown. The dual tone gives the bridge an antique look. Add in lines and other details using a darker tone of transparent brown. You can then use white gouache on the top to add in the snow settled over the bridge.

STEP 5: Paint in the next building in a similar way, using a mixture of alizarin crimson and transparent brown. Add in the windows using a darker tone of transparent brown or burnt umber. You can mix the brown with Payne's gray to make it even darker.

STEP 6: Paint the final building using the same color mixture but increase the vibrancy by reducing the amount of brown in the mixture. You can also use a mixture of quinacridone rose, sap green, and a little brown. Add in windows and doors using dark brown.

(continued)

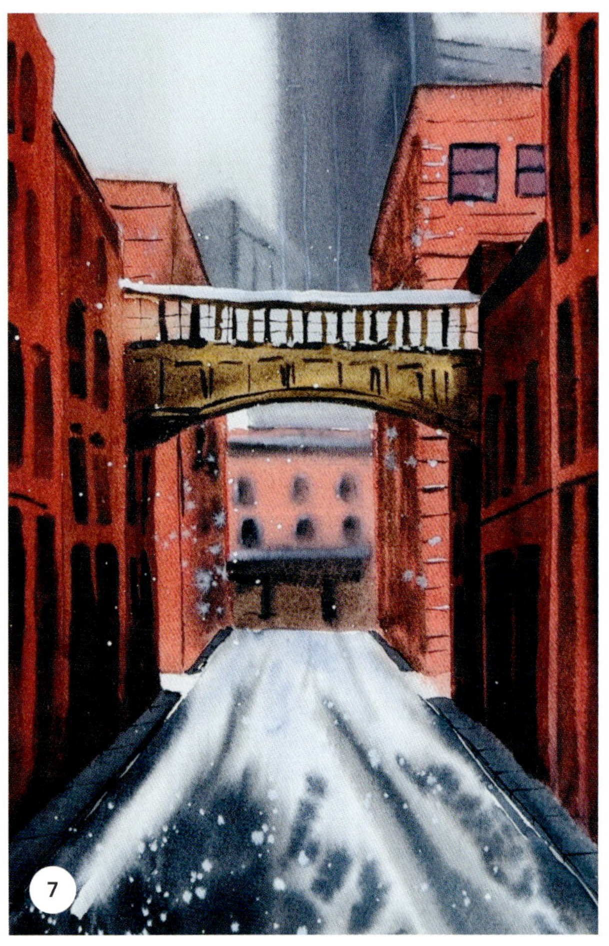

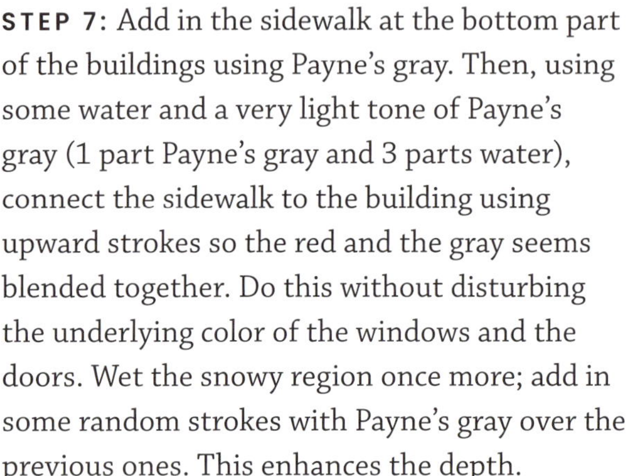

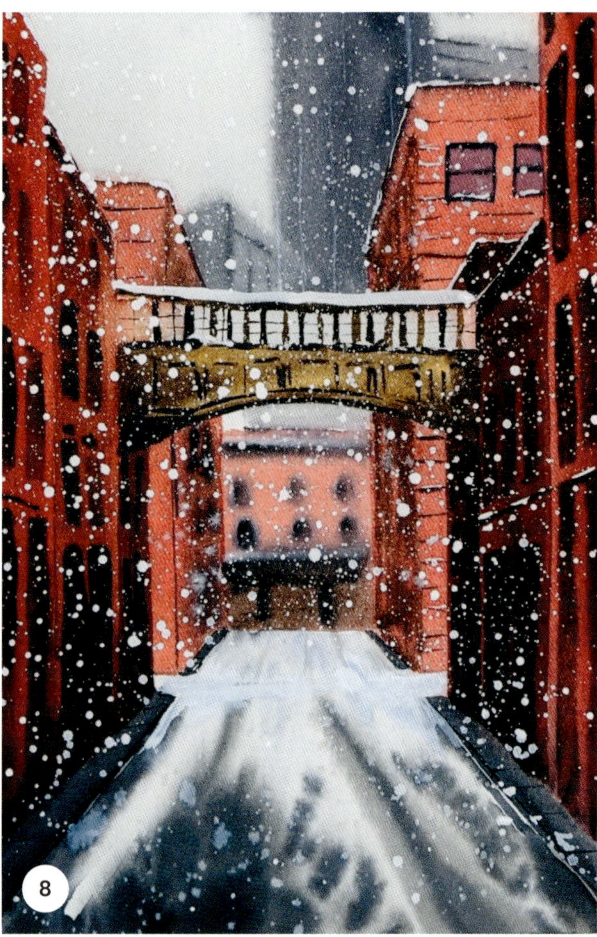

STEP 7: Add in the sidewalk at the bottom part of the buildings using Payne's gray. Then, using some water and a very light tone of Payne's gray (1 part Payne's gray and 3 parts water), connect the sidewalk to the building using upward strokes so the red and the gray seems blended together. Do this without disturbing the underlying color of the windows and the doors. Wet the snowy region once more; add in some random strokes with Payne's gray over the previous ones. This enhances the depth.

STEP 8: Splatter snow all over the painting. You can use different sizes of brushes to get different sizes of splatters, or you can use a very runny but yet creamy mixture of paint to get the larger splatters. Add in as much as you can to depict the snowy day. Observe how the wet-on-wet splatters on the background buildings enhance the depth of the snow.

PROJECT 13

SUNSET IN PARIS

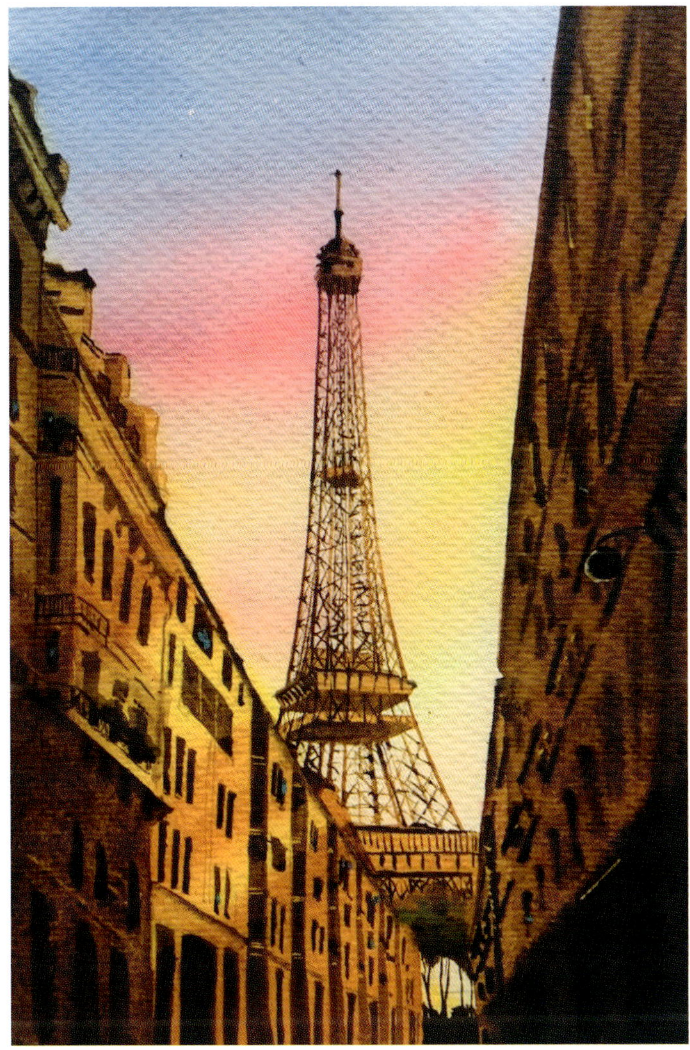

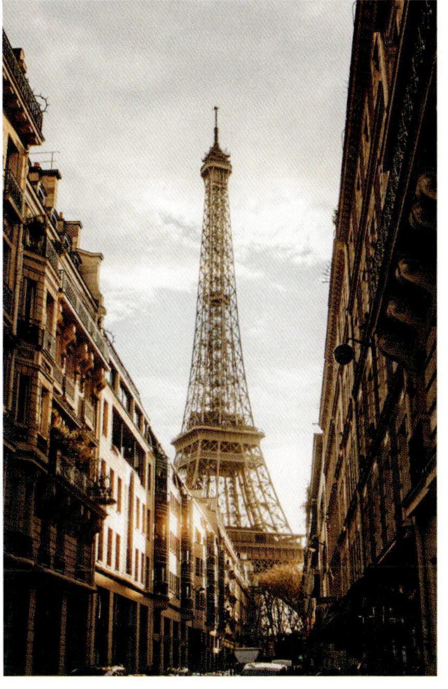

WATER TECHNIQUE: **Taped edges**

PAPER SIZE: **10" × 7" (25.4 × 17.8 cm)**

COLORS: **Transparent yellow, quinacridone rose, transparent orange, cobalt blue, quinacridone gold, transparent brown, olive green, cobalt turquoise, lavender**

(continued)

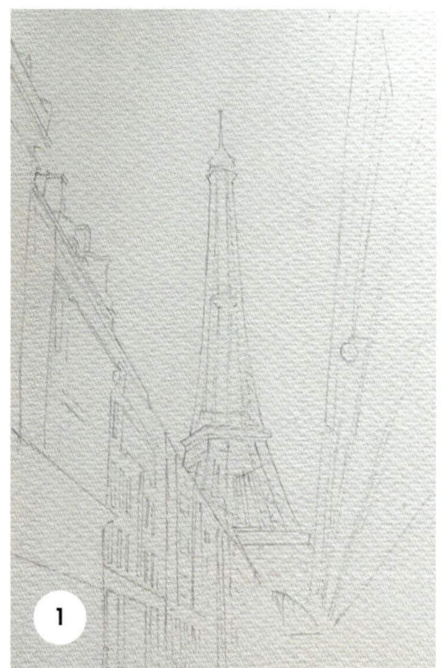

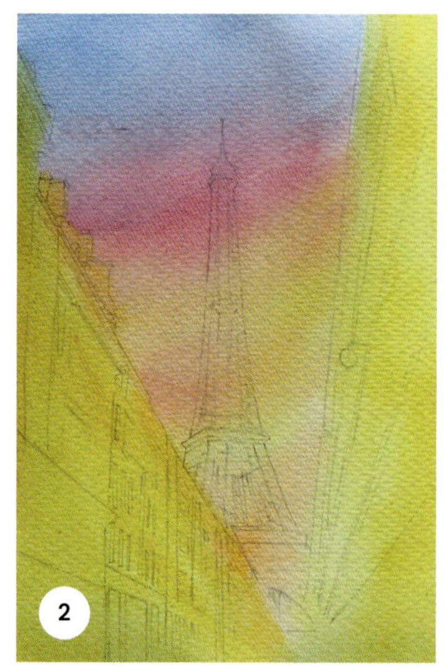

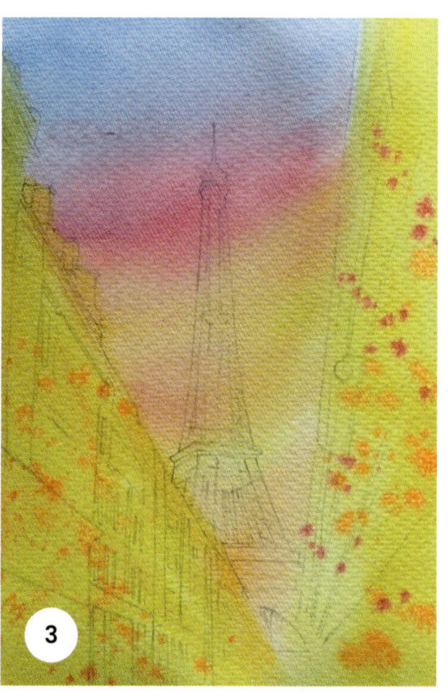

STEP 1: Sketch out the important and dominant lines in the picture using the one-point perspective. The vanishing point is at the bottom of the Eiffel Tower toward the right side. Using that point, add in all the relevant marking you think is necessary for your painting.

STEP 2: Apply to the whole of the paper and paint in the sky using the wet-on-wet method. I used transparent yellow, quinacridone rose, transparent orange, and cobalt blue to paint the sky. Use any kind of stokes you like and blend them nicely. The cobalt blue will provide a good contrasting cool tone in the painting as everything else is warm. One thing to keep in mind is to have the yellow toward the bottom in a slanted angle so that you can have this light on the building later on. Apply a complete wash of this transparent yellow over both of the buildings. This is the first layer in the painting.

STEP 3: Optional: Before the paper dries out, add in some wet-on-wet splatters with quinacridone rose and transparent orange. This enhances the final painting with subtle color changes underneath.

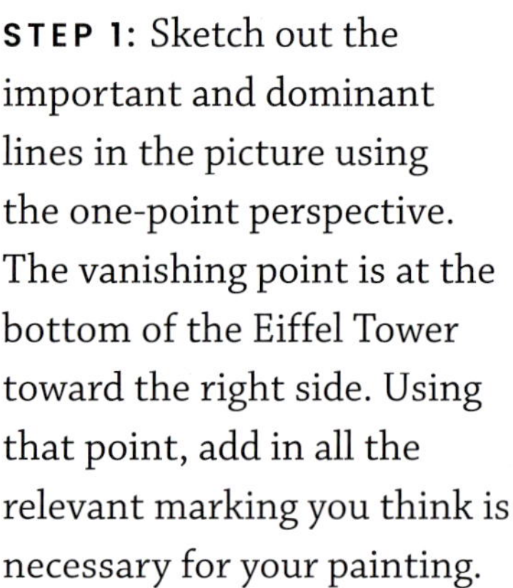

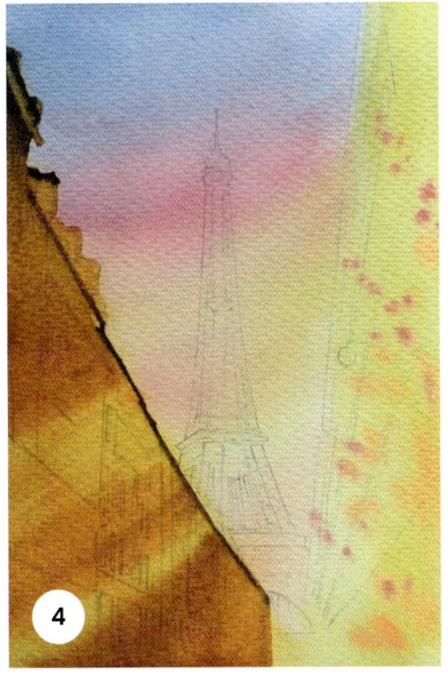

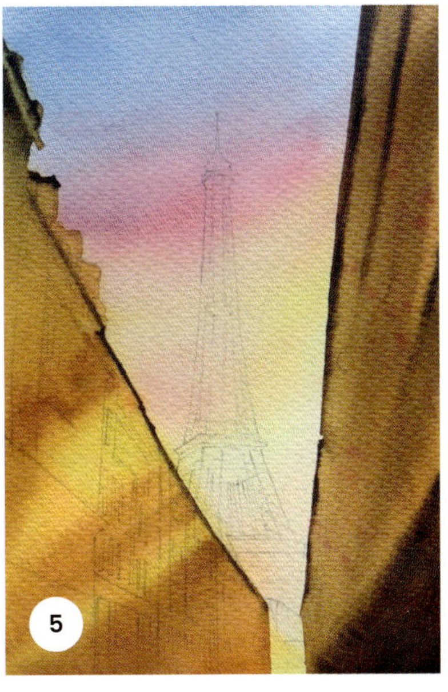

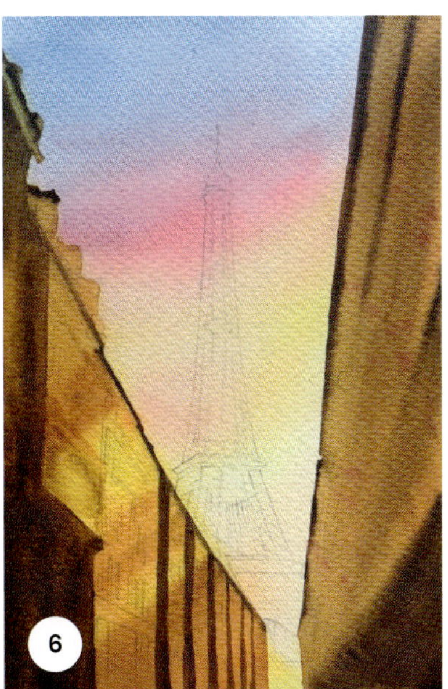

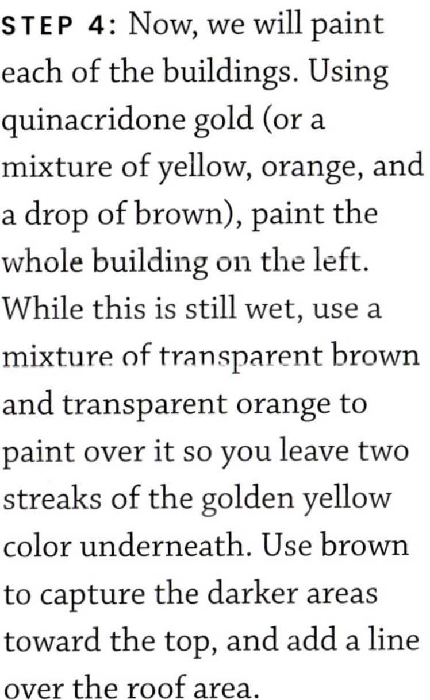

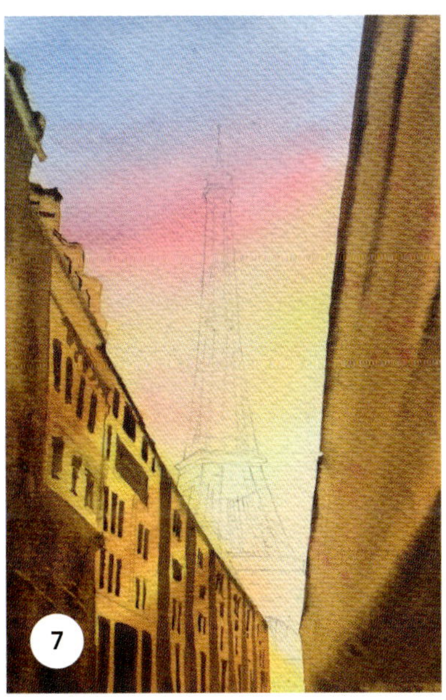

STEP 4: Now, we will paint each of the buildings. Using quinacridone gold (or a mixture of yellow, orange, and a drop of brown), paint the whole building on the left. While this is still wet, use a mixture of transparent brown and transparent orange to paint over it so you leave two streaks of the golden yellow color underneath. Use brown to capture the darker areas toward the top, and add a line over the roof area.

STEP 5: Paint the second building with a mixture of transparent orange and transparent brown (equal parts). While this is still wet, add in the darker areas, roof line, and the lines of the floors using brown.

STEP 6: Move on to the third layer once the strokes from step 4 are dry. Using transparent brown, add in the shadow areas of the buildings. These are the areas in between buildings and toward the left side, where the sunlight is not reaching.

STEP 7: Using transparent brown, add in all the windows and the doors of the left building. Remember to follow perspective for every element. All of the horizontal lines should be toward the vanishing point.

(continued)

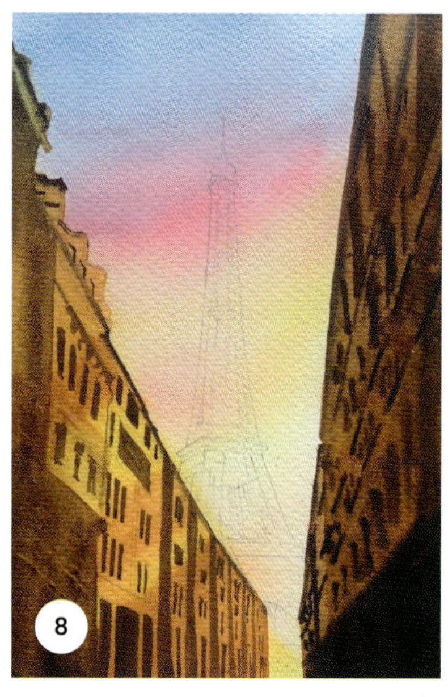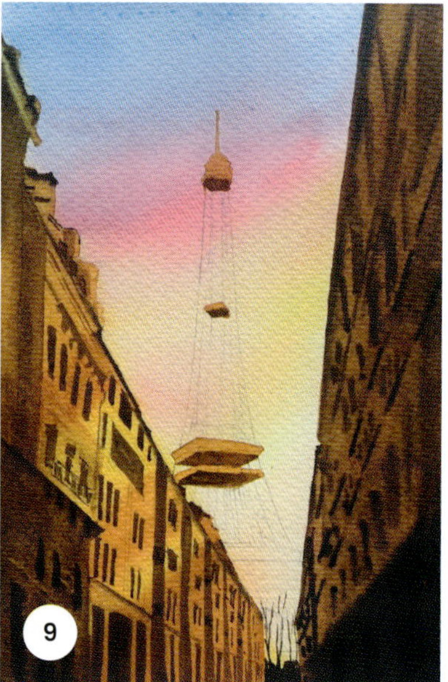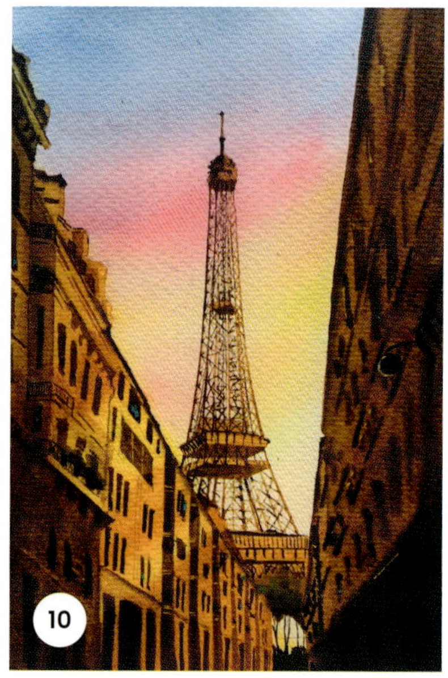

STEP 8: Repeat the process for the building on the right. However, for this building you don't need to wait for the paint from step 5 to be dry. This will make some of the windows and doors softer.

STEP 9: Using quinacridone gold and transparent brown, add in the block areas of the tower. Transparent brown would be in the darker areas. Also, add in the branches of the trees and some bushes at the bottom of the tower with darker brown.

STEP 10: Use a very thin or small brush, such as size 0 or 1, to add in the lines of the Eiffel Tower. Add darker lines toward the left with brown and lighter lines toward the right with quinacridone gold. Do not make things perfectly. You can have some lighter lines toward the left and some darker lines toward the right as well. Using olive green and brown, add in some trees toward the bottom of the tower and in some of the balconies of the building on the left. Finish with some cobalt turquoise and lavender touches to some of the windows on the left building.

QUICK TIP

The focal point on our painting is the Eiffel Tower. We are going to use the building on the left side to lead the viewer's eyes to it; hence, this building can be detailed. The building on the right can be more subtle details with softer edges to take the attention of the viewer away from it. If you were to add too many details to this one, it would look cluttered and the focus on the tower would be lost.

QUICK TIP

Do not complete every line or make every line perfectly. Incomplete lines and randomness increases the beauty of the painting. Our brain completes them for us when you look at the painting.

TRAM IN LISBON

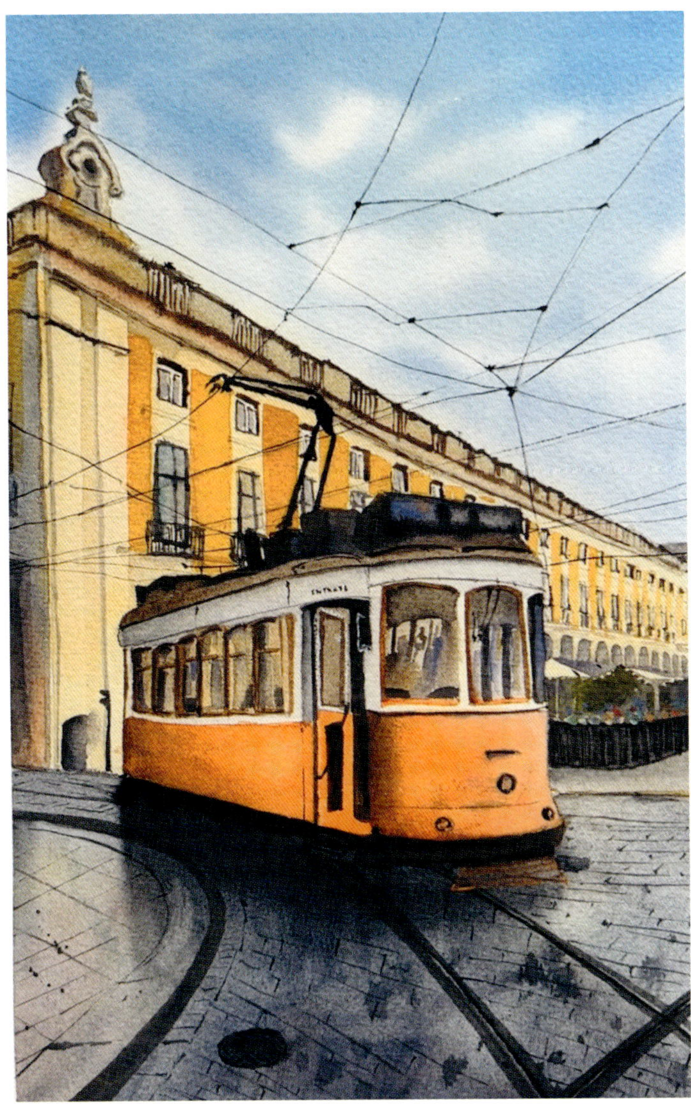

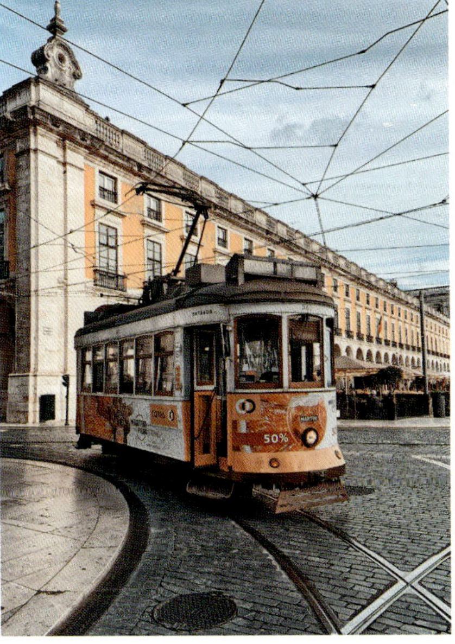

WATER TECHNIQUE: **Taped edges**

PAPER SIZE: **10" × 7" (25.4 × 17.8 cm)**

COLORS: Cobalt blue, phthalo blue, yellow ochre, ultramarine blue, burnt sienna, transparent brown, Payne's gray, olive green, transparent orange, lavender, white, cadmium orange, cobalt turquoise, cadmium red, cadmium yellow

(continued)

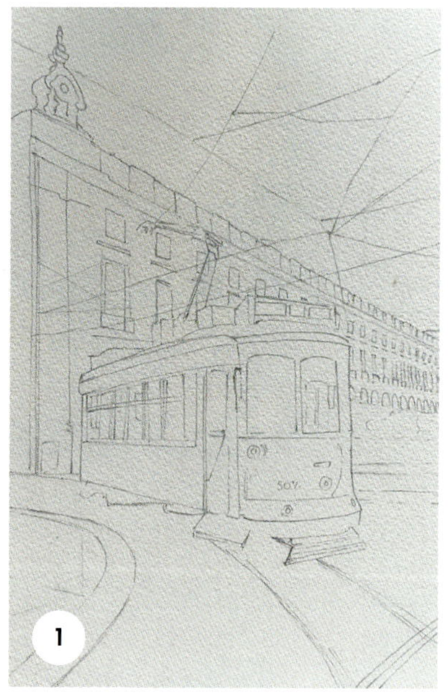

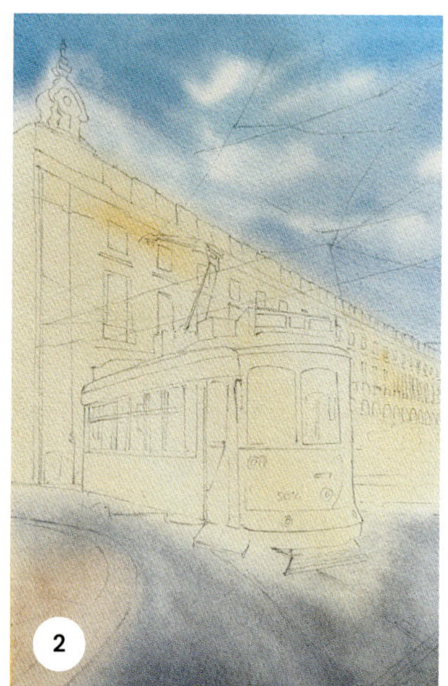

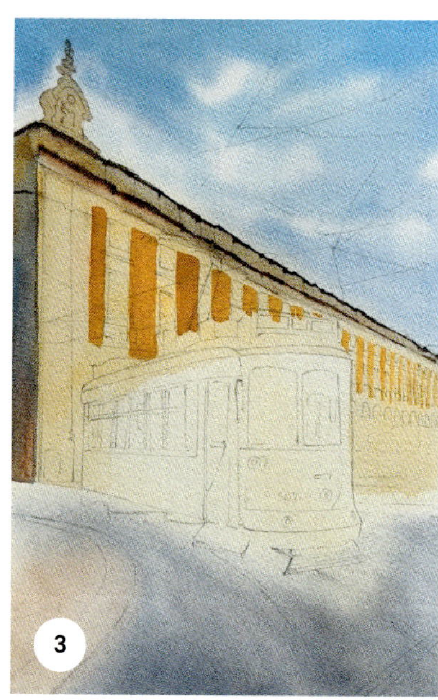

STEP 1: Sketch the outline of the entire picture using two-point perspective. Both vanishing points (VPs) are outside the paper. To get it done easily, have the paper fixed on the surface and choose two VPs, one each to the left and right side of the paper on the table. They both should be on the same line. One easy way to find the first one is to roughly estimate the position of the building on the paper and then to look at the horizontal edge going toward the further end. Trace this line all the way to the bottom of the building and that is where the first VP (on the right side) will be. The second VP will be along a horizontal line drawn from the first VP to the left of the paper. Using the two VPs, sketch the building and the tram. The roof of the building needs to be angled toward the first VP on the right, while the tram will be angled toward the VP on the left.

STEP 2: Apply water to the whole of the paper and paint in the first layer. Use a blend of cobalt blue and phthalo blue for the sky; a lighter tone of yellow ochre for the building and the tram; a mixture of ultramarine blue and burnt sienna (this creates gray) for the road; and then add more burnt sienna to this mixture for the sidewalk.

STEP 3: Add in the dark yellow accents of the buildings using a very creamy mixture of yellow ochre. Next, paint in the shadow areas of the roof and the other side of the building with a mixture of yellow ochre, burnt sienna, and ultramarine blue. Ultramarine blue creates the cool tones of the shadow. Do not completely mix all these three pigments together on the palette, but rather subtly let these colors bleed onto each other in the painting. This gives different color tones and makes the painting more attractive. Add darker edges with transparent brown.

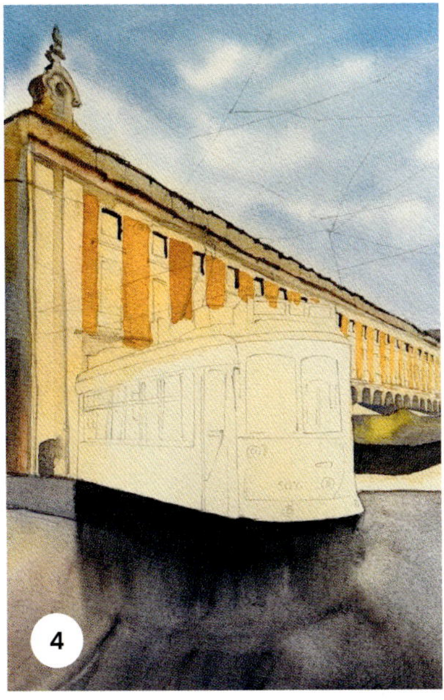

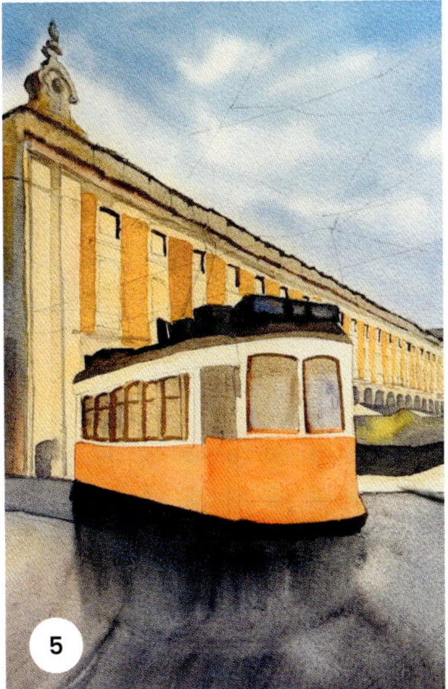

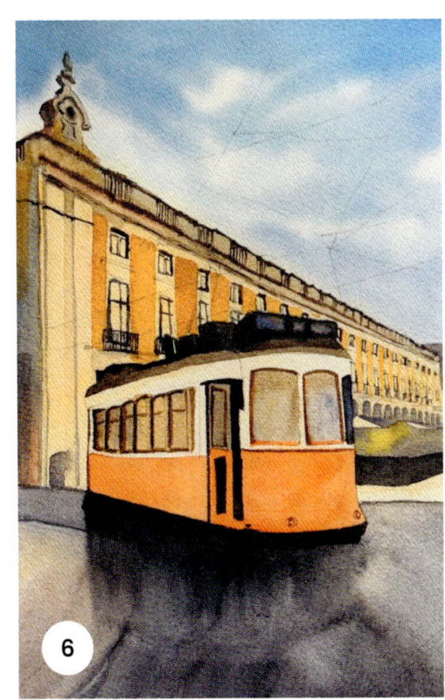

STEP 4: Wet the road area and the sidewalk. Paint the road, following along the underside of the tram with Payne's gray; add in shadows using some vertically downward strokes. Add in the doors of the building with Payne's gray and the darker shadow of the window with transparent brown. Also, paint the shadows on the crown with the shadow colors we used earlier. Add in some olive green and Payne's gray mixture for the shops on the right side. These do not need to be detailed.

STEP 5: Now, we will start painting the tram. Use transparent orange for the body, but leave the underlying lighter yellow ochre wherever it is white on the tram. Apply transparent brown for the roof, a mix of Payne's gray and lavender for the machinery on the roof, and a lighter tone of transparent brown and lavender for the windows. Once these have dried, add in the window edges with orange and brown. Using a darker Payne's gray, add shadows to the machinery on the tram's roof.

STEP 6: Add in all the lines for the windows, balconies, and doors on the building with Payne's gray. Add darker details with Payne's gray for the door of the tram and the windows as well. Remember, do not aim for perfection in each of these lines. Try to loosen up your strokes and sketch with your brush rather than carefully marking each line.

(continued)

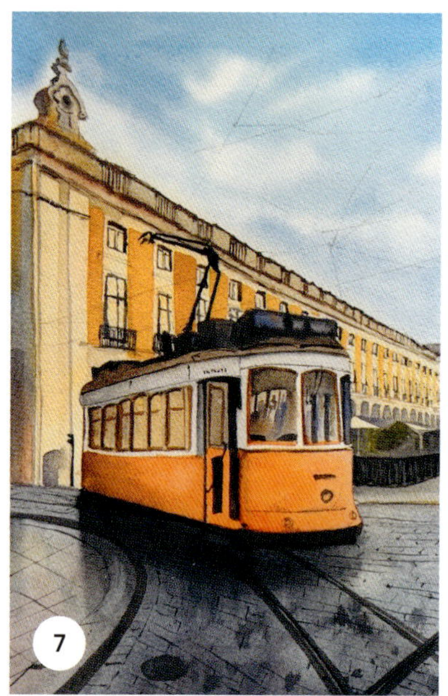 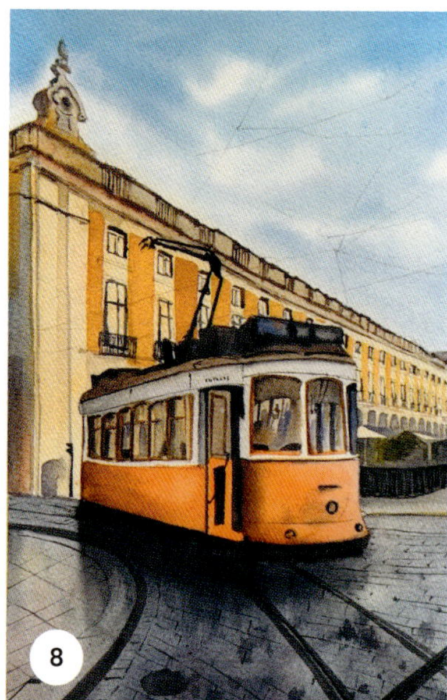 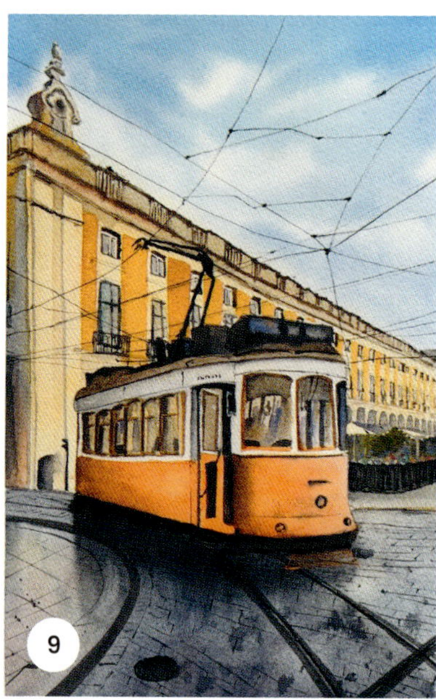

STEP 7: Make the body of the tram darker toward the left side on each face by blending in transparent brown along with orange. Add in white over the orange if you need to make any areas lighter. Paint the pantograph (the electric pole on the top) with dark Payne's gray. Complete the road with dark Payne's gray for the tram lines and then use a very thin detailer size 0 brush for the tiny lines on the road and the sidewalk. You can add the manhole and also splatter some paint for some additional dramatic effect. For the shops on the right side, add more depth with Payne's gray and a subtle olive green and Payne's gray mixture for some greenery. Look at the reference and add in smaller details as desired, like the door handle, the wipers, the small lines on the tram, and so on.

STEP 8: Paint the underside of the tram with dark Payne's gray so it looks blended with the shadow. Fill up with more tiny details as desired.

STEP 9: Add in the electric lines with a thin liner brush and darker Payne's gray. Finish off with cadmium orange for the front lifeguard of the tram and add in lots of people sitting at the restaurants and shops with cobalt turquoise, lavender, cadmium red, and cadmium yellow. These just need to be specks of paint and do not need to be detailed. Warning: This is one such painting where you can go on adding subtle details forever. So feel free to stop when you think you are done.

ACKNOWLEDGMENTS

I would like to thank my mother, Jasmin, for being the incredible human and amazing artist that she is and motivating me to paint every step of the way. You have my heartfelt gratitude for nurturing me and my creative side from my childhood.

Thank you to my father, Chandramohan, for teaching me kindness, compassion, and love. I know you would have been the happiest to know about this book if you were alive today.

It goes without saying that this book would not have been possible without the support, love, and care from my dearest husband, Sandeep, and my son, Ishaan. Thank you for patiently letting me pursue my creative passion and cheering me on every day.

Thanks also to my sister, Neenu, and brother-in-law, Aswin, for your love, patience with me, and support.

And to my dearest best friend, Pallavi, who supported me in every step of my artistic journey and showed me how to be a good friend—thank you for your support, kindness, and love from the world beyond.

I feel truly blessed to have some amazing friends supporting me and cheering me on: Sonia, Nidhi, Shraddha, Aleena, Neetha, Ramya, Christina, and Leena.

I am deeply thankful to Maggie and the entire team at Silver Brush Limited for trusting in my creativity and supplying me with all the brushes.

Thanks to Karan Sir from Sitaram Stationers for believing in me and supplying me with all necessary materials.

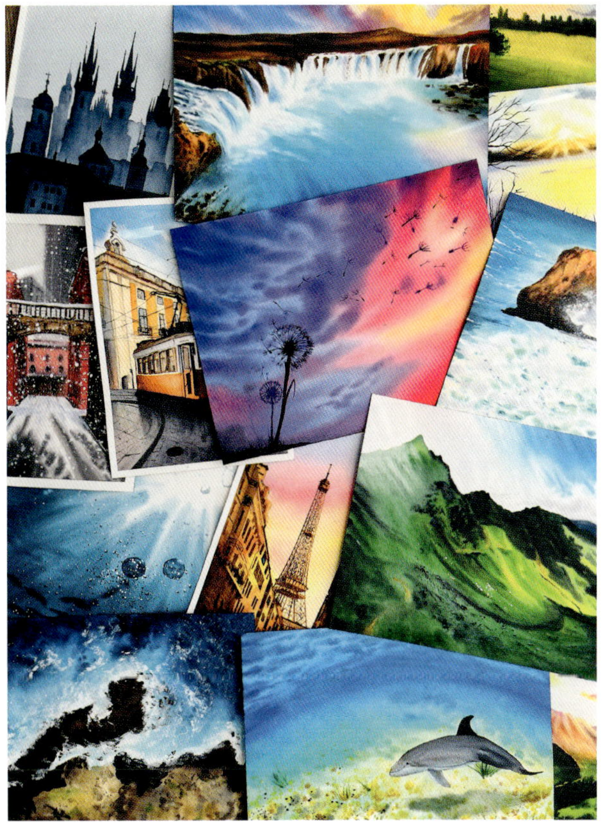

Thanks to the whole team at Quarto Publishing; my editor, Annika Geiger; and Pauline Molinari for giving me this opportunity, guiding me through the creation of this book, and helping me to achieve my dream.

Lastly, thanks to my awesome family on YouTube, Instagram, and Skillshare for immensely supporting me on my artistic journey and showering me with inspiration and motivation to paint in the last few years. A huge thanks to all of you from the bottom of my heart!

Geethu Chandramohan is the artist, illustrator, and one-woman team behind the brand Colourfulmystique. Although an aerospace engineer by profession, she manages to create vibrant and beautiful watercolor paintings on the side after her 8 to 5 job almost every day. She is a self-taught artist who started painting with watercolor right from her childhood days.

She took her painting career seriously and on a regular basis five years ago and has since created her own unique style of vibrant paintings with watercolor. As an autodidact, she breaks down the complex concepts behind creating stunning landscapes and shares her experience through step-by-step instructions and multiple techniques in this book.

She has taught thousands of students via her online classes, is a Skillshare top teacher, and dedicated herself to help students discover their passion for watercolor. Geethu has worked with brands like Artphilosophy, Nevskayapalitra, and Etchr Studio and is a Silver brush Educator.

She lives with her husband and son in Hampshire, UK. Taking on the art career along with her full-time aerospace systems engineering job has never been cumbersome for her and she is well known for her time management skills. She shares much of her processes and creativity through studio vlogs in her Youtube channel and life stories and updates in her Instagram and Threads almost every day. Both these are under the handle @colourfulmystique. For videos of some techniques found in this book, visit the artist's website, www.colourfulmystique.com/quartobook.

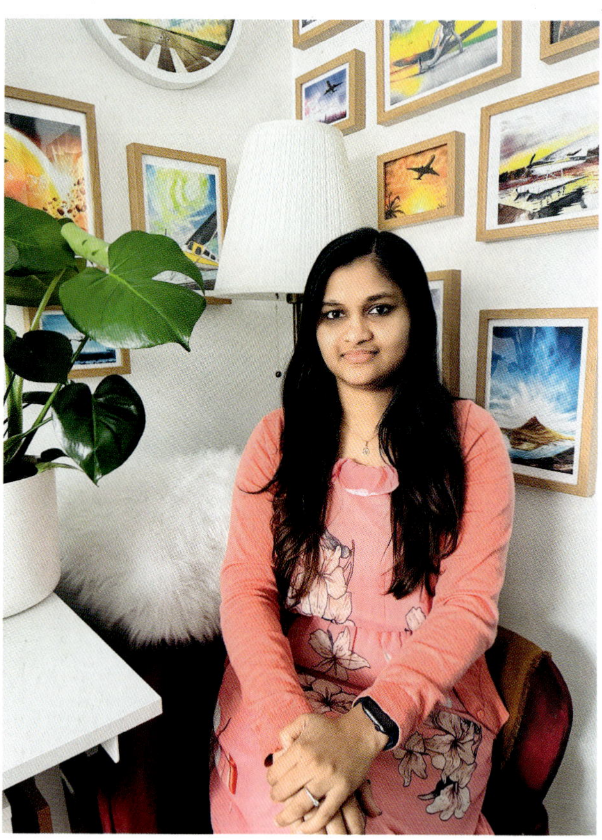